STUDIES IN AFRICAN AMERICAN HISTORY AND CULTURE

Edited by
Graham Hodges
Colgate University

D0169007

A ROUTLEDGE SERIES

Studies in African American History and Culture

Graham Hodges, *General Editor*

THE RISE AND FALL OF THE GARVEY MOVEMENT IN THE URBAN SOUTH, 1918–1942

Claudrena N. Harold

Routledge
New York & London

Routledge
Taylor & Francis Group
270 Madison Avenue
New York, NY 10016

Routledge
Taylor & Francis Group
2 Park Square
Milton Park, Abingdon
Oxon OX14 4RN

© 2007 by Taylor & Francis Group, LLC
Routledge is an imprint of Taylor & Francis Group, an Informa business

Printed in the United States of America on acid-free paper
10 9 8 7 6 5 4 3 2 1

International Standard Book Number-10: 0-415-95619-6 (Hardcover)
International Standard Book Number-13: 978-0-415-95619-2 (Hardcover)

Library of Congress Cataloging-in-Publication Data

Harold, Claudrena N.
    The rise and fall of the Garvey movement in the urban South, 1918-1942 / by Claudrena N. Harold.
        p. cm. -- (Studies in African American history and culture)
    Based on author's thesis (Ph. D.)--University of Notre Dame, 2004.
    Includes bibliographical references and index.
    ISBN 978-0-415-95619-2
    1. Garvey, Marcus, 1887-1940. 2. Garvey, Marcus, 1887-1940--Political and social views. 3. African Americans--Southern States--Politics and government--20th century. 4. African Americans--Race identity--Southern States--History--20th century. 5. Black nationalism--Southern States--History--20th century. 6. Universal Negro Improvement Association. 7. Southern States--Race relations--History--20th century. 8. Southern States--Politics and government--1865-1950. 9. City and town life--Southern States--History--20th century. 10. African Americans--Biography. I. Title.

    E185.97.G3H37 2007
    305.896'0730750904--dc22
                                                                        2006035788

Visit the Taylor & Francis Web site at
http://www.taylorandfrancis.com

and the Routledge Web site at
http://www.routledge-ny.com

For my amazing mother,

Sheryl P. Harold

Contents

Acknowledgments

Completing this book would have been impossible without the love, encouragement, wisdom, criticism, and spiritual guidance of countless family, friends, mentors, colleagues, archivists, and political activists. A number of institutions have been supportive of my research project: the National Archives, the Library of Congress, the Rare Book, Manuscripts, and Special Collections Library at Duke University, the Special Collections Library at the University of Southern Mississippi, the Schomburg Center for Research in Black Culture, the University of Notre Dame, the University of Virginia, and Temple University.

Central to the completion of this book has been the insightful work of several scholars who've produced critically important studies on the Garvey Movement: Tony Martin, Theodore Vincent, Judith Stein, Michele Mitchell, Jahi Issa, Mary Gambrell Rolinson, Wilson Moses, Barbara Bair, and Ula Taylor. An important intellectual who has contributed immensely to broadening our understanding of black radical and nationalist movements, Robert Hill created intellectual space for those of us trying to better illuminate the Garvey movement's complexities, ambiguities, and regional variations. Of course, I've drawn inspiration not only from these and other scholars, but also from the courageous women and men in the UNIA who labored toward the creation of a better world for African people. Much appreciation to the late Estelle James, Millie Charles, and Florence Borders for sharing their stories.

Special thanks to all the lovely people from my Temple University days. A basketball scholarship was responsible for my journey to the City of Brotherly Love, but selecting Temple proved to be an excellent academic decision. Three wonderful people changed my life, transformed my thinking, and launched me on this crazy career path: Mario Beatty, Valethia Watkins-Beatty, and Greg Carr. Especially enriching during these years was the friendship of Brian Jones. Lengthy discussions with Greg, Mario, Valethia, Brian, among others in Temple's African-American Studies Department, planted the intellectual seeds for this book and instilled within me a greater appreciation for the richness, diversity, *and* utility of black nationalism. Other scholars who also enriched my experience included Nathaniel Norment, Bettye Collier-Thomas, Theophile Obenga, and of course Charles Blockson. A special thanks to Nathaniel and Rose Norment and Tanya Clark for providing shelter during my research and pleasure trips to Philadelphia and New York.

Leaving Temple for graduate school in South Bend, Indiana in 1998 was a good move. I learned a great deal from several formidable scholars at the University of Notre Dame: Gail Bederman, Doris Bergen, Jay Dolan, John McGreevy, and my advisor, Richard B. Pierce. Richard Pierce deserves special thanks for providing superb mentorship during my six year stay at Notre Dame. I know that the Department of African American Studies is in great hands, for Richard has tremendous respect for the discipline and the people. Always putting me in revision mode, Gail Bederman not only pushed me intellectually, but graciously listened to my complaints when life at Notre Dame became overbearing. Notwithstanding her busy schedule, Tera Hunter was an outsider reader on my dissertation committee and her comments proved extremely helpful. A special thanks also to Myrtle Doaks.

Timely encouragement has come from my students, colleagues, and friends at the University of Virginia. To the faculty and staff at the Woodson Institute and in the History Department, your collegiality is very much appreciated. Navigating life at UVA would have been impossible without the assistance of Kathleen Miller, Ella Wood, Elizabeth Stovall, and Octavia Phillips. Octavia has provided timely advice and much laughter. A special thanks to students in my Black Nationalism, Labor History, and African American Protest courses. Thanks for enriching my teaching experience.

Speaking of enrichment, the friendships of Roderick Smith, Brian Jones, Greg Carr, Valethia Watkins, Mario Beatty, Damon Woodward, Gloria and Kent Ivey, James Collins, Corey D.B. Walker, Cheryl Hicks, Stacy Davis, Reg Jones, Arthur Jenkins, and all of my teammates at Temple University sustained me during my academic journey. An amazing scholar whose work has forced me to listen more closely to the voices of black working women, Cheryl Hicks took time out of her busy schedule to read a rather rough version of the manuscript. Moreover, she's endured my rather lengthy conversations on UVA, the perils of academic life, and the musical genius of Donny Hathaway. Much thanks to my dear friend Damon Woodward for providing encouragement ever since our workout days at the University of Notre Dame. Calling you friend is a privilege. Words can't adequately express my appreciation for Corey Walker's friendship and first-rate mind. His erudite commentary on the future of Africana studies, political economy, and liberation theology has definitely influenced my approach to black nationalism and radical politics. Corey and Carthene, you two are definitely missed on UVA's grounds. Thanks also to Reg Jones, one half of the Washington, DC-based band, Zwei. A revolutionary thinker, Reg forced me to integrate the human emotions of love, passion, faith, and disappointment into this text. Our conversations on the transcendental beauty of Me'shell Ndegeocello and Miles Dewey Davis III, religion, and the revolutionary potential of art have not only been enlightening but uplifting. I love you dearly.

An incredible human being, Roderick Smith deserves mad props for providing financial and emotional support during my college and high school years. To A.J., we don't talk much now, but your friendship still means the world to me. Another valuable friend is Stacy Davis. A talented young scholar whose work on race and religion is very important in these troubling times, Stacy is never too busy to provide much needed guidance and direction. She's definitely one of the most thoughtful people I know. Melissa and Mike, thanks for allowing me to lean on your daughter. I am also grateful to James and Tracy Collins for their friendship. James has always been encouraging and hearing his voice on the other line always buoys my spirit. I admire you more than you'll ever know.

Finally, my sincere thanks to the Buckholtz, Harold, and Crawford families for life, love, and inspiration. A few family members have been especially encouraging during my time on this planet: Joan and Samuel Owens, Eric Crawford, Jeffrey Crawford, my late brother Claude Harold, Jr., and my late brother Bruce Harold. I have had the enormous benefit of receiving much support from Joan and Sam Owens. Critical guidance was also provided by Leonard Cross, Alfred Austin, David Hudson, Gwendolyn Maxwell, Charlene Curtis, and Kelly Watts.

Last but definitely not least, my mother has been a source of strength and love from day one, always going beyond the call of duty. A hard working woman with an incredible love for black people, she has constantly affirmed my faith in humanity. After my father's death, she filled in the role of Mom and Dad, never missing a beat. Her presence and my Pop's memory have been constant sources of inspiration and encouragement throughout my life.

Introduction

Traveling from Puerto Barrios, Guatemala aboard the SS *Suriname,* the noted Pan-Africanist Marcus Mosiah Garvey arrived in New Orleans, Louisiana on the morning of July 13, 1921.[1] Over the past four months, the Justice Department and the Immigration Office had diligently labored to prevent Garvey's reentry into the United States, but various circumstances enabled the West Indian to legally return to the country after his extended stay in the Caribbean and Latin America.[2] Enormously popular among blacks living in the uptown section of New Orleans, Garvey addressed an enthusiastic crowd of fifteen hundred supporters on his first night in the city. To thunderous applause, the electrifying orator emphasized the need for race pride, improved relations between diasporan and continental Africans, and the development of black-owned industries. "The time has come," Garvey proclaimed during his opening address at National Park, "for the strongest race of people on earth, barring the Chinese, to break the bonds of oppression."[3] Developing separate and viable bases of economic and political power, he opined, was the only way for blacks to achieve true emancipation. "We have favored and aided by the hundred," he reminded women and men victimized by the most invidious forms of institutionalized white supremacy, "but favor has not been returned. Time now to pay attention to our own interest . . . The world is without sympathy. You must form your own future. Do for yourselves what others have done for themselves." Fully cognizant of the American government's efforts to undermine his influence in the United States, Garvey had a rather ambivalent message for federal intelligence agents and informants dispersed among the hundreds assembled at National Park. "I am not preaching radicalism. We are not organizing to fight the whites, but to protect what is ours, if it takes our lives."[4] Such proclamations hardly appeased federal agents who viewed Garvey and his rapidly growing Universal Negro

Improvement Association (UNIA) as formidable challenges to the racial status quo. Staying in New Orleans for three days, Garvey remained under the watchful eye of the Bureau of Investigation, the Immigration Office, and the New Orleans Police Department until his departure for the UNIA's headquarters in Harlem.

Still under heavy surveillance, Garvey arrived at New York's Pennsylvania Station on July 17. Three days later at a mass meeting in Harlem, the UNIA leader recounted his recent experiences in the West Indies and Central America, acknowledged the federal government's efforts to undermine his influence, and reaffirmed his commitment to the UNIA's Pan African agenda. Noting his recent success in New Orleans, Garvey devoted special attention to the UNIA's progress in the Crescent City. Twenty-five hundred members strong, the New Orleans UNIA was progressing remarkably under the effective leadership of the Barbadian-born activist, Adrian Johnson.[5] Strengthening the UNIA's presence in New Orleans and other cities in the South had been extremely important not only for Garvey and his associates in New York, but also for thousands of Southern women and men who vehemently rejected integration with whites as a defining goal of the black liberation struggle. Not simply committed to the eradication of racial apartheid in the United States, these Southerners sought to revolutionize global politics in such a way as to ensure a completely liberated existence for African-descended peoples in every corner of the world.

Situating their own struggles against racial discrimination and economic exploitation within an international context, Southern Garveyites welcomed the opportunity to unite politically with oppressed blacks in Europe, the West Indies, Latin America, and Africa. Envisioning themselves as members of a larger international black community, they raised money to send representatives to the UNIA's annual conventions in New York City, invested heavily in the organization's economic ventures, stood behind Marcus Garvey during his legal struggles, and stayed abreast of key political happenings in other parts of the African diaspora. To effectuate change at the local level, they created social welfare programs, established political unions, and built alliances with other grassroots activists and organizations in their respective communities. Serious engagement in local organizing work led UNIA followers in the South to develop a political praxis which at times stood in stark contrast to the agenda put forth by the Parent Body in New York. To be sure, Southern Garveyites drew tremendous inspiration and direction from the activities of their comrades in New York City; however, their political decisions often bore the imprint of their local political culture. Emerging out of local communities with their own distinctive traditions, Southern Garveyites did not always speak with one voice on such important issues as the most effective way to ensure the biological perpetuation of the race, African emigration/repatriation, community activism, or coalition building. A testament to the multidimensionality of black political subjectivity in the Jim Crow South, Southern Garveyites fashioned a politics reflective of their local, regional, and international concerns.

Only recently have scholars focused on the political activities of Southern Garveyites. To be sure, Judith Stein, Tony Martin, and Theodore Vincent in their invaluable studies on American Garveyism noted the existence of UNIA branches in the South, but their analysis of the movement and its principal leaders centered primarily on the organization's activities in New York City. Driven in part by the outpouring of scholarship on black activism in the Jim Crow South[6], several historians have challenged the common portrayal of Garveyism as a movement based exclusively in the North.[7] Notwithstanding scholars' increased efforts to extend their analysis of the UNIA beyond the North, there has yet to emerge a comprehensive study of the organization's success and failures in the urban South.

Specifically focusing on African American and West Indian communities in New Orleans, Miami, Florida, and Hampton Roads, Virginia, *The Rise and Fall of the Garvey Movement in the Urban South* provides the first detailed examination of the UNIA's emergence, maturation, and eventual decline in the urban South between 1918 and 1942.[8] It examines the ways in which laboring people fused locally-based traditions, ideologies, and strategies of resistance with the Pan-African agenda of the UNIA to create a dynamic and multifaceted movement. This complex political fusion produced incremental improvements in the lives of many Southern blacks but proved unable to transform existing power relations. Similar to other black organizations of the time, the UNIA struggled to develop a strategy to address adequately the multiple forces responsible for black political and economic inequality. Notwithstanding its limitations and eventual collapse during the depression years, the UNIA performed an integral role in the politicization of thousands of black Southerners, including such noted civil rights and labor activists as Queen Mother Audley Moore, Sylvia Woods, James B. Nimmo, and Randolph Blackwell.

Converging with recent work in the fields of Southern, urban, labor, and black nationalist studies, *The Rise and Fall of the Garvey Movement in the Urban South* chronicles how involvement in a transnational movement enabled women and men living in the nation's most racially repressive region to embrace more fully the spirit of hope and freedom under undeniably difficult circumstances. Frequently in the pages of the UNIA's official organ, *The Negro World*, black Southerners praised the Garvey movement for providing them with new ways of imagining the world, strengthening their confidence in their ability to dismantle white supremacy, and widening their political options. Left unaddressed in many of their letters was the degree to which their own financial and intellectual contributions legitimized the movement in the eyes of many outsiders, stabilized the organization during difficult times, and reminded the Parent Body of the varied ways in which white supremacy could be contested. Not at all marginal actors in Garvey's racial drama, black Southerners stood at the center of many of the UNIA's racial uplift projects, intellectual debates, and internecine fights over organizational policies.

Tracing the rise and fall of the Garvey movement in Miami, New Orleans, Lousiana and Norfolk and Newport News, Virginia, this book's significance lies not only in its attempt to elevate black Southerners to a position of importance in the history of the UNIA, but also in its detailed attention to the movement's rank and file. Not enough scholarly attention has been given to black workers' ideological and political impact on the UNIA's activities. Twenty-three years ago, Cedric Robinson, in his seminal study, *Black Marxism*, challenged scholars of the UNIA to devote more of their attention to "the masses of people involved in making the organization."[9] No scholar has made an effort to systematically analyze black laborers' contributions to the movement's success. Nor has there been a thorough documentation of their work at the grassroots level. Such an analysis will not only yield more information on working women and men's varied political and intellectual contributions to the movement, but also push forward a more nuanced reading of the UNIA's working-class constituency.

Very biased in their writings, Garvey's critics presented the UNIA's supporters as social misfits and ignorant fanatics who blindly followed an impractical visionary down the road of racial chauvinism and escapism. Not surprising given the Garvey movement's success among black laborers, the strongest critiques of the UNIA's working-class constituency came from the black Left. Writing on the Garvey movement's disruptive influence and its tendency to distract workers from "serious political engagement," A. Philip Randolph despairingly referred to the UNIA's working-class supporters as "ignorant wretches" and "dupes."[10] Strident in his criticism of the UNIA, the venerable labor leader wondered why black workers would even involve themselves with such a reactionary organization. Garveyism, in Randolph's opinion, strengthened the hegemony of the ruling class, disrupted the radicalization of the black masses, and siphoned off money which could have been used to support the more constructive and "scientific" program of the Socialist Party:

> The whites in America don't take Garveyism seriously. They dub Garvey a 'Moses of the Negro' in order to get Negroes to follow him, which will wean them away from any truly radical economic program. They

know that the achievement of his program, the redemption of Africa, is unattainable, but it serves the purpose of engaging the Negroes' brains, energy and funds in a highly nebulous, futile and doubtful movement so far as beneficial results to Negroes are concerned.[11]

Randolph provided valuable critiques of the Garvey movement during the 1920s, but this particular reading was terribly flawed. His analysis greatly underestimates the intelligence of working-class women and men, disregards their ability to discern and respond accordingly to the movement's programmatic weaknesses, and denies the existence of any substantive agency on their part. Sadly, the image of working-class Garveyites as simple minded people who lacked the political sophistication and knowledge to recognize the weaknesses in the UNIA's program surfaced in the writings of other black progressives, including Chandler Owen, Wilfred A. Domingo, Richard Moore, and Cyril Briggs.[12] "The UNIA," Chandler Owen once wrote, "is composed chiefly of the most primitive and ignorant element of West Indian and American Negroes." "Cranks, crooks, and racial bigots" with a proclivity to "violent crime," in his opinion, best described the type of people attracted to the movement and its demagogic leader.[13] One may have expected more than simplistic putdowns and myopic portrayals to emerge from the pens of these learned men, but writing balanced accounts of the association's working-class constituency was not the objective of those black activists whose principal goal was the removal of Marcus Garvey from the American scene. To advance their political aims, Randolph and Owen not only criminalized the movement's rank and file, but simplistically presented black workers' involvement in the nationalist UNIA as further evidence of their pronounced tendency toward false consciousness.

Even black radicals sympathetic to revolutionary nationalism relied on the Left's traditional invocation of false consciousness as a way to explain the movement's success among black workers. Consider the comments of African Blood Brotherhood founder and Communist Party organizer, Cyril Briggs. "The main base of the movement," Briggs pointed out, "was the Negro agricultural workers and the farming masses groaning under the terrific oppression of peonage and sharecropper slavery, and the backward sections of the Negro industrial workers." Lacking the necessary knowledge of political economy, these workers, he argued, were easily moved by the silly schemes of the UNIA. "To the advanced industrial Negro proletariat who were experienced in class struggle," he maintained, "the Garvey movement had little appeal."[14] Only six months after Briggs' article appeared in the *Communist*, Trinidadian George Padmore published a markedly similar piece in which the respected Pan-Africanist criticized black laborers for their support of the UNIA and chided "the backward sections of the Negro masses . . . still possessed of a peasant ideology [Garveyism]."[15] Unaddressed in these black leftist critiques of Garveyism was the fact that many among the UNIA's rank-and-file belonged to the industrial working class, understood the debilitating effects of capitalism, and even participated in trade union politics.

Neither ignorant wretches nor misguided dupes devoid of class consciousness, many working women and men entered the UNIA with an expansive sense of civic responsibility, extensive organizational experience, an astute awareness of class distinctions within the black community, and an understanding of the ways in which their position in the political economy negatively impacted their life chances and experiences. Very much attuned to the class dimension of their struggle, several UNIA leaders in the South simultaneously buttressed the UNIA and the labor movement during the 1920s. Southern Garveyites' organizational affiliations included the American Federation of Labor, the International Longshoremen's Association, the Tobacco Workers' Union, and the National Brotherhood Workers of America. A brilliant man with a profound commitment to improving the material condition of black workers, John B. Cary, president of the New Orleans UNIA in 1927 and 1931, would maintain his membership in the local Carpenter's Union until his death in 1945. Even though he supported the race-based politics of the UNIA, he challenged those who viewed political injustice and economic exploitation as problems encountered only by black workers. "The common people of all nations," Cary explained to readers of the *Negro World*, "have suffered great oppression. It was the common people who faced shots and shell and bore the perils of war and had their lives and property taken away in order to satisfy the wicked and selfish ambitions of men."[16] Sympathetic to the struggles of all workers, John Cary committed himself to improving the quality of life for "those of the rank and file who labor with their hands and thereby produce the wealth of the land."[17] Cary's political views should not surprise those familiar with the complexity of black political thought during the postwar period. "Left-wing ideas," Barbara Foley notes in her study, *Spectres of 1919*, "enjoyed a mass influence in the period following WWI, significantly affecting the ways in which radicals and nonradicals alike perceived historical developments and construed the relation between race and class."[18]

Situating West Indian and African American laborers at the center of its analysis, this study seeks to answer questions many black leftists refused to seriously consider in their commentary on the UNIA: Why did African American workers constitute the backbone of the Garvey movement, and in what ways did their position in the racially segmented labor market account for their conspicuous presence in the UNIA? How much did Southern black workers' concerns about modernization and mechanization factor in their decision to rally behind the cooperative endeavors of the UNIA? To what extent did their awareness of the structural inequality deeply embedded in the capitalist system and their struggles against white racism in the labor movement induce them to buttress Garvey's race-based solutions? The answers to these questions reveal a great deal about not only the Garvey movement, but also the numerous strategies Southern black workers employed in their struggles against racial discrimination and class exploitation during the postwar period.

Shaping my approach to the involvement of black workers in the Southern Garvey movement is Rod Bush's invaluable study, *We Are Not What We Seem: Black Nationalism and Class Struggle in the American Century.* Sensitive to the integral role of racial formations in the stratifying processes of the capitalist world economy, Rod Bush defends nationalist-oriented calls for Black Power as a "logical, national, and sensible response to the social structure of the capitalist world-economy, and particularly the configuration of social groups in the United States."[19] Drawing from the works of Terrence Hopkins and Immanuel Wallenstein, Bush provides a rebuttal to leftist-leaning intellectuals who questioned black nationalism as a legitimate response to the status quo.[20] Central to Bush's representation of black nationalism as a cataclysmic agent for social change is his focus on anti-systemic organizations unequivocally opposed to the logic of racial oppression and capitalist exploitation: the UNIA, the African Blood Brotherhood, the League of Revolutionary Black Workers, and the Revolutionary Action Movement. Heeding Bush's advice to avoid hasty, uninformed dismissals of nationalist politics as completely bourgeois in character, *The Rise and Fall of the Garvey Movement in the Urban South* pays very close attention to Southern Garveyites' anti-systemic intentions and their courageous efforts to dismantle systems of racial and economic oppression.[21] Taking seriously the concerns and activities of working women and men, this book seeks to provide a clearer picture of the degree to which involvement in the Garvey movement transformed the ways in which Southern laborers conceptualized race and class, evaluated the strengths and limitations of transnational political formations, and, to borrow a phrase from the German historian Alan Confino, negotiated their intimate (real) local world with a more abstract international one.

Scholarly inquiry into Southern Garveyites' political world presents us with the opportunity to not only explore the diverse ways in which African American women and men challenged white supremacy, but to also expand our knowledge of how black nationalist tropes, themes, ideas, and activities tremendously influenced black Southerners' struggle for freedom. Critically important scholarship by Winston A. Grady-Willis, Timothy Tyson, James Smethurst, Akinyele Umoja, Mary Gambrell Rolinson, Jahi Issa, and Lance Hill has detailed black nationalism's indelible impact on Southern black activists and organizations from the end of Reconstruction to the present era.[22] Even during the pinnacle of the Civil Rights Movement, ideological viewpoints and political themes commonly associated with black nationalism surfaced in the speeches and chants of Mississippi freedom fighters, the artistic productions of black college students, and the editorials of Southern-based newspapers. Later during the seventies, Black Arts Movement centers in Miami, Florida, New Orleans, Louisiana, Atlanta, Georgia, and other southern locales promoted the racial distinctiveness of black Americans, pushed forward the development of independent cultural institutions, and championed the idea of a black aesthetic. Engaging some of the issues raised in the burgeoning literature on Southern black nationalism, *The Rise and Fall of the Garvey Movement in the Urban South* participates in an ongoing conversation about Southerners' varied contributions to and unique relationship with the tradition of black nationalism, their disagreements with northern activists, and the ways in which their Southern identity shaped their unique articulations of nationalist ideas and sentiments.

ORGANIZATION OF THE BOOK

To ensure black Southerners' multiple voices and perspectives are adequately captured, this book relies on a narrative structure sensitive to how local dynamics shaped the movement and the political opinions of its participants. Organized along geographical rather than chronological lines, *The Rise and Fall of the Garvey Movement in the Urban South* is divided into five chapters. Situating the history of Southern Garveyism within the larger context of New Negro radicalism, chapter one documents Marcus Garvey's founding of the UNIA in Jamaica, his arrival in the United States, and his movement's initial penetration into the American South. The next three chapters focus primarily on the UNIA's performance in New Orleans, Miami, Norfolk, and Newport News. Investigating the UNIA's achievements in New Orleans between 1920 and 1935, chapter two analyzes Crescent City blacks' endorsement of the UNIA's Pan-African agenda, probes the complex ways in which their ideas about race, culture, and class shaped their political decisions, and details their activities at the grassroots level. Cosmopolitan in outlook, New Orleans Garveyites embraced the internationalism of the UNIA while advancing their own local and regional interests with uncompromising vigor. A major issue pursued throughout the second chapter will be New Orleans Garveyites' struggle to negotiate their dual identity as participants in a diasporan movement and members of a local community with its own problems and traditions.

No study interested in Southerners' engagement with black internationalism would be complete without an analysis of an important though overlooked geographical center of black transnational interaction: Miami, Florida.[23] Focusing on the importance of the Garvey movement to Miami's Afro-Bahamian community, the book's third chapter situates the movement's popularity within the larger context of Afro-Bahamians' struggles to negotiate the stresses of everyday life in a racially repressive environment. Scholarship by Winston James, Irma Watkins-Owen, Mark Solomon, Theodore Vincent, Tony Martin, and Michele Stephens has tremendously enriched our understanding of Afro-Caribbean politics in New York City. Viewing the black immigrant experience from the perspective of Miami Garveyites enables us to explore themes, people, and contradictions rendered invisible in many Harlem-centered narratives on West Indian life. Specifically, the story of Miami Garveyites' political engagements and compromises invites a more critical reflection on how some scholarly representations of West Indians as naturally disposed toward radical thought and activity might not be applicable to those black immigrants who lived below the Mason-Dixon Line.

Turning attention to the birthplace of Southern Garveyism, the fourth chapter details the UNIA's appeal in Hampton Roads, Virginia (Newport News and Norfolk). It analyzes the organization's triumphs in the cities of Norfolk and Newport News during the twenties, as well as locates the reasons behind its dramatic collapse in the 1930s. Opening with an analysis of the centrality of Virginian laborers to the UNIA's early success, this chapter explores the ways in which black workers' concerns about their position in both the political economy and the labor movement informed their decision to rally behind the UNIA. Significant attention will also be given to Virginian Garveyites' alliance with white proponents of federal support for African American repatriation to Liberia. Scholars who have examined the UNIA's controversial alliances' with white supremacist groups tend to focus exclusively on Marcus Garvey's 1922 meeting with Edward Young Clarke of the Ku Klux Klan, but Virginian Garveyites' involvement in the repatriation movement illustrates the extent to which the movement's participants also cooperated with some of the nation's most rabid white separatists. Virginian Garveyites' controversial alliance with Earnest Sevier Cox and the white supremacist group, the Anglo-Saxon Clubs of America reveals not only the conservative strains within the UNIA, but the complexity of white-black relations in the Jim Crow South.

Selecting Norfolk, Newport News, Miami, and New Orleans as the principal areas of concentration for this book was not a particularly difficult decision. Setting the pace for their comrades in other Southern locales, UNIA followers in the aforementioned communities formed divisions whose cultural and social activities, membership, and monetary donations to the central office in New York rivaled many northern branches. Separating UNIA divisions in these sample cities from others in the South was not only their vibrancy, but their ability to sustain massive support over a prolonged period of time. Longevity, however, was not the only reason these divisions were chosen for concentrated study. Another factor was the degree to which these divisions' histories introduced topics, themes, and issues excluded from most historical writings on the South. Studying the UNIA in Miami, New Orleans, Norfolk, and Newport News provides the historian with an opportunity to explore such important issues as the complex nature of diasporic encounters between African Americans and West Indians, black nationalists' complex relationship with white separatists, and the ideological differences and political conflict between New Negro radicals in Harlem and New Negro activists in the South.

SOURCES

To adequately capture the complex history of the Garvey movement in the South, this book incorporates data from a variety of sources: Bureau of Investigation reports; the *Negro World*; oral histories; the branch files of the National Association for the Advancement of Colored People (NAACP); local newspapers; the administrative files of the UNIA's central office in New York; city directories; and census reports. Of all the available sources, the Garvey movement's official organ, *The Negro World,* provides the most information on the activities of the southern wing of the UNIA. Over the period between 1920 and 1933, UNIA branches in various parts of the South routinely reported their activities in the section entitled "UNIA Division News." Newspaper correspondents summarized their branches' meetings, listed the names of the division's officers, provided transcripts of local leaders' speeches, and highlighted the major developments within their divisions. Significant insight into the world of Southern Garveyism was also gleaned from another important section of the *Negro World*: "The People Opinion." Starting in 1924, the *Negro World* printed letters from Garveyites in the United States, Jamaica, South Africa, Panama, and a host of other places across the globe. Enlivening the pages of the *Negro World* with their descriptive letters, Southern Garveyites explained why they supported the UNIA, discussed the progress of their divisions, and detailed their stance on such controversial issues as class divisions within the black community, the role of women in the movement, and the need for the rank-and-file to assume more autonomy over local branches.

Thirty-five years ago, historian Theodore Vincent concluded his fine study of the Garvey movement with an essay on the difficulty of conducting research on black nationalist movements. "There remains today," he opined, "a crying need for scholarly works based upon primary source materials dealing with black nationalism and other forms of black radicalism."[24] Scholars interested in Garveyism and black nationalist politics, he warned, "must be prepared to face considerable difficulty in gathering materials."[25] The availability of primary materials on the black nationalist/radical tradition has improved tremendously since Vincent's observations. So has the state of scholarship on nationalist movements in black America.[26] Fascinating research has been conducted on black nationalism's complex intersections with the political philosophies of liberalism, conservatism, and revolutionary Socialism, the gendered foundations and masculinist dimensions of black nationalism[27], and the inscription of nationalist, Afrocentric ideas in popular cultural forms. Standing at the cutting edge of black nationalist literature has been the work of Rod Bush, Claude Clegg, E. Frances White, Kevin Gaines, Michele Mitchell, James Smethurst, Ula Taylor, Komozi Woodward, and of course, the formidable intellectual historian, Wilson Jeremiah Moses. Emerging out of the work of these and other fine scholars have been important questions concerning the degree to which black nationalists imbued, reflected, and even reinforced the cultural and political ideas of white America[28], the ways in which black nationalism's tendency toward authoritarian collectivism and racial corporatism undermined its emancipatory potential, and whether nationalist activity has been beneficial or detrimental to the black liberation struggle.

Engaging many of these scholarly concerns, *The Rise and Fall of the Garvey Movement in the Urban South* provides a regional perspective on one of the most important nationalist movements, white or black, in US history. Occupying center stage of this narrative on the rise and fall of Southern Garveyism are courageous yet flawed women and men who dedicated their lives to the UNIA, developed ambitious community programs at the grassroots level, and worked tirelessly to realize political and economic freedom in their lifetime. To engage their life stories and struggles is to recognize that black nationalist activism constitutes much more than reactionary rage against ruthless white supremacy. To engage the life stories and struggles of Southern Garveyites is to come to grips with how much the emotions of love, faith, compassion, and optimism animated black nationalist activism during the 1920s.[29] Moved by revolutionary activities in various corners of the world, their Christian-influenced faith in human progress, and a heavy dose of love for and confidence in African people, Southern Garveyites never allowed their unimaginable sufferings to diminish their sense of life's beautiful possibilities, stifle their ability to imagine a much brighter future for the world, or lose their faith in the collective capacity of black people to transform the world for the betterment of all humanity.

Chapter One

Garveyism and the Rise of New Negro Politics in the Jim Crow South

The bloody war left a new spirit in the world—it has created for all mankind a new idea of liberty and democracy, and the Southern Negro now feels that he too has a part to play in the affairs of the world. A new light is burning for our brothers at this end. They are determined that they too shall enjoy a portion of democracy for which many of their sons and brothers fought for and died for in France.

Marcus Garvey, 1919[1]

Marcus Garvey benefited immensely from black Southerners' rising militancy. Engulfed by the transcendent spirit of the New Negro era, many Southerners responded enthusiastically to his efforts to dismantle global systems of racial oppression and economic exploitation. Firmly anchored below the Mason-Dixon Line during the 1920s, Garvey's UNIA garnered the support of domestic workers and longshoremen in the port cities of the Gulf Coast, tenant farmers in the cotton regions of the Black Belt, industrial workers along the South Atlantic seaboard, college students in the Carolinas, and West Indians in South Florida. Traveling to the South in the spring of 1928, J. A. Craigen, the president of the Detroit UNIA, marveled over the organization's success in the region. "The Universal Negro Improvement Association," Craigen explained to readers of the *Negro World*, "is found in practically every hamlet in the South." "It may be astonishing for some to know," he boasted, "the far reaching effects and influence that the program of Marcus Garvey exercises upon the Negroes of the South."[2] Spending considerable time in Florida, Virginia, Louisiana, and Alabama, Craigen was impressed by the large number of Southerners who had intimate knowledge of the organization's objectives and goals. "Every Negro with whom one comes in contact," he noted, "knows about Garveyism and its ideals."[3]

Claiming nearly five hundred UNIA divisions and branches by the mid-1920s, the Jim Crow South distinguished itself as a major stronghold of the Garvey movement. No small factor in the UNIA's success was the charismatic personality of Marcus Garvey. Fiercely independent, the Jamaican-born nationalist appealed not only to black women and men who had spent all of their lives under the oppressive system of Southern Jim Crowism, but also to many West Indians who settled in the South during the first two decades of the twentieth century. Moved by Garvey's Pan-African message of black pride, race unity, and economic independence, these black immigrants recognized the extent to which his personal triumphs, political struggles, and internationalist perspective corresponded with their own. Moreover, they embraced a man whose life had also been tremendously impacted by racism, economic dislocations and transformations in the Caribbean, and British imperialism.[4]

THE POLITICAL RISE OF MARCUS MOSIAH GARVEY

Three years after the Berlin Conference officially sanctioned Europe's ruthless partition of Africa, Sarah Richards gave birth to Marcus Garvey on August 17, 1887, in the seaport town of St. Ann's Bay, Jamaica.[5] Legalizing her union with Garvey's father two years after her son's birth, Sarah married Malchus Mosiah Garvey on December 15, 1889. Details on Marcus' early life are rather hazy and at times contradictory, but by most accounts, the precocious youngster received a quality education at the Anglican Church School until he commenced his printer's apprenticeship under his godfather, Alfred Burrowes. Searching for opportunities greater than those offered in his hometown, Garvey, in 1906, relocated to Kingston, Jamaica, where he gained employment at the Government Printing Office and strengthened his political skills as the vice-president of the Kingston Typographical Union. Finding himself blacklisted as a result of his involvement in trade union politics, Garvey in 1910 decided to follow the scores of Jamaican workers who searched for better economic opportunities in Central America. The twenty-three year old landed a job as a timekeeper on a United Fruit Company plantation in Costa Rica. Not long after his arrival, Garvey started to question those who portrayed Central America as a land of opportunity for West Indian laborers. "What black people had to brave sickened him," Garvey's second wife, Amy Jacques, noted in *Garvey and Garveyism*. "Daily," she continued, "they had to encounter snakes, swamps and wild tigercats. Mutilated black bodies in the rivers and bushes were common sights."[6] Shaken by the exploitative conditions under which West Indians labored in Costa Rica, Garvey pleaded with the

British Consul there to offer some type of protection to exploited Jamaican workers. Needless to say, his requests fell on deaf ears.[7] To draw attention to the plight of exploited black workers, Garvey launched a newspaper entitled *La Nation*, but his journalistic endeavor proved unsuccessful. Trekking Garvey's next steps is somewhat difficult given the paucity of primary sources on this part of his career, but according to Amy Jacques, Garvey spent some time in Ecuador, Nicaragua, Venezuela, Colombia, and Panama.[8] Life away further exposed the budding Pan-Africanist to the unimaginable levels of human suffering in the modern world, and forced him to reflect more critically on the global dimensions of white racism, colonialism, and economic exploitation.

Such reflection continued during his stay in London between 1912 and 1914. Moving to London after a brief return to Kingston, Garvey deepened his Pan-African consciousness and contacts during his brief tenure in Europe. The ambitious young man sparked a friendship with the renowned Pan-Africanist Duse Mohamed Ali, published articles in Ali's *African Times and Orient Review* and the *Tourist,* and studied informally at Birkbeck College.[9] Surrounded by West Indian and West African students in the thriving metropolis, Garvey was uniquely positioned to expand his knowledge of Pan-African politics, the similarities and differences among England's colonial subjects, and the rising levels of discontent in various parts of the British empire. Exposure to the workings of Britain's political system also contributed significantly to his leadership development. Noted Garvey biographer Tony Martin viewed Garvey's stay in London as "of great importance to his career. The workings of British democracy made a lasting impression on him, and like later generations of visitors from the colonized world to the metropolis, he noted the contrast to the autocracy which the very same colonizers maintained in their tropical dependencies."[10] London offered Garvey invaluable experiences, but financial difficulties forced him to return to his native land of Jamaica.

Sailing to Kingston aboard the S.S. *Trent* on June 17, 1914, Garvey struck up a conversation with a Guyanese passenger who had recently visited Basutoland in southern Africa. Candid in his discussions with his new friend, the Guyanese man vividly described white colonialists' inhumane treatment of the black majority. Nestled in his cabin, Garvey struggled to make sense of his recent conversation as well as his past experiences:

> I asked, "Where is the black man's Government? Where is his King and his kingdom? Where is his President, his country, and his ambassador, his army, his navy, his men of big affairs?" I could not find them, and then I declared, "I will help to make them. My brain was

afire. All day and the following night I pondered over the subject matter of that conversation, and at midnight, lying flat on my back, the vision and thought came to me that I should name the organization the Universal Negro Improvement Association and African Communities League. Such a name I thought would embrace the purpose of all black humanity.[11]

A week after his return to Jamaica, Garvey and his future wife, Amy Ashwood, founded the Universal Negro Improvement Association (UNIA) and African Commercial League (ACL) on August 1, 1914. A testament to its founders' expansive political vision, the organization's stated goals were:

To establish a universal confraternity among the race

To promote the spirit of race pride and love

To reclaim the fallen of the race

To administer to and assist the needy

To establish commissaries or agencies in the principal countries of the world for the protection of all Negroes, irrespective of nationality

To promote a conscientious Christian worship among the native tribes of Africa

To establish universities, colleges and secondary schools for the further education of the boys and girls of the race[12]

Serious attention was immediately given to the establishment of an industrial school in Kingston. Inspired by the work and teachings of the American educator Booker T. Washington, Ashwood and Garvey viewed education as the foundation for any movement designed to ameliorate the condition of black Jamaicans.[13] Writing Washington in the autumn of 1914, Garvey revealed plans to "erect several colleges at different centres in the island for the purpose of supplying free secondary and industrial education to our boys and girls."[14] Failing miserably in his efforts to mobilize local support for his educational endeavors, Garvey eventually sought assistance from sources outside Jamaica.[15,16] Thinking more support could be garnered in the United States, Garvey arrived in New York City on March 23, 1916.[17]

THE BIRTH OF AMERICAN GARVEYISM

Taking up residence in Harlem, Garvey encountered a community significantly impacted by larger developments in black America: the passing of Booker T. Washington in 1915, the intensification of America's involvement in World War I, the massive influx of Southern blacks into Harlem and other urban centers in the North, and the emergence of an increasingly radical class of black leaders strongly opposed to the accommodationist politics associated with the late Booker T. Washington and his disciples. Unproven but courageous, Garvey immersed himself in Harlem's vibrant political world. Still committed to the cause of Jamaican education, Garvey worked to raise the necessary funds for his proposed industrial school. Towards this end, he conducted his first public lecture at St. Mark's Church on the evening of May 9. Years after Garvey's death, black Harlem celebrated the West Indian as one of the most dynamic speakers of the New Negro era, but according to Wilfred A. Domingo, Garvey's first address was less than stellar:

> Shaking like an aspen leaf and with a tremor in his voice he started to deliver his oration. He hadn't gone very far when the audience began to vent its disgust by whistling and hooting. You can easily imagine the sorry figure and the pitiable spectacle the poor discomfited orator presented. He looked around in affright and pulling a manuscript from his pocket began to read. The more he read the greater was the din created by the audience . . . From all sides of the small hall came shouts of "Sit down," "Shut up," "Away with him," interspersed with catcalls and ear-splitting whistles. While this was going on one of the musicians, a Porto Rican [sic], calmly lit his cigarette from a flame not two feet from the speaker. During all of this the orator made desperate efforts to speak and then even his steel nerve snapped. He was near the edge of the stage which is about 3 feet from the floor and suddenly he began to sway backwards and forwards. Before any one in the audience could help him he fell from off the stage and lay prostrate on the floor.[18]

Still confident after his disastrous performance at St. Marks, Garvey embarked on a year-long speaking tour which included thirty-eight states.[19] Lecturing in St. Louis, Detroit, Cleveland, Cincinnati, Nashville, Louisville, and Atlanta, among other cities, Garvey gained a greater appreciation for the achievements of black Americans.[20] "I have seen Negro banks in Washington and Chicago," he recounted in an article in *Champion*, "stores, cafes, restaurants, theaters and real estate agencies that fill my heart with joy to realize that at one center of Negrodom, at least, the people of the race have sufficient pride to do things for themselves."[21] A widely traveled man who had observed the condition of blacks in the West Indies, Central and South America, and Western Europe, Garvey viewed the American Negro as more advanced than blacks in other parts of the world. "Let not the American Negro be misled," he opined, "he occupies the best position among all Negroes up to the present time."[22] Thoroughly impressed by the women and men who welcomed him into their churches, social clubs, and private homes, he returned to New York with a renewed vigor.

Success had eluded Garvey during his first few months in New York, but his popularity soared after returning from his speaking tour. Shortly after a spectacular performance at the inaugural meeting of Hubert Harrison's Liberty League of Negro Americans, Garvey started holding weekly meetings in Lafayette Hall, which drew a significant number of West Indian immigrants and recent black arrivals from the Jim Crow South.[23] Encouraged by local blacks' enthusiastic response to his lectures, Garvey switched the UNIA's base of operations from Kingston, Jamaica to New York City.

Foremost on the mind of UNIA followers in Jamaica had been the formation of an industrial school along the lines of Tuskegee Institute, but after incorporating the New York chapter of the UNIA on June 20, 1918, Garvey's political concerns shifted from educational reform to the development of black-owned enterprises and the removal of white colonialists from continental Africa. "We have to prepare against the hard times of the future," he routinely reminded his followers in New York, "and the best way we can do that is by strengthening our present economic position."[24] To improve the material existence of African-descended peoples in various parts of the world, Garvey organized the Black Star Line Steamship Corporation (BSL) in the summer of 1919. An undercapitalized venture greatly dependent upon the disposable income of the upper strata of the black working class, the BSL functioned as the cornerstone of the UNIA's ambitious plans to create an integrated community of consumers, workers, and business owners equipped with the necessary capital, expertise, work ethic, and vision to improve blacks' economic position globally. "We want an exceptionally good passenger service," Garvey informed potential shareholders, "so that in the event of any economic setback in this Western Hemisphere, we will be able through our own ships of the Black Star Line, to transport our people in the United States of America, the West Indies, and anywhere else to new industrial fields and thereby enable them to make a satisfactory livelihood."[25] Specifically targeting working-class blacks in his advertisements for the line, Garvey sold BSL shares at five dollars a piece.[26] Thanks largely to the generous contributions of blacks in New

York City, Philadelphia, Newport News, Virginia, and Colon, Panama, the BSL acquired its first ship, the SS *Yarmouth*, on November 5, 1919.

Soon after Garvey launched the BSL, he revealed plans to establish a UNIA colony in the West African country of Liberia. The political freedom of blacks in the United States, the Caribbean, and Central and South America, Garvey routinely insisted, depended upon their connection to an independent nation-state in Africa with the diasporic sensibility and political leverage in international affairs to provide protection to African-descended peoples scattered across the globe. Neither voter registration campaigns nor lobbying for the passage of anti-lynching bills would secure American blacks' their citizenship rights. "The white man," Garvey explained, "will only respect your rights constitutionally as a citizen of this country, when you have some government behind you. When you can compel a nation to respect your rights because of your connection with some government that is sufficiently strong to support you, then and only then will you be respected."[27] None of the nation-states in Africa possessed the political power to aggressively defend the rights of African-descended peoples, but Garvey cast his eyes on the nominally independent, black republic of Liberia, which, in his opinion, had the potential to develop into a world power.[28] Sending UNIA delegations to Liberia's capital city, Monrovia, in 1920, 1921, and 1924, Garvey labored earnestly to convince the Liberian government to set aside portions of its unoccupied land for UNIA settlers.[29]

Opponents of the UNIA dismissed Garvey's political goals as unattainable, but more than one million blacks in the United States believed otherwise.[30] His call for racial self-determination struck a responsive chord in the hearts and minds of West Indians and African Americans not only in the urban North, but also in the South.

GARVEYISM PENETRATES THE JIM CROW SOUTH

In many ways, the Southern political landscape was ripe for the UNIA. Several World War I developments—the urbanization and proletarianization of an increasing number of Southern blacks, the influx of West Indians into the South Florida area, rising militancy among black workers, and the heightened expectations which accompanied the black community's participation in and support of World War I—created an atmosphere where an organization led by a charismatic leader who preached the virtues of economic self-reliance, black internationalism, and race pride was certain to find a receptive audience. Observing revolutionary activities in Ireland, Russia, Hungary, and other places around the world, many black Southerners prepared for the end of the long era of white domination over African peoples. "We have been under the white people's control long enough," T.C. Glashen, president of the UNIA in Key West, Florida, complained. "The time has come for us to strike, and all of us Negroes must let the world know that we are a power, strong, and ready to defend our rights. If we can't succeed with words, we will use other methods, and never mind what happens. " "If blood is needed," he reasoned, "let it be shared. We fought to help this and other countries to be free, so let's fight to free ourselves."[31]

Cognizant of the rising black militancy in the South, Garvey and other officials of the UNIA labored to transform the fervor of the New Negro spirit into a mass-based movement for racial redemption and economic advancement. Supremely confident in his organization's ability to win the hearts of black Southerners, Garvey viewed the white South's vitriolic racism as beneficial rather than detrimental to the organization's efforts in the region. Central to the rising racial consciousness in black America, Garvey believed, was the perversity and intensity of white racism in the South. "If we had not been lynched and jim-crowed," Garvey remarked to a group of black New Orleaneans, "we would have never awakened and started a Republic of Africa."[32] Seeing race consciousness as directly linked to the intensity of white racism, Garvey anticipated success in the country's most racially repressive region.

To rally black Southerners around his political program, Garvey embarked on several tours of the South between 1918 and 1924.[33] Three months after the UNIA's incorporation in New York City in the fall of 1918, he traveled to coastal Virginia for the purpose of organizing workers in the cities of Newport News, Norfolk, and Portsmouth.[34] A critical center of black proletarian insurgency during and immediately after World War I, Virginia had been the site of numerous labor battles between African American workers and white capitalists. Moved by Garvey's Pan-African vision, black Virginians hurriedly organized UNIA branches and divisions in Norfolk, Newport News, and Portsmouth. Contributing to the early success of the UNIA's most popular venture, the Black Star Line, Virginians purchased thousands of dollars worth of BSL stock during the line's first year of existence. "Our people in Virginia," Garvey editorialized in the *Negro World*, "are doing most splendidly their part to help this Corporation fly the colors of the Negro on the high sea."[35] Sharing in many of the organization's achievements, black Virginians also participated in the UNIA's historic International Convention of the Negro Peoples of the World, held in New York during the summer of 1920. Visible at all of the plenary sessions, Virginian delegates assisted in writing the convention's *Declaration of the Rights of the Negro Peoples of the World*, recounted their struggles against racism and class exploitation, and detailed their efforts to strengthen the movement's presence in their respective communities.

Enthused over the UNIA's achievements in Virginia, Garvey pushed for greater influence in other areas of the South. Early in 1921, he dispatched some of his most effective recruiters—Reverend James Walker Hood Eason, Adrian Johnson, Arnold S. Cummings, George Tait, Jacob Slappey, and J.D. Brooks—to Georgia, Louisiana, Tennessee, North Carolina, and Arkansas. Few UNIA organizers, if any, navigated the Southern political terrain more effectively than James Eason. An Easton, North Carolina native who had attended Livingstone College and Hood Theological Seminary, Eason was very familiar with the political culture of the South. Such familiarity proved useful during his organizing efforts in North Carolina and Georgia. Working with local leaders in Georgia, Eason not only organized 17 chapters in the southwest portion of the state but he also revitalized struggling ones. Stopping through Brunswick, Georgia in the spring of 1921, Eason discovered a stagnant division with members who rarely paid dues, sparsely attended meetings, and had limited knowledge of the basic principles of the movement. Staying in the city for a week, Eason raised the division's membership to seven hundred persons, sold more than two hundred dollars worth of stock in the Black Star Line, and generated much excitement about the organization's Liberian Colonization program.[36] Similar advances were being made in the city of Winston Salem, North Carolina, where Arnold Cummings was also advancing the program of the UNIA. Late in September of 1921, Garvey ordered the New York-based activist to initiate a massive membership drive in Winston Salem. Cognizant of the large number of black, industrial workers employed at various tobacco factories in the area, Garvey had identified the manufacturing city as a fertile recruiting ground for the UNIA. Staying with the local chapter from October until February, Cummings traveled from church to church, spreading the message of Garveyism. Field representative Cummings, one Winston Salem leader informed the Parent Body, "is laboring hard in order to set the aims and objects of the association before the Negro population of the city. He has been delivering addresses since his arrival in the city."[37] Such hard labor proved beneficial for the organization, but the time away from home put a tremendous strain on Parent Body recruiters and their families. Fortunately for Garvey and others committed to building the UNIA in the South, many UNIA recruiters absented themselves from their family and friends for prolonged periods of time, courageously braved the virulent racism of the region, and shamelessly proselytized the gospel of Garveyism.

Winning the South required serious commitment not only from UNIA officials and recruiters in New York, but also from women and men who lived in the region. No discussion of the UNIA's expansion would be complete with acknowledgement of Alaida Robertson's critical work during the early twenties.[38] A masterful recruiter responsible for the formation of the New Orleans UNIA in the fall of 1920, Robertson organized chapters in Louisiana, Georgia, and Mississippi. Thoroughly impressed by Robertson's organizing work in New Orleans, Marcus Garvey in the fall of 1921 appointed the talented woman to the position of UNIA organizer for the state of Georgia. This position required extensive travel to the state's rural and urban centers, carried an enormous amount of responsibility, and included a weekly salary of fifteen dollars. A former resident of Bluefield, Nicaragua who had migrated to New Orleans in 1910, Robertson was more than equipped to provide Southerners with a first-hand account of the global exploitation of African-descended peoples in general and working-class blacks in particular. The young woman's intellectual vigor, quick wit, and charismatic presence left an indelible impression on many of her associates not only in Georgia but other Southern states. "She impresses all with whom come in contact with her fine personality," J.W. Lee, president of the Gulfport, Mississippi UNIA, wrote after Robertson delivered an inspiring address to UNIA supporters in his city.[39] Thanks to Robertson and countless other organizers' arduous and brave work, the UNIA had a strong base in the South.

Skillful recruiters definitely contributed to the spectacular growth of the UNIA in the South, but the importance of the *Negro World* in Garveyism's rising popularity should not be ignored.[40] A superbly edited weekly sold at poolrooms, dance halls, convenience stores, and beauty shops across the region, the *Negro World* introduced thousands of women and men to the UNIA, provided detailed information on the association's various programs, and cultivated a diasporic sensibility among many black Southerners.[41] Not surprising given Parent Body organizers' almost exclusive focus on the urban centers of the South, the *Negro World* was most responsible for the movement's expansion in rural Dixie. "It is impossible to say," M. Harrold of Blackton, Arkansas explained, "how much we learn from the *Negro World*. There are so many things that we would never know or understand if we did not see it there."[42] A thirty-seven year old native of Mississippi, Ashley Miller, echoed Harrold's sentiments: "I have awakened to African redemption. I did not know anything about trying to build a government until I subscribed to the *Negro World* two years ago. And I found it, so to speak, a good foundation to build on."[43] Seriously committed to the UNIA, *Negro World* subscribers worked hard to put the weekly in the hands of as many rural blacks as possible. "I received some subscription blanks some time ago," Queenie Suddith of Sunflower, Mississippi informed readers of the *Negro World*, "and I sure gave them all out to my best friends."[44] To spread Garvey's political message and agenda, Southern Garveyites not only distributed the *Negro World*, but they also organized vibrant UNIA divisions which embodied the organization's spirit of black solidarity, economic self-sufficiency, and race pride.

Fully functioning UNIA divisions existed in almost every major city in the southern United States. Striving to create a vibrant movement at the grassroots level, Garveyites in several locales purchased their own Liberty Halls, developed a variety of community service projects, and even launched their own economic cooperatives. Very attentive to the needs of their local communities, Southern Garveyites provided financial assistance to many in need of monetary support, fed and clothed the hungry, and offered medical services to the community. Even smaller divisions in the South implemented many, though definitely not all, of the programs found in the larger locals. Consider the work of the Winston Salem UNIA. A manufacturing city with a black population of twenty one thousand, Winston Salem possessed the largest concentration of Garveyites in North Carolina. The Winston Salem UNIA had only two hundred dues-paying members, but the division provided a wide range of social services for black working people. Quite serious about its image in the local black community, the UNIA division in Winston-Salem organized an employment bureau, an adult night school, a charity department, and a free legal service.[45]

All across the urban South, UNIA branches and divisions not only provided invaluable social services, but also functioned as centers of black art and culture. Southern Garveyites worked earnestly to transform the segregated spaces of their urban environment into liberated zones where black women and men effectively countered many of the negative stereotypes regarding individuals of African descent, developed and displayed their artistic talents, and temporarily escaped the rigors and pressures of everyday life. UNIA followers, it should be noted, did not view cultural activity as a substitute for political mobilization; rather, creative art, in their opinion, functioned as a tool to inspire people to work toward social change. Fully aware of the political potential of culture, Garveyites in the urban South relied on artistic expressions to generate interest in the movement, familiarize folks with the basic principles of the UNIA, and create a sense of unity between diverse groups. Very early, Southern Garveyites identified music as an effective medium through which they could spread their message of racial uplift and empowerment to their respective communities. More concerned about content than form, UNIA musicians articulated the organization's agenda through spirituals, jazz tunes, blues numbers, and choral arrangements. Songs such as *On with the Fight Negroes, I Am A Stranger Here, Africa Is My Home, O'Africa Awaken,* and *Somebody Knows It's Garvey* directly expressed the nationalistic aims and objectives of the organization.[46] Typically, UNIA music centered on five interrelated themes: race pride, the need for black unity across international lines, the pernicious effects of global white supremacy on African descended peoples, the rank-and-file's devotion to Marcus Garvey, and African redemption. Music constituted an important vehicle for political expression, but Southern Garveyites also articulated their frustrations, political desires, and collective ambitions through drama, poetry, and street celebrations.

Far away from Harlem, the geographical center of the New Negro Renaissance, Southern Garveyites created a thriving cultural world in which the humanity of black people was defended, promoted, and affirmed. UNIA locals endowed black Southerners with a sense of self-confidence and inner security, race pride, and collective purpose. Under the oppressive system of Jim Crow, African Americans endured daily assaults on their humanity and dignity, but inside the walls of their Liberty Halls, Southern Garveyites discovered, if only momentarily, a safe space for retreat, healing, and resistance.

OPPOSITION TO THE SOUTHERN WING OF THE UNIA

Needless to say, the UNIA significantly enriched the lives of thousands of black Southerners, but not everyone enthused over the UNIA's success in the region. Vigorous opposition to the movement erupted in various corners of the South. Writing to the United States' Attorney General Harry Daugherty in the spring of 1921, George Washington of Key West, Florida expressed concern over the organization's growing popularity among black Bahamians in the South Florida city. "These people," Washington complained, "are displaying a red, black and green flag; this they hoist on a mast at their meetings, and each of them are wearing in the lapels of their coats an emblem of their flag and going around preaching to other Negroes that it is the only flag that they honor."[47] Viewing the organization as a threat to local and national security, Washington urged Daughtery to "send to this city at once some government investigators in order that they may run down these West Indie [sic] aliens that are connected with this organization as they are fomenting a lot of unrest amongst ignorant Negroes in this city against our government."[48] Not at all oblivious to the critical role of the *Negro World* in the growth of the UNIA, many whites sought to prevent the paper's circulation in the South. "Such literature," C.B. Treadway of Cocoa Beach, Florida complained to Bureau of Investigation Chief Frank Burke, "is causing a great deal of unrest among the Negroes in this section and particularly those Negroes who are trying to find some grievance against the white people."[49] Sharing many of Treadway's concerns, R.J. Watkins of Fort Smith, Arkansas was particularly worried about the *Negro World's* impact on younger blacks. "There is no danger," Watkins informed federal agent E.J. Kerwin "immediate or otherwise from our old time darkey but from the present younger crowd."[50] Convinced that the continued distribution of the black nationalist weekly would "cause riots, revolutions, rebellions and finally chaos," W.W. Bailey of Nashville, Tennessee urged the Postmaster General, Albert Bureleson, to ban the sale and distribution of the *Negro World*.[51] Frequently white Southerners suggested that the further spread of the *Negro World* and the UNIA would push black women and men to violent revolt, but Garveyism's penetration below the Mason-Dixon Line provoked violence from the white rather than black populace.

Violent attacks on UNIA followers occurred in Dallas, Texas, Fort Smith, Arkansas, Miami, Florida, New Orleans, Louisiana, Charlotte, North Carolina, and Chattanooga, Tennessee. A group of Klansmen in Dallas, for example, kidnapped UNIA organizer R.B. Mosley, brutally beat him, and then ordered the Garveyite "to get out of town and to stay out."[52] Troubled by the UNIA's growing popularity among black workers, Commissioner Bryan of the Chattanooga Police Department (CPD) ordered a raid on the local division in the summer of 1927.[53] Late Thursday night, on August 4, the CPD raided the local Liberty Hall where approximately one hundred blacks had gathered for a mass meeting. Tearing down the back door of the division's meeting place, the officers opened fire on the division's paramilitary group, the Universal African Legion (UAL). To protect themselves, several AUL men fired back at law enforcement officials. Amazingly, despite the close range in which the CPD and the AUL fired shots at each other, only five people—two police officers and three Garveyites—were seriously wounded. [54]

The following day, law enforcement officials indiscriminately rounded up several UNIA followers for questioning as well as arrested Ira Johnson, Emory Bailey, James Jackson, and Louis Moore for attempted murder.[55] Convinced that the UNIA fanned the flames of revolt in the black community, the Chattanooga Police Department banned the UNIA and all of its auxiliary groups. The CPD's ban baffled the organization's leaders. "The Universal Negro Improvement Association [in] Chattanooga," Minton Milyard explained to his comrades across the country, "has never committed a single discredible act, it has always obeyed the law; it has never created any disturbance of any kind."[56] One of the more powerful leaders in the Parent Body, William Ware, the president of the Cincinnati division and personal representative of Marcus Garvey, discussed the possibility of testing the constitutionality of the city's ban of the UNIA, but all of the movement's defense funds were devoted to providing legal assistance for the four Chattanooga Garveyites charged with attempted murder.[57] Not equipped with the financial resources necessary to legally fight the city's ban on the UNIA, the Parent Body conceded defeat in Chattanooga.

Overcoming white opposition was not the only challenge for UNIA followers in the South. Writing off the Garvey movement as a negative influence on black workers, many African American ministers, business persons, newspaper editors, and community activists openly declared war on the UNIA. Talking to the *Chattanooga Times* about the local UNIA, Reverend C.K. Brown of Wiley Memorial Church derided the "ignorant class of laborers" who buttressed the UNIA. Stating that there "was no place for such an order in this city or country," Brown approved all efforts to break up the organization. [58] Even though many of these leaders routinely stressed the need for group unity, they had no problem working with law enforcement officials in their efforts to undermine the UNIA. In fact, one Bureau of Investigation agent in Florida identified "the better class of the negro element" as law enforcement officials' most valuable ally in their fight against the organization. [59] Undeterred by those who sought to undermine the movement, many Southern Garveyites remained firmly committed to the UNIA. Staying committed was not always easy for those diehards who not only endured external attacks but lived in communities where interest in the movement was either lukewarm or episodic.

A comprehensive analysis of Southern Garveyism must also acknowledge those areas where the UNIA struggled to build consistent support over a sustained period of time. Strong opposition from the white community, lack of interest, the predominance of accommodationist and liberal integrationist strategies, and ineffective leadership posed serious problems for UNIA organizers in Nashville, Tennessee, Birmingham, Alabama, Charlotte, North Carolina, among other locales. Troubled divisions and branches in these cities often endured periods of prolonged inactivity when leaders proved unable to collect dues, failed to communicate with the Parent Body in New York, and stopped holding weekly meetings. Let's look briefly at the chronically unstable Nashville UNIA. Only a few months after its formation in the fall of 1920, the Nashville UNIA started to lose many of its members as a result of its leadership's ineffectiveness and fiscal dishonesty. The local division was thrown into a serious crisis in the spring of 1921 when the president stole funds from its treasury and moved to another city. "Chaos," one Garveyite noted, "covered the association." [60] Frustrated with the dishonest practices of the division's leaders, hundreds of women and men fled the organization, cancelled their subscriptions to the *Negro World*, and ceased communication with the Parent Body. To revitalize the troubled Nashville UNIA, Garvey assigned George Tait to the Nashville chapter in the fall of 1921. Canvassing the black community, Tait stopped by the homes of former UNIA members and assured them of the Parent Body's resolve to bring stability and order to the local branch. Slowly but surely, folks returned to the division. Within weeks of his arrival, the Nashville UNIA held a general election for new leaders, secured a new building for the division's weekly meetings, and added seventy persons to its membership rolls. Satisfied with his work in Nashville, Tait headed back to New York. The Parent Body representative predicted continued growth for the division, but this would not be the case. Never able to sustain support for any prolonged period of time, the Nashville UNIA collapsed in 1923. This drama of stagnation, renewal, and then collapse plagued other UNIA branches.

CONCLUSION

Clearly, there were areas in the South where the UNIA's performance fell below the Parent Body's expectations, but for the most part, the organization performed remarkably below the Mason-Dixon Line. Faithful UNIA followers could be found in Atlanta, Georgia, Charleston, South Carolina, Natchez, Mississippi, Mobile, Alabama, Key West, Florida, New Orleans, Richmond, Virginia, Fort Smith, Arkansas, Raleigh and Greensboro, North Carolina, among other urban and rural locales in the South. Firmly entrenched as the dominant expression of Pan-African nationalism, Garveyism had a profound impact on black social and cultural life in many rural areas, small towns, and major cities across Dixie. No matter the frequency in which critics condemned the Garvey movement, the UNIA enriched the social, political, and economic life of many Southern black communities. "Every Sabbath at 4 p.m.," one Winston Salem Garveyite boasted, "Liberty Hall is crowded to the utmost capacity."[61] Offering much more than social entertainment on Sunday afternoons, the UNIA widened its members' circle of friends and political comrades, assisted women and men in their time of financial, medical, and even spiritual need, and strengthened ordinary folks' confidence in their ability to effectuate social change. More than previously recognized, the UNIA also provided invaluable political training for several women and men who would become important civil, labor, and human rights activists after the demise of the UNIA. A noted civil rights activist who served as the director of the Mississippi Voter Project during the transformative sixties, Randolph Blackwell gained his earliest political training in the Greensboro, North Carolina UNIA. Fair housing activist, Marie-Ann Adker's profound love and concern for the black poor was nurtured inside the walls of the Miami UNIA's Liberty Hall. Queen Mother Audley Moore learned the importance of Pan-African unity, grassroots activism, and black solidarity as a member of the New Orleans UNIA during the early twenties. Southern Garveyism may not have dismantled white supremacy, but it definitely transformed many of its victims.

A major aim of this chapter has been to demonstrate the UNIA's influence in the South, but there are many questions about the Garvey movement's presence in the region which still need to be answered. How can we think with more specificity about the ways in which the UNIA and its programs changed over time and place? To what degree did the philosophical tenets of Garveyism correspond to the lived experiences and political traditions of local people in the south? How successful were local Garveyites in their efforts to draw from the strengths as well as transcend the weaknesses of an international movement whose leaders occasionally ignored the importance of local issues? To what extent did local contexts and circumstances lead black Southerners to question some of Garvey's political activities? How much did Garveyites involve themselves in the social and political struggles of their local community? Turning to New Orleans, Louisiana, Miami, Florida, and then Norfolk and Newport News, Virginia, the next three chapters seek to answer these and other complex questions.

Chapter Two

"We Are Constantly on the Firing Line": The Garvey Movement in New Orleans, 1920–1935

> I must say that the World War has furnished the common people of the Negro race with much food for thought. They are thinking as they never thought before. They are beginning to realize that they must think and act for themselves. The Negroes have been so often deceived by their supposed leaders that they have reached a conclusion not to be fooled any longer. During the World War they were told by those who represented selfish interests that the war would make the world safe for Democracy. Have such promises benefited the Negro? With the ending of war practically all the liberties of the Negro people have been taken away. Big business and professional politicians, supported by faithless clergy, have fastened the shackles upon the Negro people, and we continue to suffer under the terms of our deceptors [sic]. Now we are seeking relief and freedom through the principles of the Universal Negro Improvement Association, sponsored by Marcus Garvey.
>
> John B. Cary, New Orleans Garveyite[1]

Nowhere in the Jim Crow South was the influence of the Garvey movement more visible than New Orleans. A permanent fixture in the black community between 1920 and 1935, the Universal Negro Improvement Association (UNIA) achieved widespread popularity in the Crescent City.[2] Working-class blacks, in particular, responded enthusiastically to the UNIA's valiant efforts to transform dispersed Africans into a diasporan community with the collective power to advance those political and economic issues of significance to black people across the globe. Garveyites in New Orleans financially supported the many economic ventures of the UNIA, rallied around Marcus Garvey during his legal problems, and performed an indispensable role in the growth of the UNIA in other parts of the South. Of course, local blacks did not passively wait for directives to be handed down to them by the central office in New York City; nor did they acquiesce to all of the Parent Body's demands. Strong believers in the principle of self-determination, they asserted their right to develop their own locally-based programs, maintain autonomy over the movement at the local level, and determine for themselves their relationship with other racial advocacy organizations. Their assertiveness and independence enabled them to have a far wider influence in New Orleans than would have been possible had their politics been limited to the strategies and programs emanating from the association's headquarters in Harlem.

Tracing the history of the New Orleans UNIA from its meteoric rise in the early 1920s to its decline during the 1930s, this chapter documents local Garveyites' struggle to negotiate their dual identity as participants in a diasporan movement and members of a local community with its own problems and traditions. Opening with an analysis of the developmental stages of the Garvey movement in New Orleans, the first half of the chapter focuses on the UNIA's presence in the Crescent City between 1920 and 1924. It explores why the association achieved so much success among black workers and evaluates the complex relationship between New Orleans Garveyites and the Parent Body in New York. Exploring an issue seldom discussed in Garvey studies, the second half of the chapter details Garveyites' response to some of the major problems in black New Orleans: the maldistribution of wealth, inadequate health facilities and medical services, political inequality, and limited educational opportunities for the black working class. Serious in their commitment to improve the quality of life for blacks in New Orleans, Garveyite women and men established a community health clinic, offered a wide array of social service programs, and built an adult night school which provided leadership training courses for working-class blacks. Such activities legitimized the UNIA in the eyes of many people who initially dismissed Garveyism as an utopian movement totally detached from the lives and quotidian concerns of ordinary people.

THE FOUNDING OF THE NEW ORLEANS UNIA

An extraordinary activist, Alaida Robertson organized the New Orleans Division (NOD) of the UNIA at her home on October 12, 1920.[3] Over the next four months, Robertson familiarized her family and friends with the UNIA's political objectives, secured the division's charter from the Parent Body, and supervised the election of NOD officers. As was the case with most branches in the South, the NOD's leadership cadre was solidly working class. A porter at a local bank, Alaida's husband Sylvester served as the division's president.[4] Occupying the important office of division treasurer was Mamie Reason. Smart, outspoken, and extremely confident, the forty-year-old domestic worker supervised the NOD's financial affairs and provided exemplary leadership during her two-year tenure with the organization. These women and men worked earnestly to build up support for the division, but New Orleans would not become a major stronghold of the movement until the Parent Body assigned its own recruiter to the city in early 1921.

Not particularly satisfied with the UNIA's progress in the South's largest city, Marcus Garvey dispatched Adrian Johnson to New Orleans in February of 1921 for the purpose of launching an extensive membership drive there. Fully supported by the NOD's founding members, the charismatic Barbadian achieved substantial success in the Crescent City.[5] A strong believer in the need for local divisions to develop amicable relationships with other organizations in the community, Johnson conducted a series of lectures at various churches, fraternal orders, and mutual aid societies. At these meetings, he encouraged local leaders to view each other as co-workers in the struggle for black liberation rather than rivals battling for members. "It was time that all Negro organizations," Johnson explained to members of the West Indian Seaman Association, "should take up the fight for a better day for the race by uniting their efforts, without losing their specific identity."[6]

Johnson's approach was extremely successful. Five months after his arrival, the number of dues-paying members in the NOD swelled from a modest seventy persons to twenty-five hundred people.[7] The growing popularity of the UNIA in the Crescent City was a source of pride for UNIA officials in New York. "When I arrived in New Orleans," Marcus Garvey proudly told his Harlem followers during the summer of 1921, "I found hundreds of loyal men—good men and true men—who were waiting to receive me through the great work that Johnson had done preparatory [sic] to my getting there."[8] Quickly establishing itself as one of the major centers of American Garveyism, New Orleans claimed more than four thousand UNIA members by the fall of 1921.[9]

Central to the Garvey movement's popularity among black New Orleaneans was its unapologetic embrace of Pan-African nationalism. New Orleans native Millie Charles, the granddaughter of a domestic worker who proudly "donated her dollar to the Garvey movement," attributed her grandmother's support of the UNIA to its emphasis on black pride and African repatriation: "The whole movement back to Africa was what intrigued her, and that kind of philosophy caught her fancy because she always had a sense of curiosity about where she came from and that sort of thing. Even though she worked for whites, she was a proud black woman."[10] Situating the UNIA's popularity within the larger context of the city's cultural and spatial dynamics, particularly the social divide between 'American blacks,' who lived in uptown New Orleans, and Creoles of Color, who resided in the downtown section of the city, Charles was not at all surprised by the movement's success: "It was kind of easy that a movement such as that would take hold, especially uptown. I'm not talking about downtown."[11] A preexisting race consciousness, forged out of their encounter with Creoles of Color and virulent white racism, in Charles' opinion, disposed many uptown blacks toward the racialism of the UNIA. To be sure, not all uptown blacks pledged their support to the organization, but Marcus Garvey's promotion of race pride resonated deeply in the hearts and minds of many who struggled to navigate the city's complex color line.[12] His exaltation of blackness and celebration of those physical characteristics—dark skin, broad noses, and full lips—that were often portrayed as aesthetically unattractive in white popular culture—appealed to many blacks who wanted to counter pejorative images of blackness, develop a more positive self-concept, and publicly articulate their own standards of beauty. One group of women in the New Orleans UNIA welcomed the opportunity to celebrate their race pride:

> We are not members of the Negro 400 of New Orleans, composed of the class spending their time imitating the rich white, with card parties, eating parties, and studying Spanish so as to be able to pass for anything but a Negro. We are not ashamed of the race to which we belong and we feel sure that God made black skin and kinky hair because He desired to express Himself in that type as well as in any other.[13]

Opponents of the UNIA frequently offered such sentiments as evidence of the ways in which Garvey implanted a spirit of divisiveness in black America, but these women's ideas about race, color, and caste were formulated in the cultural, spatial, and racial politics of their local context.[14]

THE SEARCH FOR ECONOMIC INDEPENDECE

Organizers found local blacks receptive not only to the UNIA's emphasis on race pride but also to its economic agenda. The year 1921 witnessed an outpouring of local support for the UNIA's two major economic ventures: the Black Star Line Steamship Company (BSL) and the Liberian Construction Loan (LCL). "Investment in the Black Star Line," Garvey guaranteed potential shareholders, "will be the safest value in the hands of Negroes in another few years."[15] Very soon, Garvey also promised, the BSL would be in a position to employ thousands of women and men. Such promises appealed to many struggling black workers. Substantial decline in the volume of foreign trade, production cutbacks, and business closures had resulted in decreased employment opportunities and severe wage reductions for black and white laborers in New Orleans' leading industries. The elections of John M. Parker to the Louisiana governorship and Andrew McShane as mayor of New Orleans provided additional ammunition to the city's commercial elite in their ongoing war with labor over wage increases, the work process, and the use of non-union employees.[16] Increasingly uncertain about their economic future, working women and men in the NOD rallied behind the central office's economic initiatives. The NOD's treasurer, Mamie Reason, earned little money as a domestic worker and part-time seamstress, yet she purchased twenty-five dollars worth of shares in the BSL and encouraged her comrades to stand behind the steamship company with their "financial guns."[17] Viewing the development of racially-based economic cooperatives as an effective way to improve their material condition during the economically depressed years of the early twenties, New Orleans Garveyites invested nearly eight thousand dollars worth of BSL stock and Liberian Construction Loan bonds between January and July of 1921.[18]

Enormously supportive of the UNIA's pan-African vision, black New Orleaneans also displayed tremendous interest in Garvey's efforts to establish an African paradise in Liberia. Not all UNIA followers desired to leave the United States, despite their extreme hatred of white supremacy, but most supported the association's efforts to establish an autonomous colony of industrial workers and farmers in the independent, black republic of Liberia. Negotiations between the UNIA and the Liberian government officially opened in May of 1920 when Elie Garcia, Auditor General of the UNIA, traveled to Monrovia.[19] Garcia aimed to familiarize government officials with the UNIA's program, communicate the association's willingness to provide the virtually bankrupt country with developmental funds, and ascertain the government's position on black emigration to the country. Quite desirous of foreign investment, Liberia's Secretary of State, Edwin Barclay, assured Garcia of the government's plan to "afford the Association every facility legally possible in effectuating in Liberia, industry, agriculture, and business projects."[20] Encouraged by Barclay's promise of assistance, the Parent Body launched the Liberian Construction Loan in the fall of 1920. "The purpose of this loan," Garvey editorialized in the pages of the *Negro World*, "is to start construction work in Liberia, where colleges, universities, industrial plants, and railroad tracks will be erected; where men will be sent to make roads, and where artisans and craftsmen will be sent to develop industries."[21] An industrially developed Liberia, Garvey insisted, would "offer great opportunities to all men and women who desire to start off independently to build fortunes for themselves and their families."[22]

Starting anew in Liberia captured the attention of many black New Orleaneans, especially those who harbored serious doubts about the attainability of freedom in the United States. "The time has come," Elenore Brown declared at the NOD's anniversary celebration in October of 1921, "for every nation to look to his own country for a place of safety." "We are looking forward to our home, 'Africa for the Africans,'" the domestic worker exulted. "We are proud of the Messiah that God has sent us, and the message of the Great Marcus Garvey is come home; where we shall no longer possess the name nigger, but we shall be a nation respected by the world."[23] Substantially influenced by the symbolism and rhetoric of nineteenth-century Ethiopianism, Brown and other black New Orleaneans viewed the organization's activities in Liberia as an integral part of God's design for the redemption of Africa and its people.[24]

A labor activist who looked favorably upon the UNIA's projects, T.A. Robinson was equally excited about the association's work in Liberia. One of many in the movement who simultaneously supported the black nationalist politics of the UNIA and the class-based agenda of the labor movement, Robinson, an officer for the New Orleans Black Longshoremen's Association, served as vice-president of the NOD in 1921.[25] Buoyed by the prospects of a better economic life in Liberia, he expressed tremendous confidence in the UNIA's ability to achieve its goals of economic independence and African redemption. "This movement," Robinson predicted, "will grow commercially and financially in such an extent that the day may not be far distant that we may return to Africa, our home and we will be able to exclaim, we came, we see, and we are satisfied."[26] Unfortunately for those who pinned their hopes on the UNIA's business ventures and colonization scheme, Robinson's prediction for future success proved widely off the mark.

A recurring conundrum in the early history of the New Orleans UNIA was the vast difference between NOD followers' expectations of the movement and UNIA realities. Take for example the organization's Liberian program. While visiting the Crescent City in the summer of 1921, Garvey spoke confidently of the association's African plans: "We are going to put up in Africa a Negro government—the greatest government on earth—to protect the Negroes from the world." "If we get power," he assured an audience of two thousand black New Orleaneans, "the whites will respect us. There will be no more race prejudice because you will be too powerful."[27] Interestingly enough, at the time of this speech, the UNIA's negotiations with the Liberian government were at a virtual standstill. Worried that their association with the Garvey movement would negatively impact their already fragile relationship with the governments of England, the United States, and

France, Liberian officials, especially President Charles King, backed away from their initial endorsement of the UNIA's colonization plans.

Further complicating matters for the association was the collapse of the Black Star Line, which had been in negotiation with the US Shipping Company for the purchase of a ship that would provide inexpensive transportation for those who desired to migrate to Liberia.[28] The BSL had been a valiant attempt at economic integration and co-operation between African descended peoples, but the line and its officers were not equipped with the financial capital, nautical experience, political connections, and business contacts necessary to survive, let alone turn a profit, during the postwar recession. The line's vessels, the SS *Yarmouth,* SS *Kanawha,* and SS *Shadyside,* were constantly plagued with mechanical problems and financial difficulties.[29] Over the period between 1918 and 1922, UNIA supporters across the globe contributed close to one million dollars towards the BSL's purchases and operations, but more money was needed to succeed in the shipping industry. On February 20, 1922, Elie Garcia, treasurer of the Black Star Line, ordered all divisions to cease the sale of BSL shares. Several weeks later, on April 1, *The Negro World* announced the line's suspension.[30]

Notwithstanding the BSL's critical role in building support for the movement, the UNIA remained quite popular among black New Orleaneans. Stopping through New Orleans during a nationwide speaking tour in June, Garvey drew thousands of women and men to his nightly lectures at the Negro Longshoremen Hall. Small turnouts in several West Coast cities had dampened Garvey's spirits, but the enthusiasm of NOD supporters was a source of inspiration for a man who in recent months had probably endured more setbacks than any leader in black America. Only five months before his visit to New Orleans, Garvey had been arrested on the charge of using the federal mails to defraud. Vilified as the most dangerous Negro in America, Garvey had been under the watchful eye of the Justice Department for nearly three years. Leading the investigation was the recently appointed head of the General Intelligence Division, J. Edgar Hoover. A man who would wreak havoc on the black liberation struggle for more than fifty years, Hoover viewed the removal of Marcus Garvey from the United States as integral to the maintenance of the status quo. Employing several black informants—Dr. Arthur Craig, James Wormley Jones, William A. Bailey, Herbert S. Boulin, and James Edward, Hoover hoped to uncover criminal activity within the leadership ranks of the UNIA. Writing Hoover's assistant, George F. Ruch, in 1919, Bureau of Investigation Chief Frank Burke was forthright regarding the agency's motives and intentions:

As Marcus Garvey is an alien, it is particularly desirous of establishing sufficient evidence against him to warrant the institution of deportation proceedings. Any advocation [sic] by him of opposition to law and order would be ground upon which to have a request for deportation. Therefore, kindly have the informant give particular attention to this phase of the question.

Sloppy accounting and promotional practices by Black Star Line officials eventually provided an opening for Hoover and the Justice Department. The department's examination of UNIA records revealed the promotion and sale of stock in a non-existent ship, which according to advertisements purportedly planned to transport prospective colonists to Africa. To the delight of the UNIA's black and white opponents, Marcus Garvey and three other UNIA officials were arrested on mail fraud charges on January 12, 1922. Fourteen days later, a New York grand jury indicted Garvey and his associates on twelve counts of using the federal mails to defraud potential BSL stockholders.

Even with all of Garvey's legal struggles, black New Orleaneans remained firmly committed to the UNIA and its embattled leader. Needless to say, their devotion to Garvey and the UNIA's pan-African agenda confounded some of the movement's critics. Why would black New Orleaneans remain supportive of an organization whose most important venture had failed, and a leader who had been arrested for mail fraud and vilified by the black press as a fiscally dishonest lunatic? Was their continued support of Garvey and the UNIA proof of their fanaticism and irrationality? The answer to these question lies in the evolution of the New Orleans UNIA from an ad hoc organization comprised of BSL investors and emigrationists into a vibrant social institution providing its members with a much needed outlet for self-expression and leadership development.

THE SOCIAL WORLD OF NEW ORLEANS GARVEYISM

To understand why the NOD stayed afloat after the BSL's demise and Garvey's legal struggles, it is necessary to explore the social world of the UNIA. No one can deny the fact that the association's entrepreneurial pursuits and colonization endeavors brought many into the NOD, but women and men also derived much enjoyment from the organization's social activities, mass meetings, late night dances, and excursions to nearby towns. Visiting New Orleans in the summer of 1921, Garvey himself was impressed by the numerous cultural activities offered by the local division. "We had a time in New Orleans," Garvey boasted after returning from the city in 1921. "I spoke for two nights in the National Park in New Orleans, where we had thousands of people. They had a large plaza and they had midnight dances and other amusements. They had music, and they danced all night."[31] An important cultural center, the New Orleans UNIA provided an institutional space where men and women could listen and dance to the syncopated sounds of the division's jazz band, showcase their various talents, debate the meaning of human existence, laugh and cry over life's joys and pains, and criticize the ways of white folks and the black elite without fear of reprisal. Within the confines of the division's Liberty Hall, women and men communed with individuals who shared their political viewpoints, cultural tastes, and working-class status. UNIA functions offered members of the community temporary respite from the drudgery of work, household duties, parental responsibilities, and the general demands of everyday life.

Of course, the movement's appeal and importance extended beyond its leisurely pleasures. Systematically denied the opportunity to participate in the mainstream political culture, New Orleans Garveyites also appreciated the opportunity to further develop their leadership skills. Few organizations offered more leadership opportunities to working blacks than the NOD. Education, occupation, and social background were not determining factors in an individual's eligibility for office in the New Orleans UNIA. Washerwomen, carpenters, cooks, longshoremen, porters, and common laborers held positions of authority within the division and its various auxiliaries.[32] A glimpse at the occupations of those women and men voted to the division's top offices in March of 1922 proves this point. T.A. Robinson, a longshoreman, was elected president; Mamie Reason, a domestic worker, was chosen as the division's treasurer; and Hiram Workman, a screwman on the local docks, served as the assistant-general secretary. Marshall Crawford, a plasterer, and Myrtle Baptiste, another domestic worker, headed the Committee on Boards and Auxiliaries, while Theresa Fleming, a cook, was elected to the Black Cross Nurses Committee.[33]

Occupying leadership positions within the movement was a source of pride for many laboring people in New Orleans and elsewhere. No one recognized this more than the noted sociologist E. Franklin Frazier. "A Negro might be a porter during the day, taking his orders from white men," Frazier perceptively noted in a 1926 article in *The Nation*, "but he was an officer in the black army when it assembled at night in Liberty Hall." Quenching black workers' thirst for "self-magnification," the UNIA with its numerous offices "made the Negro an important person in his immediate environment."[34] Surely, NOD supporters appreciated public recognition, but their embrace of the UNIA was rooted in much larger class dynamics within the black community.

A central motif in black nationalist thought was and continues to be the belief in a corporate racial interest; however, NOD supporters did not necessarily see their concerns as the same as those of the black elite. Nor did many believe that the black elite always had a genuine interest in the welfare of black laboring people. "The common people of the Negro Race," John B. Cary, one of the division's more popular leaders, once remarked, "have suffered great oppression; their real defenders have been very few."[35] Frustrated with the direction of many of the leading racial advocacy groups in black America, Cary and other workers searched for (and created) new institutional spaces where their concerns could be articulated, their voices heard, their ideas taken seriously, and their leadership skills developed in order to ensure a better future for themselves and their children. For many, the NOD constituted such a political space. Thus, despite Garvey's legal difficulties, the failure of the Black Star Line, and the stagnation of the Liberian scheme, the UNIA continued to hold considerable value for many blacks in the Crescent City.

Speaking in New York after visiting New Orleans two months after the BSL's suspension, Garvey applauded the NOD's commitment to the movement: "The Universal Negro Improvement Association is anchored forever, as far as its dignity and honor are concerned, in the city of New Orleans."[36] Later that year however, Garvey's faith in the NOD's loyalty to his vision and leadership abilities would be greatly tested. Dramatic developments at the UNIA's Third Annual International Convention of Negro Peoples of the World in August not only severely destabilized the NOD but strained the relationship between New Orleans Garveyites and Parent Body officials in New York.

A MOVEMENT IN CRISIS: NEW ORLEANS GARVEYISM, THE 1922 CONVENTION, AND THE EASON CONTROVERSY

No convention in the history of the UNIA was more tumultuous than the 1922 gathering. Delegates fiercely debated the role of women in the UNIA, the reorganization of the Black Star Line, Garvey's recent rendezvous with the Ku Klux Klan (KKK)[37], and the sending of an UNIA delegation to the League of Nations' Peace Conference in Geneva.[38] The constant bickering among delegates at the convention deeply troubled two New Orleans Garveyites, T.A. Robinson and Mamie Reason. Nothing disappointed them more than Garvey's strong criticism of Reverend James Eason, the second highest ranking official in the organization.[39] Only three months before the convention, Eason had spent considerable time in New Orleans working with local leaders and giving well-received lectures at various venues in the city. "With his eloquence," one New Orleans Garveyite remarked, Eason "left the members of the association in this section with greater courage to press on until there shall be established a great culture and empire upon the continent of Africa."[40] Loved by many women and men in New Orleans and elsewhere, Eason found himself under serious attack for his recent criticism of Marcus Garvey's management of the BSL affairs, overtures to the KKK, and general leadership style.

Several days into the UNIA's 1922 convention, Thomas Anderson, Garvey's right hand man, accused Reverend Eason of not only participating in an inside conspiracy to undermine the influence of the UNIA's chief officer, but engaging in sexually inappropriate behavior during his recruiting trips across the country.[41] Two weeks after Anderson's startling allegations, Garvey, who had delayed his public response to the developing controversy, recommended the impeachment and expulsion of the 'American Leader' on grounds of financial dishonesty, conduct detrimental to the interests of the association, disloyalty to the UNIA, and violation of "the constitution of the UNIA against the instructions, advice, and warning not only of the president but of the entire Executive Council."[42] Three days after his recommendations, Garvey received enough votes from the convention's delegates to expel Eason. Not everyone, however, was happy with Eason's expulsion. "Nearly every American," Bureau of Investigation agent Andrew M. Battle noted in his remarks on the convention's most heated controversy, "is against the management of Garvey except those who are getting salaries from him."[43] Surely, there was a degree of exaggeration in Battle's statement, but Garvey's authoritarian style disturbed many delegates in attendance.

Garvey's handling of the Eason affair, the impeachment of two other members of the central office's executive council, Adrian Johnson and J.D. Gibson, and the general disorder at the convention proved too much for T.A. Robinson, the New Orleans UNIA's president. "To follow Garvey any longer," he bluntly told *New York Age* correspondent W.P. Thomas, "one would have to be a rank fool." "The New Orleans branch of the U.N.I.A.," Robinson reasoned, "will either quit following Garvey and the outrageous methods he employs in handling the affairs of the association and line up behind some other fairer man who will organize a similar movement in opposition to it, or split up in factions aiming at the same end for the good of the Negro people of the United States."[44] Equally upset with Garvey's behavior was Mamie Reason, who after the close of the convention immediately scheduled a meeting with the UNIA leader in order to voice her concerns. Not one to suppress her opinions, the NOD's outspoken treasurer charged Garvey with "ruining the colored race," and vowed to return to New Orleans to tell the people "exactly what he stood for."[45] Firing back at Reason, Garvey called her a "traitor to the cause" and summarily dismissed her from the organization.[46]

Seldom did organizational conflicts at the association's headquarters in New York City disrupt the internal politics of local divisions, especially those in the South, but the Eason drama had huge implications for Garveyites in New Orleans. Shortly after returning to New Orleans, Mamie Reason and T.A. Robinson rallied behind the Reverend Eason, who, after his expulsion from the UNIA, formed an off-shoot group called the Universal Negro Alliance (UNA). Spurred on by his previous success in the city and the endorsement of Reason and Robinson, Eason trekked to New Orleans in early October for the purpose of building a local branch of his new organization.[47] Conducting several lectures at local churches, Eason blasted Garvey for his handling of the organization's administrative and financial affairs.[48] Unwilling to respond to the very serious charges leveled against him at the UNIA convention, the ex-Garveyite attributed his expulsion from the UNIA to his criticism of Garvey's fiscal mishaps rather than any wrongdoing on his part: "I could today be still in the Garvey group of the Universal Negro Improvement Association and the Factories Corporation, and other concerns if I would only keep my mouth shut, not come out publicly and call upon Mr. Garvey, as I have done, as I intend to continue to do, to tell the truth to the members of the association as to what has become of the nearly one million dollars collected from the members, with absolutely nothing to show for it."[49]

Over the next two weeks, Eason continued his attacks on Garvey and the UNIA's program. Instead of raising money to send delegates to Liberia, Eason insisted, the organization needed to focus its attention on securing civil rights for blacks in the United States.[50] His comments ruffled the feathers of many NOD supporters, especially those who recognized the sudden change in the minister's position on several key issues. Writing in the pages of the *Negro World,* the NOD's secretary, Lemansley Hall, dismissed Eason as an opportunist whose recent criticism against the UNIA contradicted his previous pronouncements:

> When this person was getting paid by the Universal Negro Improvement Association he said it was the greatest thing in the world for Negroes, and he wanted his bones to be taken to Africa to rest in the soil of his motherland, but since we have cut off his salary he is saying that the Back to Africa movement is a wild scheme . . . A man who contradicts himself any time he wants to is a dangerous character, and we have no respect for him.[51]

All of the chaos surrounding the Garvey-Eason feud had a discernable impact on the New Orleans UNIA. Fragmentary evidence suggests the division lost approximately one thousand members in the months following the 1922 convention.

Further contributing to the NOD's problems was the arrival of one of Garvey's most loyal and volatile followers: Esau Ramus. Few, if any, Garveyites disliked James Eason more than Ramus. The former third-vice-president of the Philadelphia UNIA and leader of its paramilitary group, the Universal African Legions, had been arrested in Philadelphia for inciting a riot and carrying a deadly weapon at one of Eason's rallies in late September.[52] Not long after Ramus' arrest, Garvey informed NOD officials of his desire to send the firebrand to New Orleans. "Mr. Ramus," Garvey explained to the NOD's executive secretary, William Phillips, in a letter dated November 10, "is going to live in New Orleans and desires to work in the interest of the Association. I ask that you be good enough to help him in whatsoever way you can to serve the Association. I will appreciate it very much if you can find some organizing work for him to do for the division in going around enlisting new members and helping generally."[53] Recruiting new members for the NOD, however, was not particularly appealing to the newcomer. Not at all interested in canvassing the community for potential recruits, Ramus set out to organize a police force, which would engage in acts of intimidation against Garvey's critics, specifically Eason.

Support for Ramus' plans was extremely low. "Mr. Ramus is endeavoring to organize a police and secret service unit," William Phillips immediately notified Enid Lamos, Garvey's secretary, "but it has not met the approval of the majority of officers."[54] Phillips failed to offer any explanation for NOD leaders' objection to Ramus's plans, but quite possibility, New Orleans Garveyites' negative response was related to their growing disgust at the Parent Body's increased involvement in local affairs. Only two weeks before dispatching Ramus to the Crescent City, Garvey had infuriated some of the NOD's rank and file by refusing to allow the division to hold a general election after the Parent Body declared all of the division's offices vacant.[55] Quite possibly, those frustrated with the Parent Body latest actions interpreted Ramus' arrival as evidence of the central office's desire to gain complete control over the movement. Another factor possibly contributing to the community's lukewarm response to Ramus was his ethnicity. Several weeks before Ramus' arrival, some NOD members had reacted rather negatively to news of the central office's plans to send "another West Indian Negro to live on the people of New Orleans."[56] Offended by the complaints emerging out of the NOD, Thomas Anderson, assistant secretary-general of the central office, chastised the division for "making distinction between the various groups of black people when we are classed by the world, and even high Heaven as Negroes. We do not wish to hear any such a thing again from the New Orleans Division." An infuriated Anderson denied any intention on the part of the central office to dispatch another West Indian to New Orleans. "If another man is sent to the New Orleans division," he informed Phillips in his fiery letter, "he will not be a West Indian."[57]

Less than a month after Anderson's letter reached New Orleans, Ramus, a native of St. Kitts, arrived in the city. Only a handful of folks in the division welcomed him. Seemingly undisturbed by New Orleans Garveyites' opposition to Ramus' arrival, Garvey's personal secretary, Enid Lamos, ordered the division's executive secretary to do "all you can to assist Mr. Ramus as it is our desire that he continue work in the cause of the Association as he has always done."[58] Immediately, Ramus started monitoring and intimidating Garvey's New Orleans critics. His endeavors interested around thirty to forty men in the division, who held several meetings at the home of Constantine Dyer.[59] One of the founding members of the division, Dyer had befriended Ramus, rented a room in his home to the new arrival, and encouraged him to continue with his plans.[60] Not the least bit concerned about protecting the NOD's relatively positive image in the black community, Ramus and his cohort focused their attention on Reverend Eason, whom they heckled during his lectures at various churches in the city.

Sadly, the conflict between Ramus' cohort and Eason turned violent on the evening of January 1, 1923. Late in December, a group of black New Orleaneans invited Eason to participate in New Year's Day ceremonies at St. John's Baptist Church.[61] The minister was scheduled to testify for the federal government in its mail fraud case against Garvey and three other BSL officials on January 4, but he accepted his colleagues' invitation. Eason arrived in New Orleans on December 31 and delivered a stirring address on New Year's Day. Unfortunately, the joyous occasion would be disrupted by violence. Shortly after his speech, Eason, who had endured verbal abuse and physical threats in the months following his departure from the UNIA, was brutally gunned down outside St. John's Baptist Church.[62] A small group accompanying the minister chased three men in the general vicinity of where the shots had been fired, but the assailants fled the scene of the crime. Seriously wounded, Eason was immediately rushed to Charity Hospital where he was listed in serious but stable condition. The following morning in an interview with Captain George Reed of the NOPD, the minister mustered up enough strength to implicate the UNIA in the shooting. "I am positive," he purportedly informed Reed, "that my assailants were acting on the instructions to put me out of the way and prevent my appearing as a court witness against Garvey at the trial."[63] Two days after his interview with Reed, Eason, a key witness in the federal government's mail fraud case against Garvey, took a turn for the worse and died of internal injuries.[64]

LOCAL RESPONSE TO EASON'S DEATH

Law enforcement officials immediately arrested Constantine Dyer and William Shakespeare, a painter who rented a room in Dyer's home, on murder charges.[65] Then, NOPD officers issued a warrant for the arrest of Esau Ramus, but their attempts to locate him proved futile. A petty criminal well experienced in running from the law, Ramus had already boarded a train for New York City, where he met with Garvey and allegedly received sixty dollars to flee to Detroit.[66] Interpreting the recent turn of events as further evidence of Garvey's negative impact on black America, several civil rights leaders encouraged the federal government to press ahead in its mail fraud case against the UNIA leader.[67] Coupled with calls for Garvey's deportation was a strong critique of the activities of the New Orleans branch. "The assassination," W.P. Thomas editorialized in the *New York Age*, "has not helped the Garvey movement in this city. It has instead, hurt it very much among the people of the race and in the eyes of the law."[68] Several leaders condemned the UNIA for its alleged role in the murder of James Eason. Leading the attack on the UNIA, the Black Baptist Ministerial Alliance vowed to help law enforcement officials "bring the guilty to the bar of justice."[69] Likewise, the New Orleans NAACP's president, George Lucas, who had been very supportive of the NOD during its first year of existence, agreed to work with the NOPD. "New Orleans citizens are aroused about the affairs and will take a special interest in seeing that these parties are punished," Lucas told Robert Bagnall, the director of NAACP branches. "Mr. Eason was very well thought of here," he continued, "and in November he delivered a strong address to the NAACP."[70]

Outrage on the part of the black leadership class was the least of the NOD's concerns. Far more serious were the attacks on the division by the Bureau of Investigation and the New Orleans Police Department (NOPD). Worried about the strength of the federal government's mail fraud case against Garvey, the Justice Department hoped to acquire incriminating evidence connecting the UNIA leader with Eason's murder. If Garvey was acquitted at his upcoming trial, he would then be tried for involvement in his former associate's murder. Caught in the middle of the US government's war against Garvey, New Orleans Garveyites endured constant harassment from the Bureau of Investigation and local law enforcement officials.[71] Three weeks after Eason's death, the Justice Department raided a NOD meeting, seized membership lists and other records, and arrested nine of the division's leaders.[72] Another raid followed on Sunday night, February 11. Twenty police officers, armed with guns and tear gas, broke up the division's meeting at the Negro Longshoremen Hall, ordered everyone to evacuate the building, and confiscated additional documents. Then, according to detailed reports in the *Negro World* and the local newspaper, *The Times Picayune*, the NOPD arrested ten of the division's leaders, including two women, on the charges of inciting a riot and unlawful assembly. The arrestees were hauled off to a nearby jail, where they were held until an unidentified white attorney from Woodwell and Woodwell law firm posted their bond.[73]

Coupled with the disruption brought about by the NOPD's raids, the NOD struggled to overcome growing internal strife over the Parent Body's increased involvement in the local division's affairs. An increasingly vocal group of New Orleans Garveyites complained about their loss of autonomy.[74] Local blacks expressed disgust not only at Garvey's decision to place the selection of all of the New Orleans division officers in the hands of the central office, but also at the Parent Body's choice of leaders for the division.[75] Not much was said about the central office's selection of Lawrence Davis, a steel worker, as the division's treasurer, and John Cary, a carpenter, as president of the Board of Trustees, but according to *New York Age* reporter W.P. Thomas, the appointment of Isaiah Chambers, a teacher at a local public school, as president, and Isaac Whitmore, a professor at New Orleans College, as vice-president enraged more than a few of the division's members.[76] Their frustration with the central office's latest moves was understandable. Neither Chambers nor Whitmore had any experience with the organization.[77] So why given the fragile state of the NOD did the Parent Body appoint two unproven leaders to positions of authority? W.P. Thomas viewed the appointment of Whitmore and Chambers to the positions of president and vice-president as a strategic attempt to "give the organization here standing and respectability." Some NOD loyalists believed the move represented the "shutting of the door of hope to all but college men for leadership and the filling of high offices in the U.N.I.A."[78] Anger over the Parent Body's recent actions gripped many division's members. "See what they have done to men we elected to office in the organization," one disgruntled Garveyite complained in the *New York Age*, "just put them aside and put college men over us . . . why it looks as if government in the Garvey movement is not to be of the people, by the people, for the people, but to be a government of the people by the classes for the classes."[79]

A major stronghold of Southern Garveyism, the New Orleans UNIA was in serious trouble. The ingredients for organizational collapse—internal dissension, leadership changes, external opposition, and legal problems—were plentiful, but loyal Garveyites were determined to fight for the survival of the NOD, despite all of the drama of the past six months. One group of women in a fiery letter of protest to Mayor McShane declared the division's innocence with regards to the Eason murder, criticized the NOPD for their unwarranted raids, and affirmed their commitment to the division. "The Universal Negro Improvement Association is our church, our clubhouse, our theatre, our fraternal order and our school, and we will never forsake it while we live; neither will our men forsake it."[80] Signed by Grace Davis, Effie Hathaway, and Florence Watterhouse, the letter, which was published in the *Negro World*, communicated fully UNIA followers' unwavering loyalty to the movement.

Surviving the storm would not be easy. Securing Constantine Dyer's and William Shakespeare's release from prison exacted an incredible emotional and financial burden on the NOD.[81] One week after Dyer and Shakespeare's arrest for Eason's murder, Garvey ordered William Phillips, who had been appointed the division's executive secretary in the summer of 1921, to retain legal services for the two men. Friendly with Eason before and even after his expulsion from the UNIA, Phillips initially hesitated to provide legal assistance for the men, but local supporters demanded their fellow Garveyites have adequate legal counsel. A reputable white lawyer named Loys Charbonnet, who would provide legal counsel for the NAACP in its successful fight against a local housing segregation ordinance, represented Dyer and Shakespeare at their trial in late March. After deliberating for twelve hours, the jury found the two men guilty on the compromise charge of manslaughter and sentenced them to eighteen to twenty years in prison. A year after the jury's decision, however, the Louisiana State Supreme Court ordered a new trial. According to the Supreme Court, Judge Eschesabal's refusal to allow Loys Charbonnet to present evidence linking Esau Ramus to the murder was unconstitutional. At the retrial, Charbonnet, according to the *New Orleans Picayune*, "intensively and industrially by many devious ways and turns, centered his efforts on getting before the jury the links in a chain of alibi evidence that Esau Ramus killed Eason." Thanks to his service, Dyer and Shakespeare were acquitted on August 3, 1924.

THE REVITALIZATION OF A MOVEMENT

Vindicated in court, the New Orleans UNIA now aimed to increase its membership rolls, strengthen its treasury and, most importantly, regain the respect of local people. Slowly but surely the division started to show signs of recovery between 1924 and 1926. An aggressive membership campaign resulted in the addition of five hundred persons to the NOD's membership rolls by the spring of 1925. "The New Orleans Division is growing by leaps and bounds," Philip Clinton, the executive secretary of the division, reported in the *Negro World*, "and bids fair to rival some of her Northern sisters in membership."[82]

Contributing to the division's revitalization during this period was the central office's announcement of the formation of the Black Cross Navigation and Trading Company (BCNTC) in April of 1924.[83] The BCNTC's first ship, Garvey announced, would carry "the first organized group of colonists to Liberia," but other ships would also be purchased to develop "a trade relationship between Negroes of Africa, the United States of America, the West Indies and South and Central America."[84] Critics questioned whether the BCNTC possessed the resources to survive in such a competitive market, but Garvey pointed out to his followers the many economic opportunities in Africa, the Caribbean, and the Americas. "There are hundreds of shiploads of cargo waiting for us in Africa, in the West Indies, [and in] South and Central America to convey back to the United States of America. Millions can be made for the race in the conveying of raw materials from one part of the world to the other, and the return to them of our finished products." Within a year, Garvey assured his supporters, the line would be in "a position to employ millions of our own people in America, West Indies, and Africa, thereby making our race industrially independent."[85] Five months after Garvey revealed his plans for the newly organized line to the UNIA's rank-and-file, BCNTC officials purchased the *General Goethels*, rechristened as the *Booker T. Washington*, for $100,000. Extremely supportive of the Parent Body's latest venture, New Orleans Garveyites rejoiced at the news of the organization's latest purchase.

Organizational controversies and legal battles had consumed the energy of NOD supporters between 1922 and 1924, but Garvey's announcement of his plans to reenter the shipping industry enabled UNIA followers in the Crescent City and elsewhere to refocus their attention on the organization's principal agenda: building a strong Pan-African empire. Still committed to the idea of racial enterprise as an effective method of economic uplift, New Orleans Garveyites contributed roughly one thousand dollars towards the purchase of the line.[86] Feeling more should be done to respond to the economic needs of black Southerners, black New Orleaneans also initiated discussions about the formation of regionally-based cooperatives. Speaking to delegates at the UNIA's Fourth Annual Convention in 1924, Isaac Chambers, president of the NOD at the time, suggested that the central office and local divisions organize cooperatives to empower black sharecroppers in the rural South. These cooperatives, according to Chambers, would be the means "through which cotton and other produce of the Negro could be bought, thereby preventing white capitalists from obtaining this produce at a ridiculously low figure, as was the case at present to the undoing of the farmer."[87] Such an ambitious enterprise would have undoubtedly benefited farmers laboring under exploitative conditions in the South; unfortunately the New Orleans UNIA lacked the necessary funds to realize their economic dreams. To the disappointment of Garveyite women and men in the Crescent City, the New York office was also unable to realize its economic dream of operating a successful shipping company. Unable to attract much business, the *Booker T. Washington* was taken out of service in the summer of 1925 and sold at a fraction of its original cost in March 1926.

None of the division's reports published in the *Negro World* provide detailed insight on local blacks' response to the BCNTC's demise, but the NOD's activities after the line's collapse suggest that supporters had not given up on the movement. An optimistic Philip Clinton (the New Orleans UNIA's executive secretary) reported that the division was determined to "retain its prestige as leader of the South."[88] To achieve this end, the division in the summer of 1926 launched an ambitious membership drive, which netted the division two hundred additional members by the end of the year. Another achievement of 1926 was the division's purchase of a new building in uptown New Orleans. Ever since the division's formative years, its meetings had been held at the Negro Longshoremen Hall, but in late 1926, the *Negro World* announced the division's acquisition of a building on South Rampart Street. A hotspot during the 1920s, Rampart Street, according to Florence Borders, a New Orleans native who grew up in the uptown section of the city during the twenties, "was considered one of the prime black streets; jazz, parades, everything you associated with black culture was probably centered on Rampart Street."[89] The UNIA was located in the center of the city's black cultural world, and very soon, the sights and sounds of the Garvey movement blended in well with those of the nearby juke joints and clubs. Late Saturday night, one could stroll into Liberty Hall and enjoy the syncopated sounds of the division's jazz band, the Holy Ghost Band, which served as the house band for a local jazz club in uptown.[90] A gathering place for many musicians, Liberty Hall also featured such local acts as Freddie "Harmonica Genius" Small[91], the Rang Tang Boys, the Crescent Brass Band, the Banner Orchestra, and the Lions Original Jazz Band.[92] Of course, the new Liberty Hall offered much more than cultural entertainment. An important institutional space where working-class blacks engaged in lengthy discussions on important political issues, Liberty Hall also featured locally-based and nationally respected leaders who delivered moving lectures on the most effective solutions to the problem of global white supremacy, the future of the UNIA, the political role of the black church, and the strategic limitations of the civil rights leadership.

Visiting New Orleans in the spring of 1927, J.A. Craigen, Garvey's personal representative and president of the Detroit UNIA, was impressed by the NOD's progress, its vitality, and its commitment to the Parent Body. "A more faithful group of Negroes," Craigen noted, "cannot be found anywhere."[93] Carrying on the work of the Parent Body was important to New

Orleans Garveyites, but they also demonstrated a new resolve to have a more visible presence in their local community.

NEW ORLEANS GARVEYITES AND COMMUNITY ACTIVISM, 1927–1930

No public statement on a change in the division's policy was released, but during the second half of the 1920s, the NOD entered a new phase of engagement with local issues and regional concerns. The inability of the national office to develop a program of action enabled many divisions, including the NOD, to devote more of their time and resources to local issues.[94] Less focused on activities in New York, UNIA followers in New Orleans focused on problems— limited health care facilities, insufficient municipal and social services, and inadequate educational opportunities—of particular importance, though definitely not confined, to black New Orleans. To improve the quality of life for black New Orleaneans, Garveyites opened an adult night school, constructed a medical clinic in the back of their meeting hall, expanded the division's social welfare programs, and reached out to other racial advocacy organizations in uptown New Orleans. "Let us put far away from us," Garveyites pleaded with local activists, "those bits of prejudice and misunderstanding which have held us back for too long."[95] Verbal calls for racial solidarity, however, were not enough. To truly regain the respect of local organizations and activists, the division had to demonstrate its willingness to provide financial and moral support to racial advocacy groups in their fights against poverty, racial discrimination, and disfranchisement. Their opportunity would come in the spring of 1927 when various racial uplift and civil rights organizations responded to the physical and human devastation brought about by the Mississippi Flood.

The catastrophic Mississippi flood of 1927 inundated nearly thirty thousand square miles of land, cost two hundred and fourteen people their lives, and damaged more than two hundred million dollars worth of property. All of the Delta's residents struggled to rebound from the disaster, but the recovery process was particularly difficult for the region's black majority, forced to contend with white racism and violence. Unscrupulous planters sold free Red Cross supplies to dispossessed blacks who found themselves in greater indebtedness to the planter class; white mobs inflicted violence on many blacks attempting to flee the region; and the federal government turned a blind eye to the deplorable situation.[96] Leading spokespersons in black America not only challenged the federal government to ensure that black flood victims received their share of the available relief aid, they also pressured Northern politicians to put an end to the institution of peonage. Veteran journalist and editor of the *Negro World*, Timothy Thomas Fortune forcefully registered his complaint against the situation in the Mississippi Delta:

> The Mississippi flood showed the uplift agencies of the country, as well as the protective agencies of the Federal Government, that a system of slavery has grown up in the Mississippi River States which it is necessary to run down and root out. They now know and can have no excuse for not doing the work of correction, redress and protection which the victims call loudly for and are entitled to receive as a matter of constitutional right and as an act of human justice. The white employers of labor in the Southern States must not be allowed to develop another condition of Negro slavery which might grow into a cause for another bloody civil war.[97]

Saddened by the plight of their brothers and sisters affected by the flood, New Orleans set in motion a plan to provide assistance to flood victims in the Delta.[98] Leading the NOD's relief efforts was the Black Cross Nurses (BCN). An all-female auxiliary comprised of mostly laywomen and a few professional nurses, the BCN responded quickly to the crisis. Supervisor of the BCN at the time of the flood, Mrs. R.J. Wall handled the administrative and financial planning of the relief efforts. One of the few professionals in the NOD, Wall had worked extensively with her working-class sisters in the division on numerous community service projects. A nurse and superintendent of the New Orleans Colored Maternity Home, Wall possessed the skills, contacts, and experience necessary to effectively carry out the division's plans.[99] "The Black Cross Nurses are being prepared to do all in their power in assisting the needy community with necessaries for relief," S.E. Buchanan, the division's executive secretary, reported to readers of the *Negro World*.[100]

Women in the BCN drew on their experiences with other community organizations, but they also benefited immensely from the reservoir of knowledge acquired during their labors within the division.[101] Much more than the helpmates of the movement's male leaders, women in the NOD supervised meetings, held positions of authority, represented the division at the association's annual conventions in New York, and traveled to nearby towns and cities to mobilize support for the UNIA.[102] Skills acquired or further developed during these activities—handling internal conflict, writing letters, public speaking, learning the specific needs of certain locales, managing money, and so forth—proved invaluable when planning and executing a community service venture as challenging as their flood relief initiative.

Once the division formulated its stated objectives, Mrs. R.J. Wall immediately launched a fundraising drive within the NOD. Using the space allotted to the division in the *Negro World*, Wall appealed to the international community of UNIA supporters for assistance in the division's relief efforts in the Delta: "At this time we request the members of the Universal Negro Improvement Association the world over to know that thousands of its members, active, and otherwise, of the race are severely suffering from flood disasters along the Mississippi Valley. Critical conditions exist among our people. For humanity sake we are appealing to all of our brothers and sisters to help with food and money and whatever possible for the sufferers."[103] Responding rapidly to the NOD's call for assistance, Garveyites in Miami, Los Angeles, New York, and a host of other cities in the United States donated money, clothes, shoes, and other articles, all of which the BCN immediately distributed to families affected by the flood.

Fully aware of the ways in which membership in an international organization made their work at the regional level possible, NOD members expressed their appreciation to UNIA followers across the country for their financial support in a letter to the *Negro World*: "The New Orleans Division wishes to give thanks through the *Negro World* to the divisions and chapters throughout the United States who did what they could to help out the suffering of the Mississippi. Everything sent was distributed directly through the division and over three hundred people benefited. Those of the organization who helped will have our everlasting gratitude."[104] Such cooperative efforts did not simply alleviate the suffering of aid recipients, they strengthened New Orleans Garveyites' bond with UNIA followers in various parts of the United States.

Over the next few years, New Orleans Garveyites engaged in other activities which gained the respect of their comrades in other parts of the country, as well as non-UNIA members in their local community. To improve the quality of life for black women and men in uptown New Orleans, the NOD not only developed an impressive array of social programs; it also buttressed the work of other groups in the city. Symbolic of New Orleans Garveyites' willingness to pursue a course of action independent of the Parent Body in New York, the NOD even financially supported one of the New Orleans NAACP's legal cases. Standing on the front line in black New Orleans' perennial battle against white supremacy was the NAACP, which thrived under the guidance of George Lucas.[105] Walter White, executive secretary of the NAACP's national office, depended greatly upon the local branch for assistance in the association's fight to dismantle the social and legal foundations of white supremacy. According to historian Adam Fairclough, White's confidence in the New Orleans branch was well deserved:

The New Orleans NAACP scored some notable successes during its early years. In 1927 it achieved a legal triumph when the United States Supreme Court struck down the city ordinance establishing segregated residential areas. Three years later it hired a white lawyer to assist in the prosecution of Charles Guerand a white man who shot and killed a fourteen-year–old girl, Hattie McCray, who had resisted his sexual advances. In a courtroom hushed into stunned silence, an all-white jury found Guerand guilty—probably the first time that a white had been sentenced to death for the murder of a Negro.[106]

None of the NAACP's legal victories would have been possible without the financial assistance of local clubs, churches, mutual aid and benevolent societies, and civic organizations. Among the local groups donating money towards the litigation efforts of the NAACP was the New Orleans UNIA.

A remarkable leader who worked earnestly to unite the various factions within black New Orleans, Lucas enlisted the aid of local Garveyites during a drive to raise money for the attorney fees of a black sharecropper whose two daughters had been brutally murdered by a group of drunken white men in Eros, Louisiana, on Christmas Day, 1928.[107] Suspecting that "the conviction of these cold blooded murders could have a profoundly salutary effect not only upon Louisiana but throughout the South," Walter White ordered Lucas to initiate an intensive fundraising drive for the legal fees of the sharecropper.[108] One does not know the extent of White's knowledge of the internal politics of black New Orleans, but news of the UNIA's donation to the branch's defense fund probably surprised him. "Have received a few dollars from local sources" Lucas reported to White, "among which is a check for twenty dollars from the local Branch of the U.N.I.A., and they promise more help."[109] The significance of the NOD's contribution lies not in its monetary but symbolic value.

Supporting the NAACP in any form or fashion constituted treason in some UNIA circles.[110] Marcus Garvey despised the organization and many of its leaders. On numerous occasions, he dismissed the NAACP's political strategies as ineffective, even though he relied on its most popular tactics—litigation and petitions—in his personal struggles with the federal government.[111] Sounding markedly similar to the rabid segregationists of the Jim Crow South, Garvey accused NAACP leaders of teaching racial amalgamation and inter-marriage. "They would make it appear," the UNIA leader hissed, "that they are interested in the advancement of the Negro people of America, when in truth, they are but interested in the subjugation of certain types of the Negro race and the assimilation of as many of the race as possible in the white race."[112] Such venomous comments infuriated several

NAACP leaders. Countering Garvey's attacks against them, NAACP leaders lambasted the UNIA and his followers as ignorant racists who lacked the intelligence to meaningfully contribute to the black freedom struggle. Writing in the pages of the NAACP's mouthpiece, *The Crisis*, W.E.B. Du Bois dismissed Garvey as a "racist demagogue" who "easily throws ignorant and inexperienced people into orgies of response and generosity."[113] Sinking to a personal low, Robert Bagnall, director of branches for the NAACP, poked fun at Garvey's physical characteristics. In the *Messenger*, Bagnall vilified Garvey as a "Jamaican Negro of unmixed stock, squat, fat and sleek, with protruding jaws, and heavy jowls, small bright pig-like eyes and rather bull-dog face" always "devising new schemes to gain the money of poor ignorant Negroes."[114]

Occasionally, the animosity between the two organizations surfaced at the local level. Consider the battles between NAACP supporters and Garvey-ites in Key West during the early 1920s.[115] Envious of the UNIA's success in the city, NAACP leaders cooperated with local law enforcement officials in their efforts to destroy the UNIA division there. Fortunately, the NOD and the New Orleans NAACP, led by individuals who truly believed in the idea of racial cooperation, managed to achieve a peaceful coexistence in the Cres-cent City.[116] Not allowing the vicious battles between black nationalists and integrationists in New York to determine the ways in which they interacted with NAACP leaders in New Orleans, many NOD followers drew their own conclusions on the nation's most respected civil rights organization.[117] NOD leaders not only rallied behind the branch in its efforts to convict the white men in Eros, Louisiana; they also labored alongside the organization in vari-ous community relief projects during the depression years.

Even though the NOD financially backed the NAACP's litigation case in Eros and occasionally spoke out against the exclusion of blacks from the political process, New Orleans Garveyites never fully committed themselves to any organized effort to reverse Louisiana's racially discriminatory policies and laws. Instead, the division devoted most of its resources to the creation of black-controlled institutions and social programs designed to counter the deleterious effects of blacks' political powerlessness. Under the guidance of such able leaders as John Cary, Beulah McDonald, Mrs. R.J. Wall, Odella Spears, and Jay Peters, the local division granted financial assistance to those in need of monetary support, distributed food and clothing to the needy, constructed an adult night school, and offered medical services to the community. Such institutions and programs were designed not only to respond to the immediate social problems confronting black New Orleans, but to facilitate the creation of the ideal, modern Negro subject, intellectually and physically equipped to advance the UNIA's larger pan-African agenda.

THE OPENING OF THE UNIA FREE COMMUNITY MEDICAL CLINIC

Ensuring the perpetuation, integrity, and progress of the race was extremely important for Garveyite women and men. Frequently, Garveyites' discussions on racial survival and progress elicited controversial debates regarding miscegenation and the regulation of the black body. "Garveyites," Michele pointed out in *Righteous Propagation*, "could not realize any of their goals with out the actual biological perpetuation of the race. If the UNIA was to be successful in promoting—and ultimately creating—a strong, healthy nation, sexuality had to be monitored and controlled so that it benefited the race; if the nation were to be "black," Garveyites would need to enforce racial purity as well."[118] A few New Orleans Garveyites expressed interest in the association's racial purity projects and its anti-miscegenation rhetoric, but for the most part, their discussions on the possibility of racial extinction rarely broached the topic of miscegenation.[119] Living in a city where the black population had the highest morbidity and mortality rate in the country during much of the first half of the twentieth century led many concerned about the biological perpetuation of the race to focus their attention on the issue of health care.[120] Threatening the future of the race was not interracial, sex, in the opinion of many New Orleans Garveyites, but the infusion of diseases into a *body politic* disproportionately impacted by poverty and the unequal distribution of medical services. Of course, Garveyites were hardly alone in their concern about the health status of the black community.

Lively discourses on race and health disparities occurred throughout black and white New Orleans during the 1920s. Influenced by the pseudo-scientific scholarship of the leading eugenicists, New Orleans whites often cited African Americans' purported moral laxity, cultural backwardness, and unfitness for urban life as the principal causes for their health problems. Countering whites' racist claims, black activists attributed their communities' health problems to the limited medical facilities and health services available to the city's black population, the local government's unequal distribution of municipal services among the city's white and black populace, and politicians' general indifference to the medical needs of its impoverished residents (both white and black).[121] An unresponsive city government forced black activists to rely on their own resources to solve their health care issues. One of the many organizations placing the black community's health crisis at the top of its priority list during the 1920s was the New Orleans UNIA, which implemented several programs to fight against the community's climbing mortality and morbidity rate.

On January 21, 1928, the NOD announced plans to open up a medical clinic in the back of the division's 'Liberty Hall.' "Within the next few days," Lillie Jones, secretary of the NOD, proudly informed readers of the *Negro World*, "we shall open a first class-medical clinic for the poor of our community."[122] Nine months after the NOD publicized its plans, the UNIA Free Community Medical Clinic opened for service under much fanfare. Logan Horton, a young African American doctor in the city, directed the clinic and the Black Cross Nurses volunteered their services. Incredibly excited about their local work, New Orleans Garveyites were determined to provide first-rate service to uptown's poor blacks. "Courtesy and efficient care will always be given to everyone," division leaders promised the community."[123]

Community leaders showered local Garveyites with praise. An editorial in the *Louisiana Weekly*, the city's black newspaper, applauded the work of the NOD and challenged other organizations to follow in the division's footsteps: "Too much credit cannot be given to this organization for its forward step towards the uplift of fallen humanity. This city and State needs many such clinics to cope with the rising death rate of the colored group in this section."[124] A testament to the community's changing perception of the NOD, the *Louisiana Weekly's* laudatory editorial illustrates the extent to which the UNIA had become a respected institution in the black community. Four years prior, during the Eason controversy, few outside of the UNIA would have had anything positive to say about the local branch, but now, Garveyites received praise on the front page of the city's black weekly.[125]

Crucial to the success of the NOD's public health agenda was the service of Black Cross Nurses. In addition to working in the clinic, BCN disseminated information on disease prevention, promoted and observed National Negro Health Week, and sponsored informative exhibitions on diet, sanitation, and other disease preventive measures.[126] Occasionally, women convened weekend symposiums devoted exclusively to health care issues.[127] Like so many grassroots organizations, the NOD lacked the financial resources to provide the full range of health care services so desperately needed in the black community. Nonetheless, when one takes into account the limited funds of its working-class constituency and the lack of outside support in the form of white philanthropy, the division's work in the field of public health was quite impressive.

EDUCATING THE MASSES

Saving black bodies was an integral component of New Orleans Garvey-ites' political project; however, significant attention was also given to the development of powerful institutions and programs which would provide African American people with the intellectual foundation to be victorious in their struggles for political freedom, economic justice, and social equality. One of the proudest moments in the history of the New Orleans UNIA was the opening of its adult night school on October 21, 1928.[128] A permanent fixture in the division well into the New Deal years, the night school, which received a boost with the assignment of Works Progress Administration (WPA) teachers during the 1930s, offered classes in basic reading and writing skills.[129] Literacy classes were definitely needed in the Crescent City. Of the major southern cities with a population of more than 100,000, New Orleans ranked second in the percentage of blacks, aged ten or over, classified as illiterate.[130] Such statistics hardly troubled whites desirous of maintaining the status quo by any means necessary. Vigorously opposed to any potential catalyst for social change, municipal officials were indifferent and, at times, downright hostile to the cause of black education. Nothing revealed whites' hostility more than the Orleans Parish School Board's 1930 rejection of the Rosenwald Foundation's offer to build a black secondary industrial school in the city.[131] Convinced that educated blacks would try to obtain 'white jobs,' local politicians deemed it necessary to keep trade schools out of the black community.

Strong believers in the power of black education, Garveyites vowed to provide the necessary educational opportunities for African American children and adults. Teaching men, women, and children basic literacy skills, however, was only one component of the NOD's educational program. School instructors focused a significant amount of attention on leadership training and development. "A course in public speaking and leadership," according to Doris Busch, was offered for "those students whose abilities and fraternal and social connections warrant the need of the course."[132] One theme often stressed at the adult night school was the need for working-class people to construct their own solutions to societal problems. Leadership training and intellectual stimulation were not to be confined to the educated elite. "Everyone," Lucille Hawkins reminded members in an announcement for an upcoming lecture series during the division's 'Education Month,' "is expected to make a special study of race problems."[133]

Most of the instructors at the night school were affiliated with the NOD but local educators occasionally taught classes for the division. Garveyites invited high school teachers as well professors from two local black colleges, New Orleans College and Straight University, to participate in discussions about the strengths and weaknesses of the Garvey movement. One particular debate, for example, was structured around the following questions:

1. Is Garvey a Thief?

2. Is Garvey crazy?

3. Is Garvey a fake?

4. Is Garvey diplomatic?

5. How can Marcus Garvey get into Africa?

6. How can Negroes build for themselves a mighty nation?

7. Isn't the Negro's progress in the Western world a sufficient indication that he is going to enjoy equality with the white people within the next few years?

8. How does the U.N.I.A. propose to stop lynching?[134]

These types of questions, which division leaders drew in order to induce a lively dialogue between the visiting educators and NOD members, illustrate the willingness of movement supporters to engage in a critical analysis of the UNIA. Individuals with doubts about certain aspects of the organization's program or the leadership skills of Marcus Garvey were allowed to voice their opinions without fear of a physical or verbal lashing.[135] No topic was off limits. Lest we err on the side of idealism and distortion, everyone in the division did not take kindly to criticism of the association's work, but many welcomed the free exchange of ideas. Working people, in particular, appreciated the opportunity to discuss issues of importance to them, articulate their views on various racial matters, and engage in critical dialogue with others about the best way to uplift themselves.

Even though the night school directed much of its curriculum to the needs of adults, the division also created educational opportunities for the community's youth. NOD leaders placed tremendous value on the intergenerational transmission of knowledge and the preparation of young people for leadership roles within the UNIA. In keeping with the spirit of the times, Garveyite children learned a great deal about African and African American history.[136] Viewing the teaching of African and African American history as integral to their political project, New Orleans Garveyites displayed an unwavering commitment to expand their children's knowledge of black history and culture. To achieve this end, UNIA leaders in New Orleans organized an Educational Forum to "offer a chance to everyone to get an education on Negro life and history, with emphasis on Africa."[137] Similar to Afrocentric and African-centered scholars of today, Garveyites focused mainly on the Nile Valley civilizations of Egypt as well as the West African empires of Songhai, Mali, and Ghana.

Not an exclusive group, the NOD encouraged children and teenagers whose parents did not belong to the NOD to participate in its educational and cultural activities. A group of teenagers with the Progressive Youth Club, for example, showcased their knowledge of African American history by staging a "race conscious" play at one of the division's meetings.[138] Essay contests were frequently held to provide an opportunity for politically-conscious youngsters to express ideas not particularly welcomed in more formal academic settings. One contest, for example, offered a monetary prize to the high school student who wrote the best essay "on some phase of Negro life and activities."[139] By participating in a wide rage of educational activities, young children and teenagers gained invaluable lessons on race pride, group solidarity, and social responsibility.

The second half of the 1920s was an extremely productive time for the New Orleans UNIA, despite the chaotic state of the central office in New York. Fully integrated into the institutional structure of the local community, the NOD not only provided invaluable social services to local blacks, but the division solidified itself as an important cultural center in uptown New Orleans. Committed to providing uptown New Orleans with quality entertainment, NOD leaders organized barbeques, sponsored excursions to nearby towns and cities, held elaborate parades, and threw lively social dances. Few events drew larger crowds than the NOD's late night dances. A brief look at a *Negro World* report reveals the type of fun and excitement enjoyed by NOD party goers. "On Monday night," Lucille Hawkins proudly reported, "an exquisite Red, Black, and Green dance was given in the hall. The people were dressed in their gorgeous costumes, which made a beautiful sight as they danced under the reflection of the lights. The music was rendered by the Lions Aid and Pleasure Club Association. When the dancing was over everyone went away rejoicing over the jolly time they had."[140] The NOD with its dances, parades, and lively meetings significantly enriched the social lives of the many women and men who traveled in and out of Liberty Hall during the second half of the 1920s.

Garveyites in New Orleans were incredibly excited about their ability to provide the local community with much needed cultural and social services. Stagnation and internal conflict had plagued so many UNIA branches during the late 1920s, but the NOD had been able to accomplish many of its goals. Working women and men constructed an adult night school, built a health clinic, provided relief to blacks in and outside of New Orleans, and offered a safe space for wholesome entertainment. "Great things," Lucille Hawkins boasted to readers of the *Negro World*, "are being carried on by the New Negroes in this section. We are constantly on the firing line—the line that leads to true and lasting emancipation." [141] Garveyites vowed to continue their community service work in uptown New Orleans, but the onset of the Great Depression stalled the division's progress and led many to question the self-help strategies of the UNIA. Sadly, many of the social programs developed during the late 1920s had to be eliminated as the division struggled to withstand the hardships brought on by the depression.

THE GREAT DEPRESSION AND THE DECLINE OF NEW ORLEANS GARVEYISM

Few organizations were exempt from the hardships accompanying the Great Depression. "The general financial depression," NAACP leader George Lucas told Walter White in response to complaints about the New Orleans branch's failure to pay its dues to the central office, "put New Orleans in the worst fix ever witnessed, by even, the oldest citizens." [142] More dependent on the patronage of the black working class than many cared to admit, African American businesswomen and men suffered immensely from the economic crisis. "The depression quickly undermined even the modest progress that black business witnessed during the 1920s," historian Donald Devore writes in his analysis of New Orleans' black business community after the economic collapse. "In the six years between 1929 and 1935, 482 black owned retail stores went out of business, and the net sales of the remaining 289 stores totaled only 574,000 dollars." [143] One of the basic tenets of the UNIA had been the ability of racial enterprise to solve African Americans' economic problems, but the closing of hundreds of black businesses in New Orleans during the depression demonstrated vividly the limits of black entrepreneurship as a strategy for collective economic advancement.

Life was particularly difficult for black laborers. African Americans' unemployment rates hovered around ten percent in the first year of the depression and then skyrocketed to forty percent in 1931. Totally insensitive to their plight, Mayor T. Semmes Walmsley vowed to further circumscribe blacks' employment opportunities by enforcing the "twenty-three year-old ordinance that forbade the hiring of individuals who were not qualified voters by city contractors except when there was excess work and a lack of eligible labor."[144] Walmsley's proposal to reserve employment on publicly owned wharves to eligible voters never passed but he successfully restricted employment on an extensive bridge project to registered voters, which automatically eliminated most blacks because of their disfranchised status.

Struggling blacks had no recourse but to turn to their own institutions during these trying times. Municipal penuriousness coupled with private charities' indifference toward the needs of the black poor placed the tremendous burden for their care squarely on the shoulders of black organizations.[145] Since its formation, the NOD had dispensed aid to members during times of financial distress, but the number of people in need of monetary assistance increased exponentially during the depression years. In response, women in the division created a new auxiliary, the Sons and Daughters of Ethiopia, to coordinate more effectively the division's relief program. One of many auxiliaries within the division, the Sons and Daughters of Ethiopia, according to Doris Busch, served those who "through economic needs, usually demand some form of material aid from any organization with which they happen to be connected."[146] Leading the auxiliary in its relief efforts was Odella Spears, who monitored the distribution of food baskets and monetary assistance to the needy within the organization and in the general community.[147] No longer isolated in their community work, Garveyites also collaborated with other organizations during the depression years. The NOD was quite active in the Negro Division of the Community Chest (NDCC), which distributed thousands of dollars to unemployed black women and men. A brilliant leader who constantly encouraged the division to build coalitions with other organizations in the local community, Jay Peters, the president of the New Orleans division between 1927 and 1930, served on the executive committee of the NDCC.[148] One of the NOD's more popular presidents, Peters possessed an acute sensitivity to the cultural and internal politics of the local community and worked hard to develop a strong relationship with local leaders. His placement on the executive committee of the NDCC symbolized how much the NOD had become an integral component of the institutional life of the black community.[149]

The varied efforts of the NOD to alleviate the material suffering of the black poor were impressive indeed, but ineffective since the elevation of the masses of black folk out of their impoverished condition was impossible without systemic economic changes and political empowerment. NOD leaders tried their best to maintain a positive outlook as the depression wreaked havoc on the black community: "Despite the industrial handicap through which the colored folk in this section have been passing, the New

Orleans Division is yet keeping the fires of loyalty and progress burning," the division's secretary assured the central office.[150] Two years later, Odella Spears gave a less glowing report on the state of the NOD: "The people have very little or no money at all. The president, Mr. John Cary Jr., is doing his best to make the New Orleans Division what it used to be and to financially straighten her out with the Parent Body."[151] Unfortunately for those who had invested their time and financial resources into the NOD, the division would never return to "what it used to be." To be sure, a small group of committed nationalists carried the torch of Garveyism well into the sixties, but as was the case for most UNIA branches after 1930, the NOD functioned along the margins of black political and social life.

CONCLUSION

The early demise of the UNIA does not diminish its importance as a major force in the lives of thousands of black New Orleaneans. An integral part of the institutional fabric of the local community during the 1920s, the NOD provided many women and men with an outlet for self-expression and leadership development, enabled them to develop substantive relationships with people outside of their immediate environment, and most importantly, strengthened ordinary people's belief in their ability to effectuate change. Of course, New Orleans was not the only Southern community in which the UNIA significantly impacted the lives of black women and men. A major bastion of black nationalist activity during the 1920s, Miami, Florida claimed hundreds of loyal Garveyite women and men. Not all but the vast majority of Miami Garveyites had recently migrated from the Bahamas. Struggling mightily to adjust to the South's particular form of racial apartheid, these immigrants turned to the New York–based UNIA for political direction and self-affirmation. Studying the Garvey movement in the ethnically diverse city of Miami provides us with the opportunity to explore blacks' perennial struggle against not only vicious white supremacy, but invidious ethnic divisions within their own communities.

Chapter Three

"I Am a Stranger Here": Black Bahamians and the Garvey Movement in Miami, Florida, 1920–1933

> What shall I do to be saved from the political oppression that is common to the Negro everywhere, from economic depression so universally arranged against the Negroes? What shall I do to be saved from inhuman treatment that is committed on the Negroes in every country; from humiliation that Negroes are so apt to encounter anywhere regardless of their character and ability? What shall I do to be saved from the false propaganda that makes the Negro think he is inferior to all other men? What shall I do to save the manhood and womanhood of this race, to make men self-respecting, to make women more dignified and honest, and to save the youths of our race? I have resolved to support and defend the principle of this organization, and adhere to its founder, His Excellency, Hon. Marcus Garvey.
>
> John Hurston, Miami Garveyite, 1929[1]

Frequently during the 1920s, Miami Garveyites enlivened the pages of the *Negro World* with their commentary on racial politics in the United States. Not afraid to voice their opinions, they condemned white supremacy, offered incisive critiques of ethnic divisions within the black community, and encouraged their comrades to be more supportive of the UNIA. Few were more effusive in their praise of the UNIA's work than John Hurston. Outspoken in his support of Pan-African nationalism, Hurston championed the Garvey movement as the most viable political response to the myriad social and economic problems faced by African-descended peoples. A native of the Bahamas who labored hard to transform Miami into a major stronghold of the UNIA, Hurston lived among hundreds of black immigrants moved by Garvey's audacious vision of a transformed world in which black people exercised full control over their political, social, and economic lives.

This chapter examines the centrality of the Garvey movement to Miami's Afro-Bahamian community. It contextualizes the rising popularity of the UNIA within the larger framework of Afro-Bahamians' struggle to negotiate the stresses of everyday life in a racially repressive environment. Occupying the center of this story are complex women and men whose response to white racism calls into question portrayals of West Indians as invariably more radical than American-born blacks. Neither obsequious accommodationists nor hardnosed radicals, Garveyites in Miami searched for a middle ground on which they could maintain their dignity and self-respect, while avoiding any open conflict with powerful whites.

To understand fully the political behavior of Miami Garveyites, it is necessary to analyze, if only briefly, the social position of black Bahamians in South Florida's largest city. Ethnically diverse from the moment of its inception, Miami was incorporated in July of 1896, the same year the US Supreme Court handed down its historic *Plessy v. Ferguson* decision, which codified in law the South's racial caste system. Three months before the city's incorporation, railroad magnate Henry Flagler delivered on an earlier promise to extend his Florida East Coast Railroad passenger train into the sprawling town. Shortly thereafter, Miami and its immediate environs experienced an unprecedented land and construction boom along with tremendous growth in its tourist industry.[2] News of the high availability of wage employment quickly spread to the Bahamas, where oppressive labor systems locked most blacks in a perpetual cycle of indebtedness and poverty.[3] Scores of Bahamians from Harbour Island, Nassau, Crooked Island, Rum Cay, Inagua, Mayaguana, Bimini, Eleuthera, and Abaco trekked to Miami between 1900 and 1930.[4] Working as seasonal laborers in the rich agricultural fields of Coconut Grove, a small community south of the city, most Bahamian workers cleared land, picked fruit, and harvested vegetables. Individuals employed in Miami labored as domestic servants, hackers, draymen, porters, cooks, bellmen, and laundry workers. Earning wages three times higher than their counterparts in the Bahamas, many black islanders amassed enough money to achieve a considerably improved material existence, send remittances back home, and even start their own businesses.

Newly arrived Bahamians discovered numerous employment opportunities in Miami, but they also encountered racial bigotry, police brutality, capricious enforcement of vagrancy laws, inadequate housing and insalubrious living conditions, and limited educational opportunities. To be sure, relations between whites and blacks in the Bahamas were far from perfect, but in Miami, legal segregation and racial discrimination prevailed in every aspect of life.[5] Not long after their arrival in South Florida, West Indian immigrants discovered the power of race and the ways in which the color line permeated every facet of Southern society. One Afro-Bahamian in an interview with noted sociologist Ira Reid discussed his initial encounter with Miami and its Jim Crow social order:

> Having passed the immigration and customs examiners, I took a carriage for what the driver called "Nigger Town." It was the first time I had heard that opprobrious epithet employed, and then, by a colored man himself. I was vividly irked no little. Arriving in Colored Town, I alighted from the carriage in front of an unpainted, poorly-ventilated rooming house where I paid $2.00 for a week's lodging. Already, I was rapidly becoming disillusioned. How unlike the land where I was born. There, colored men were addressed as gentlemen; here, as 'niggers.' There policemen were dressed in immaculate uniforms, carried no deadly weapon, save a billy; here, shirt-sleeved officers of the law carried pistols, smoked and chewed tobacco on duty. Colored Miami was certainly not the Miami of which I had heard so much. It was a filthy backyard of the Magic City.[6]

Navigating the troubled waters of racial politics in the Magic City was not an easy task for black immigrants. "Coming to Miami," James B. Nimmo bitterly recalled, "was like coming into slavery." "If you didn't have a job," he explained, "they would lock you up. Farmers would come and bail you out. They would take you to their farms and work you for a period of time. The farmers would give you a minimum salary. This was common practice."[7] Seventeen years of age at the time of his arrival in Miami, Nimmo, born in Acklins Island, Bahamas on December 15, 1898, dedicated his life to improving the conditions of blacks in the city. Over the course of his adult life, the Bahamian embraced black nationalism, trade unionism, and revolutionary socialism. A committed activist who worked extensively with the Congress of Industrial Organizations (CIO) and the Communist Party during the 1940s and 1950s, Nimmo acquired many of his political and organizing skills as head of the UNIA's paramilitary group, the Universal African Legions (UAL), during the post-World War I years.[8] "I despised and hated the treatment of the Black man," Nimmo recounted, "and was determined to fight for the hopes and aspirations of Black people. I was impressed and strongly motivated by the Garvey movement."[9]

Garveyism with its message of black pride, racial solidarity, and self-determination strengthened the psyche of Nimmo and hundreds of other Bahamian immigrants who encountered dehumanizing acts of brutality, racial epithets, disfranchisement, and a dual legal system. Denied the privileges and benefits of American citizenship on account of their race, many black island-ers who permanently settled in Miami adopted the UNIA as their nation and pledged their allegiance to the association's President-General, Marcus Garvey. Garvey's nationalistic symbols resonated deeply with many whose migration experience and encounters with racism opened them to new ways of imagin-ing community and national identity. Followers not only clung to the UNIA's nationalist rhetoric but they strongly identified with the movement's empha-sis on economic empowerment. Living in an economically thriving city where making money and get-rich-schemes consumed the minds of nearly everyone during the boom years of the early twenties, many Bahamian immigrants were especially intrigued by the materialist ethos of the UNIA. It is no coincidence, therefore, that economically stable working-class people who aspired to and saw within their grasp the opportunity for business enterprise and land and homeownership formed the backbone of the movement.

THE FOUNDING OF THE MIAMI UNIA

Two weeks after attending the UNIA's First International Convention of the Negro Peoples of the World, held in New York City in August 1920, Rev-erend John A. Davis of Ebenezer AME Church summoned sixty blacks to Bethel AME for the purpose of organizing a local chapter of the UNIA.[10] Three months later, on November 14, the Miami division, which at the time claimed more than four hundred members, elected its first slate of officers.[11] Common laborers and artisans held most of the division's key leadership posi-tions. George A. Brown, a blacksmith, was voted to the position of First-Vice President; Samuel C. McPherson, a tailor, occupied the position of Second Vice-President; Oscar Johnson, also a tailor, was the division's financial secre-tary; and Percy A. Styles, listed in the 1920 census as a common laborer, was the Assistant Secretary and traveling organizer.[12] The class composition of the Miami UNIA was markedly similar to branches in New Orleans and other areas of the South, but the absence of women in key leadership positions dis-tinguished the local division from most in the United States. Unlike the New Orleans division, the Miami UNIA never elected a woman to the position of president, vice-president, treasurer, or general secretary.

Another distinguishing feature of the Miami UNIA was the predomi-nance of Bahamian immigrants in the division. Even though an African Amer-ican founded the Miami UNIA and served as its first president, the division proved unable to garner the support of native-born blacks. Writing J. Edgar Hoover in 1921, Leon Howe, director of the Florida division of the Bureau of Investigation, was taken aback by the lack of African American involvement in the Miami UNIA. "Of the membership in Miami, which numbers around

1,000, I have found only seven American Negroes . . . all the active work of the organization was in the hands of Bahama [sic] Negroes."[13] This ethnic imbalance was a source of disappointment for several of the division's leaders. Founding members, according to George Carter, president of the division's board of trustees, envisioned the UNIA as a "medium through which the people from the Bahamas and native Americans could support a common cause, and realize that we were children of one common parent stock, who were transplanted at different points in America."[14] Much to Carter's disappointment, the Miami division and smaller chapters in the area never attracted considerable interest from the African American community.

One should not be surprised by native-born blacks' reluctance to become members of the Bahamian-dominated UNIA. Ever since the incorporation of Miami in the late nineteenth century, ethnic antagonisms and divisions in the black community had been a major problem for community activists seeking to build a united front against white supremacy. Coming from northern Florida, South Carolina, and Georgia, the vast majority of Afro-Americans had minimal, if any, contact with West Indians prior to their arrival in Miami. African Americans lived with, married, and conducted their primary social relationships with blacks born in the United States. They created ethnically exclusive churches, fraternal orders, social clubs, and benevolent and mutual aid societies. The same can be said of black islanders.

Turning inward socially and culturally, Afro-Bahamians also established ethnically exclusive institutions, socialized primarily with other Caribbean immigrants, and had minimal contact with African Americans. Culturally different than native-born blacks, Bahamian immigrants generally spoke with a distinctive, British accent, engaged in a more reserved style of religious worship, and usually possessed more formal education than US born blacks. No matter the frequency in which Miami Garveyites stressed the need for Pan-African unity, they could not ignore the cultural differences between Afro-Bahamians and African Americans. Nor could they ignore the ways in which their varying positions in the local economy deepened these fissures. In the ethnically diverse cities of the North and Midwest, the world of labor occasionally functioned as a mediating force between opposing ethnic/immigrant groups, but this was not the case in Miami since Bahamian immigrants and African Americans were employed in different occupations.[15]

Two groups whose cultural differences and variant positions in the economy frequently led them to view each other with suspicion and disdain, Afro-Bahamians and American blacks could be extremely hostile towards one another.[16] Trying to appease the white ruling elite, African American leaders occasionally assisted local authorities in the suppression of perceived radicals within the black immigrant community. Thinking cooperation with the Bureau of Investigation or the local police department would prove their fitness for full participation in the body politic and civil society, several black Americans readily supplied local authorities with critical information on controversial Bahamians in Miami and surrounding environs. On one occasion, the Colored American Legion, comprised of native born blacks, provided assistance to local authorities in their search for a Bahamian immigrant who had purportedly raped a white woman.[17] Only a small number of African Americans participated in the white community's surveillance of black Bahamian activists; nevertheless, their involvement reinforced many black islanders' stereotypical image of native-born blacks as docile and totally content with their lot as second-class citizens. Moreover, their actions engendered distrust in the hearts of the few black Bahamians who genuinely desired to improve their relationships with African Americans.

A telling example of the way in which the Garvey movement often proved unable to transcend local realities, the UNIA, even with its emphasis on black unity across ethnic boundaries, failed to unite Bahamian immigrants and African Americans.[18] To achieve such an objective would have required the organization's leaders to devote more of their time and resources to the problem of fissures within the black community. Such a project does not appear to have been embraced by the UNIA at the local or national level. Nowhere in the Bureau of Investigation records or in the division's weekly reports is there any mention of an attempt on the part of Miami Garveyites to aggressively recruit African Americans into the various chapters and divisions in the city. Nor is there any indication of serious distress on the part of the central office in New York over the lack of African American support for the Miami UNIA. So long as the Miami division maintained a sizable membership and poured money into the central office's coffers, Parent Body officials remained comfortable with the Bahamian-dominated local movement.

THE EXPANSION OF MIAMI GARVEYISM

Even without the support of the African-American community, the Garvey movement in Miami grew dramatically during the postwar years. Slightly less than one year after its formation in 1920, the Miami UNIA claimed more than one thousand members, possessed nearly two thousand dollars in its treasury, and gained recognition as one of the most vibrant black organizations in the city.[19] Modeled along the lines of the Parent Body in New York, the local division, along with smaller chapters in the outlying communities of Coconut Grove and Homestead, held mass meetings, developed male and female auxiliaries, and sponsored a wide range of social activities. Financially secure, the Miami division leased the Airdrome building in Colored Town for its meetings as well as purchased a motion picture machine in order to provide entertainment for movement supporters.[20]

Weekly meetings at the UNIA's Liberty Hall provided a forum where women and men strategized over the most effective ways to respond to the various forms and manifestations of white supremacy. Lecturers outlined the objectives of the UNIA, offered incisive critiques of the limits of certain political strategies, and engaged in spirited debates with the audience on the most effective method to ameliorate blacks' material condition. Speakers electrified crowds with discussions on subjects as diverse as the Haitian Revolution, the Easter Rebellion in Ireland, the Chicago race riot, the Bolshevik revolution, and Jim Crow legislation. Noted speakers who addressed UNIA audiences included Alonzo Potter Burger Holly[21], the son of the well-known nineteenth-century black nationalist Dr. James Theodore Holly; international socialist Jothar Nishada[22], a native of Honolulu who had been arrested under the California State Syndicate Law in 1919; and J.H. Le Mashey, a radical black Bahamian whose name was high on the Bureau of Investigation's list of most dangerous activists in Florida.[23] Since most black Miamians had minimal contact with blacks in other parts of the country, UNIA leaders in the city worked hard to expose local blacks to the ideas and thoughts of African Americans and West Indians in other parts of the United States.

Several prominent leaders in the New York UNIA conducted lectures in the city. Amy Jacques Garvey, William Le Van Sherrill (Second Assistant President-General and titular leader of the American Negroes), Fred A. Toote (Acting president of the UNIA during Garvey's incarceration for mail fraud), and Madame M.L.T. Ebimber (Assistant International Organizer) spent time in Miami.[24] Fully aware of his popularity in South Florida, Garvey made plans to visit Miami in February of 1921, but James Holly advised the UNIA leader to stay away from the city on account of local police officers' opposition to the movement. Taking Holly's advice, Garvey cancelled his visit to Miami, deciding instead to conduct three lectures in nearby Key West.[25]

Even though Garvey never visited the Magic City, Miami Garveyites' love for the UNIA leader was as strong as those black New Yorkers who encountered the charismatic nationalist on a weekly basis. True to the cause, UNIA followers in Miami diligently read Garvey's editorials, regularly paid their dues to the Parent Body, sent delegates to the UNIA's annual conventions, and contributed financially to the Black Star Line and the Black Cross Navigation and Trading Company.[26] "Ever since I came to the Miami division," one Garveyite remarked in the *Negro World*, "I have never seen them fail to answer a call from the Parent Body when called to duty."[27] Indeed,

Miami Garveyites buttressed the work of the central office in New York, but they also invested their time and financial resources to building a vibrant movement at the local level.

MIAMI GARVEYITES STRUGGLE FOR ECONOMIC INDEPENDENCE

Very early, Miami Garveyites placed tremendous energy into becoming economically self-sufficient. Organizing locally-based cooperatives was a stated objective for most, if not all, UNIA divisions, but faced with numerous economic hardships, most Garveyites, especially those in the South, lacked the capital to create small-businesses. Owing in large part to Florida's economic boom during the early twenties, UNIA followers in the southern region of the Sunshine State were able to launch several economic ventures. Garveyites in Key West, for example, put the theory of economic preparedness and racial cooperation to practice by establishing a bakery and a delivery service in 1921.[28] Taking part in the real estate craze of the early twenties, the Miami UNIA purchased several plots of land on which they built their Liberty Hall as well as constructed an unspecified number of houses from which, according to J. A. Craigen, "they derive rentals and on which not one penny is owed."[29] Due to the paucity of evidence on the business undertakings of local divisions, it is impossible to assess the profitability of these cooperatives. Nonetheless, their existence illustrates the degree to which Miami Garveyites, as well as their Key West counterparts, applied the organization's economic philosophy at the local level.

Individually, Miami Garveyites also engaged in their own business endeavors during South Florida's economic boom. Treasurer of the division's ladies department in 1920, Alicia Johnson, a Bahamian who arrived in the United States in 1890, owned a small restaurant in Colored Town.[30] A native of Jamaica, Maxwell Cook was the owner of Kingston Pressing Club, a small dry cleaner located on 1834 Northwest Fourth Street. Cook had been a porter at a hardware store before accumulating enough money to start his own business.[31] To strengthen their financial standing, other Garveyites sought to achieve economic independence through the buying and selling of land. Traveling to Miami in 1910, Albert Gibson, a native of Eleuthera, a tiny island ninety miles west of Nassau, worked as a farm hand in Coconut Grove. Struggling mightily to adapt to the intensity of white racism, Gibson had no intentions of making Miami his permanent home. "I filled out an alien card every year," he recalled. "I didn't take no [any] citizenship. I kept thinking, I'm not going to stay here because of the way white people treat you."[32] An avid supporter of the UNIA, Gibson not only stayed in Miami, but he profited considerably from the land boom of the early twenties. After ten years of diligently saving his money, the farmer purchased four acres of land for six hundred dollars in 1923. Later, Gibson, like other Miamians who managed to acquire "a piece of land," resold a portion of his property for a handsome profit of five thousand dollars. Similar to other upwardly mobile laboring people, Gibson and many of his UNIA cohorts measured economic success in terms of one's ability to purchase a home, open up a business, or acquire a small amount of land. In this regard, their economic aspirations were not very different than similarly situated blacks and whites striving for the quintessential American dream of economic independence and homeownership.

WHITE OPPOSITION TO THE UNIA

Quite proud of their collective and individual accomplishments, Garveyites in Miami viewed themselves as the paragons of respectability; but not everyone in the city shared their perspective. Turned off by the organization's symbolic militancy as well as its call for economic self-reliance, many whites worked incessantly to undermine the movement. Law enforcement officials planted informants in several branches, interrupted UNIA meetings, and interrogated the organization's more outspoken supporters.[33] No small factor in law enforcement officials' intensive surveillance of the Miami UNIA was the predominance of West Indian immigrants in the division. Ever since their influx into Miami, Bahamian immigrants had been portrayed by the white populace and a select group of American-born blacks as fiery radicals who refused to acquiesce to the racial status quo. Nearly every summer, rumors of a Bahamian-directed plot to murder massive numbers of whites circulated in Miami and surrounding areas. Viewing the city's black immigrant community as a disruptive force, the Miami Police Department and the Bureau of Investigation monitored closely the activities of black immigrants, especially those in the UNIA who criticized city officials for denying blacks their civil and political rights.

Another opponent of the UNIA was the Ku Klux Klan. Vigorously opposed to the UNIA's promotion of race pride, group solidarity, and economic empowerment, the Miami KKK initiated a plan of attack against one of the UNIA's most vocal supporters, Reverend Ritchie Higgs. Very outspoken, Higgs was the minister of St. James Baptist Church in Coconut Grove. Serving also as the president of the Coconut Grove UNIA, the Harbour Island native promoted the use of armed-self-defense as a method of resistance against white terrorist attacks on the black community.[34] Much to the chagrin of local whites, he also encouraged his followers to work toward the overthrow of Jim Crow segregation by devoting more attention toward building the educational institutions needed to politically and economically uplift themselves. "Reverend Higgs," longtime Miami resident Lourena Smith remembered, "was preaching to the people that they should give their children a good education so as to prevent them from having to work inside a white person's house and so that they can find a better job."[35] Worried about the Baptist preacher's growing influence, the KKK vowed to rid the city of one of its most outspoken activists.

More assertive in his demands for social justice than most of his comrades, Higgs eventually had to square off against the white racists whom he so sharply criticized in his speeches. On Friday night, July 1, 1921, four white Klansmen captured and handcuffed Higgs outside his home, shoved him into their parked automobile, and drove westward to an undisclosed location. Details are rather hazy, but the men apparently stopped at a local store and added four more Klansmen to their party. Once the white men reached their final destination, they removed Higgs from the car, threw him on the ground, and mercilessly whipped the handcuffed minister with a rope for more than two hours.[36] "They beat him up good," his fellow Garveyite Albert Gibson recalled "and gave him 48 hours to leave town."[37]

Screaming for assistance, Higgs had tried to alert his neighbors during the initial moments of his capture, but by the time his friends exited their homes, the car in which the minister had been placed was already moving down the street at an extremely high speed. Anticipating the worst, a large crowd of black Bahamians, including the minister's frightened brother, Reggie, swarmed the streets with guns in hand, more than ready if the white kidnappers decided to return to the area. Word of Higgs' abduction and the ensuing unrest within the black community immediately reached law enforcement officials. Sensing the potential for a race riot, the Coconut Grove Police Department requested immediate assistance from Miami's police force and the American Legion. Law enforcement officials, according to the *Miami Herald*, prepared for an all-out race war:

> Every police officer and deputy sheriff in the city with the exception of the beat officers, was immediately dispatched to Coconut Grove, and the officers arrested and disarmed more than 25 negroes, arresting nine Negroes . . . Following the dispatching of the officers to Coconut Grove, A.J. Cleary, commander of the Harvey Seeds Post, No. 29, American Legion, called out every member of the local legion here who could be located and these men were ordered to report at police headquarters where they were armed with rifles and shotguns. The door to Chief Raymond Dillon's office containing the cases of rifles and shotguns kept by the police for riot duty was unlocked and the cases broken open and

the arms distributed among the legion men. Cleary then opened the two classes containing two Lewis automatic rifles and a squad of men were led into a truck and rushed to Coconut Grove where one machine gun was mounted in the center of the town in order to command all approaches. Guards of ex-servicemen and others were placed on every bridge in and near both Miami and Coconut Grove with orders to hunt down every person.[38]

Local Garveyites seethed with discontent over the abduction of their leader as well as local authorities' siege of their community; however, their anger subsided when Reverend Higgs staggered home in the early morning hours. Badly battered, Higgs informed family and friends of his intention to leave for Nassau, Bahamas. On July 5, local Garveyites with tremendous sorrow, according to Gibson, "put him [Higgs] on a boat, gave him a couple of hundred dollars and let him get lost."[39] Not sure of how the local black community would react to the forced departure of their beloved leader, white officials braced themselves for a wave of rebellion within the black community. "The situation is very strained between white and colored citizens of the Miami district," federal agent Leon H. Howe informed his supervisors in the nation's capital, "and agent is expecting a recurrence of the race troubles which occurred during July and August last year."[40]

No major disturbance occurred within the black community in the aftermath of Higgs' expulsion from the city. Yet whites remained on heightened alert, largely due to a *Miami Herald* story on Higgs' purported involvement in a recently discovered, mass murder conspiracy in Key West. Months before his kidnapping, Higgs had allegedly planned a scheme whereby domestic workers in Key West would poison their white employers. Once the domestics murdered their employers, according to the newspaper, the city would be transformed into an independent, black republic governed by members of the UNIA.[41] Supposedly Higgs, a former resident of Key West who traveled often to the city for various UNIA functions, had designed the mass murder plot with the assistance of the Key West division's fiery president, T.C. Glashen.[42] A Jamaican born in British Honduras, Glashen was also known for his advocacy of armed-self defense against white aggression. Infuriated by Glashen's open advocacy of armed self-defense, the president of the local Chamber of Commerce ordered the UNIA leader to leave the United States in twenty four hours or face imprisonment and then deportation. "There is . . . some question of the legality of ordering Glashan [sic] to leave Key West," Bureau agent, Leon Howe, admitted, "but it was done by a judge of the Circuit Court, Judge Hunt Harris." Unwilling to leave, Glashen was arrested and imprisoned on June 16, 1921. Shortly thereafter, an unidentified central office representative convinced Glashen to leave the city in order to ease the tensions between Garveyites and local whites.

Was the story of Higgs' scheme true, or simply the invention of a frightened white populace? To what extent were other Miami Garveyites involved in the alleged conspiracy? Unfortunately, Bureau of Investigation records and local newspapers do not provide us with enough evidence on which to draw any conclusive answers to these questions. When questioned by the local police, Higgs denied any knowledge or involvement in any mass murder conspiracy.[43] Curiously though, nearly sixty years after the minister's kidnapping, James Nimmo in an interview with Marvin Dunn admitted to the division's involvement "in a number of plots aimed at retaliation for wrongs done to blacks." Nimmo never mentioned specifically any scheme to poison white families.[44] Nor did he discuss Higgs' plans to cooperate with blacks in Key West.

Whether factual or contrived, the existence of these rumors guaranteed that white surveillance of the UNIA would continue. Trying their best to maintain a handle on the movement, law enforcement officials continued to disrupt meetings, monitor outspoken leaders, and frequently deny the division the necessary permit to hold meetings when Parent Body officials from New York visited the city.[45] "The police would sit in on meetings," recalled Nimmo, "attempting to intimidate us and see what we were up to, but we would proceed with the meetings as planned to show them what we were about."[46] Like many former Garveyites, Nimmo, in his recollections of the Miami division, always related in wondrous terms the ways in which local Garveyites defied white authorities; but he obscured a much more complex reality. More specifically, he downplayed the movement's conservative tendencies. Consider the Miami division's actions after the Higgs' incident in 1921.

Obeying the instructions of the central office in New York, which wanted to ensure that funds continuously rolled in from Miami, conservative leaders within the division arranged private meetings with local politicians and law enforcement for the purpose of assuaging white fears.[47] At these meetings, UNIA officers disavowed any desire to integrate into white society, stated strongly their disapproval of interracial marriage, differentiated their goals from those of the liberal integrationist NAACP, and generally presented themselves as racial separatists who desired the exact same things as their white counterparts.[48] No leader donned the mask of conservatism more willingly than George Emonei Carter. One of the few African Americans members of the division, Carter, at a gathering attended by the city's police chief, counseled UNIA followers on the need to accept segregation as a permanent feature of the Jim Crow South. To the delight of his white listeners, he promised to expel any individual who refused to respect "the white man's laws."[49] A week later in the pages of the *Negro World*, Carter issued a warning to Garveyites in Miami who had taken issue with his statements at the meeting. "We need men," he declared, "who are loyal to their people yet understand the community in which they labor and will always seek to keep down race antipathy."[50] Sounding markedly similar to white racists who advised Caribbean immigrants to leave the country if they could not respect the racial mores of the Jim Crow South, Carter instructed those who desired "integration," which of course was always loosely defined in the South, to "seek other climes, where you may live without antagonizing your neighbor."[51] Organizational survival in the racist region, he believed, required a certain degree of capitulation to white racism or at least avoidance of any confrontation with white extremists.

Few in the Miami division acquiesced completely to the prevailing social order, but at the same time, they did not aspire to become revolutionary martyrs for the cause of black liberation. Ever mindful of the dangers involved in any frontal assault on white supremacy in the racist South, Garveyites, especially after the Higgs' incident, tempered their verbal attacks on the white power structure, refrained from public advocacy of armed self-defense, and grudgingly donned the mask of acquiescence when local circumstances called for a more evasive style of politics.

A brief glance at the African Universal Legion's occasional conflicts with the local police sheds additional light on the ways in which even the most symbolically militant Garveyites delicately treaded the shaky ground of racial politics. A paramilitary group who vowed to defend the black community against white violence, the Universal African Legions (UAL), comprised of roughly two hundred men, drilled on Sunday afternoons at Dorsey Park in Colored Town.[52] Men in the legion, according to the UAL's leader, James Nimmo, drilled weekly with wooden rifles, even though most of the men possessed firearms. Visible at most, if not all, UNIA's functions and gatherings, the African Legion embodied the militant spirit of the New Negro Manhood Movement. A precursor, in many ways, to the Nation of Islam's paramilitary group, the Fruit of Islam, the UAL instilled within its members a sense of pride as well provided male role models for Garveyite boys. The UAL, writes historian Barbara Bair, "represented the ideas of power and dominance and the military might necessary to achieve and maintain Negro Nationhood."[53] Opposed to the Legion's militaristic displays, law enforcement officials frequently interrupted their practices and ordered them to disperse. Interestingly, Nimmo and his men never retaliated against the local police when they interrupted the UAL's practices and confiscated their rifles; but at the same time, the African legion refused to cease their activities. "We would just go home," Nimmo explained, "make new rifles, and drill next week."[54] Never would Nimmo and other members of the UNIA become completely comfortable with constant interference from whites; however, they learned to maneuver under these conditions.

Dealing with criticism from the black community constituted another challenge for Miami Garveyites. Threatened by the success of the Garvey movement, African American and West Indian opponents of the movement instructed the black populace to stay away from the UNIA, ridiculed the division's working class leaders for their purported lack of refinement, and encouraged law enforcement officials to arrest UNIA recruiters from the North. No group was more strident in their criticism of the Miami UNIA than the community's religious leaders. "Just about the time when the doctrines of the U.N.I.A. were beginning to take hold on the Negroes of Miami," one unidentified Garveyite explained to readers of the *Negro World*, "some of our so-called preachers thought their end had come. So to lengthen their hold on the people, a little longer," the writer continued, "they got hotheaded, and went down to the authorities of the city and made a dangerous vicious statement concerning the U.N.I.A."[55]

Even under critical scrutiny and external opposition, the Miami UNIA thrived during the early 20s. Such perseverance impressed UNIA followers in other parts of the country. "With all of the persecution it has suffered from the hands of the authorities," Jo A. Craigen of the Detroit division noted after a visit to Florida, "[the] Miami division is one of the largest and strongest divisions of the association. The members are loyal to the core."[56] Indeed, the UNIA followers in the Magic City financed the Black Star Line and the Black Cross Navigation and Trading Company, subscribed to and diligently read the *Negro World*, and dutifully answered the central office's many calls for financial assistance. Above all else, they built a strong and viable movement at the local level. Miami Garveyites held elaborate meetings, sponsored parades and excursions, and provided an array of musical entertainment for the local community. UNIA branches with their bands, choirs, and quartets significantly enriched the lives of the many women and men who traveled in and out of Liberty Hall during the heyday of the Garvey movement. A predominantly Bahamian organization, the local branch also provided a space for black immigrants to reflect on their West Indian heritage as well as transmit their history and culture to their children. A native of Miami whose father had been born in the Bahamas, Ann Marie Adker fondly remembered her experiences in the movement:

> The Garvey people had a great big hall just around the corner from
> where we lived. On Sundays after church my father would take us there.
> Every Sunday that's where we would be. You had all kinds of people,
> from schoolteachers to just everyday people. They were all right in there

learning about our history. They would tell folk tales. Now these were mostly people from the Bahamas. They told us stories that were told to them at their knees. It was the most amazing thing.[57]

The UNIA was an important part of many black Miamians' lives, and between 1920 and 1925, the organization assisted numerous immigrants in the resettlement process. Consequently, hundreds of black Bahamians were dedicated to building and sustaining strong UNIA branches and divisions in their neighborhoods. Standing strong in the face of white opposition constituted the primary challenge for these Garveyites between 1920 and 1925, but in the second half of the decade, UNIA followers faced a new set of challenges: the end of the city's economic boom, the development of factions within the division, and the onset of the Great Depression. If the first half of the decade was a period of tremendous growth for the Miami UNIA, the second half was one of constant readjustment and then decline.

SHIFTING POLITICAL PERSPECTIVES AND THE QUESTION OF AFRICAN REPATRIATION, 1925–1930

Changes in the local economy during the second half of the 1920s led many Garveyites to reexamine their politics. The early years of the 1920s had witnessed a dramatic rise in real estate activity in the Greater Miami area. Financially secure Miamians enjoyed unprecedented prosperity but the local economy began to show signs of faltering in 1925. A "national backlash of hostility against the excesses of the real estate boom" coupled with the Bureau of Internal Revenue's ruling that the entire sum of the purchase price for real estate had to be reported as income resulted in a drastic decline in land sales in Miami and other parts of South Florida.[58] Then, in October of 1925, the Interstate Commerce Commission issued an embargo on the shipment of all freight coming in carload lots as a result of an unanticipated workers' strike on the Atlantic Coast Line Railroad. Later, on January 10, 1926, the *Prins Valdemar* sank in Miami harbor and further disrupted the flow of supplies. An already bad situation worsened on September 17, 1926, when a hurricane of devastating strength hit Miami in the early morning hours.

Skimming the pages of the *Miami Daily News* on the sunny afternoon of September 16, most Miamians ignored meteorologist Richard W. Gray's warning of "destructive winds in the late evening and early morning hours of the next day."[59] Darkening skies and heavy winds at nightfall, however, convinced locals of the imminence of a serious storm. Thirty minutes before midnight, Gray, the city's weather bureau chief, raised the hurricane flags atop the Ameri-First Building and prepared for the worst. Wreaking havoc on an unprepared community, winds, registered at 115 miles per hour by 3:00 am, ripped through Miami. "You could sit down," one Garveyite recalled, "and hear big trees tumbling down and a sound went through like a train . . . Thought the Lord was going to wipe the world out."[60] When the hurricane passed around 9:00 am, Miamians were shocked at the human and physical devastation, especially in the black sections of the city where poorly constructed wood-frame homes and buildings proved unable to withstand the destructive storm. Roughly four hundred people lost their lives; more than seven thousand were injured; and property damage in homes alone totaled an estimated five million dollars. [61]

No longer viewing Miami as a secure place for financial investment, wealthy realtors and entrepreneurs withdrew from the Magic City in massive numbers. Unemployment and homelessness increased exponentially, especially among the city's African American and Afro-Bahamian population. Observing conditions in Miami during a visit in March 1927, the UNIA's Parent Body representative J.A. Craigen was deeply saddened by the level of poverty and human misery: "Negroes are walking the streets by the thousands, and because of being unable to secure employment I have seen them arrested by the wholesale, carried to jail, and only those fortunate to be able to pay the fine imposed are allowed their freedom. The others are taken out of the city limits and ordered to leave town. What a condition!"[62] Declining economic opportunities in Miami did not merely alter the material condition of many Garveyites but prompted a significant shift in their position on the question of African repatriation. Suddenly, Miami Garveyites opened up to the idea of a massive relocation to Liberia or another part of West Africa.

Far too often, historians treat UNIA followers as a monolithic group who invariably agreed on the most effective strategies to secure blacks' political and economic rights, but Garveyites had different opinions about a wide variety of issues, including the matter of resettlement in Africa. Garvey's Liberian plans had always received substantial support in New Orleans, Norfolk, Newport News, and other southern cities, but during the first half of the twenties, his followers in South Florida demonstrated little interest in relocation to Liberia or any other part of Africa. Let me say that black Miamians' lack of interest in relocation to Liberia should not be interpreted as disapproval of the organization's nation building efforts in the West African country. Over the period between 1920 and 1925, Miami Garveyites wrote several letters of support for the UNIA's Liberian scheme. Writing to the *Negro World* in 1924, Hattie Huggins of the Miami UNIA communicated her division's support for the organization's efforts to establish a colony in Liberia: "Our members are keeping up the fight for African redemption and all are doing everything possible to aid the U.N.I.A. to put over the program."[63]

Optimistic about their economic future in South Florida, Miami Garveyites had been content to remain in the United States, but their position changed dramatically after the local economy collapsed in 1926. Increasingly after the hurricane, Miami Garveyites promoted repatriation as the panacea for blacks' many woes. "We need each and every Negro in our race to line up with us in the Universal Negro Improvement Association and help in the struggle to [find] a government in our mother country," Samuel Culmer, the division's second vice-president exhorted his comrades. [64] Only by leaving the United States, in his opinion, could blacks achieve complete political and economic freedom. Africa, Culmer, declared, "is the only safe refuge for us."[65] Anti-emigrationists across the country denounced calls for the massive relocation of Afro-Americans to Africa as foolhardy, but Culmer questioned the sanity of those who predicted the future absorption of blacks into American society:

> Many men are telling us to let down our buckets where we are, I want to know what Negroes expect to get by letting down their buckets in America or any place else than Africa. For three hundred and fifty years these Negroes have let down buckets and they can't afford to draw these damnable buckets up. Old grandmammies [sic] and old granddaddies have let them down so long as now they are decrepit. What are the results? Jim Crowed, segregated, lynched, burned, shot to death, and it is all over. Wake up, Negro! Try and get into Africa and let down your buckets there and your tubs, and everything else you have, and when your buckets have been down three hundred and fifty years you will be able to draw them up with satisfaction. [66]

Ever since the UNIA's incorporation in 1918, Culmer's basic premise, that resettlement in Africa was the best solution to America's racial dilemma, had been forwarded in the pages of the *Negro World* and at speeches in Liberty Halls around the country. Years before most black Miamians seriously promoted the idea of repatriation, the central office in New York had worked toward the creation of an autonomous colony in Liberia, but the Parent Body failed miserably in its negotiations with the West African government. Fully aware of his followers' growing impatience, Marcus Garvey promised to eventually strike a deal with Liberia, but in 1927, thousands of rank-and-file Garveyites in the Deep South, including black Miamians, who desired to repatriate to Africa, placed their faith in the program of a charismatic woman named Laura Adorkor Kofey.[67]

A dynamic speaker who initially claimed to be a close friend and representative of Garvey, Laura Kofey, alias Laura Champion, arrived in

Miami on May 29, 1927 and addressed roughly three hundred people at her first lecture in Liberty Hall. [68] Thrilling her audience with a passionate discourse on the struggles of black Americans, Kofey stressed the need for the development of black-owned enterprises and cooperatives, a solid emigration plan, and pan-African unity. Kofey struck a responsive chord in the minds and hearts of hundreds of local blacks pessimistic about their future in America. "Over 800 members enrolled during the week," Vernon Parkinson Greenslade informed the central office. "Mrs. Coffey is marvelous. Garveyism is spreading like wild fire down here in Miami."[69] Scheduled to stay in the city for only one week, Kofey extended her visit for an additional week in order to "convince 800 more that they need freedom and Africa needs them."[70] Leaving Miami Garveyites in a state of great anticipation for the day when the children of Africa would return to their motherland, Kofey spent the rest of the spring and summer giving lectures in Jacksonville and Tampa, Florida, New Orleans, and Mobile, Alabama. In these and other southern locales, she collected thousands of dollars from frustrated blacks who had grown tired of life in racist America.[71]

The dynamic Kofey returned to Miami in the fall of 1927 and proceeded to collect money for her African colonization scheme.[72] Now claiming to be the daughter of King Knesipi of the Gold Coast, she unveiled an elaborate plan whereby African kings would dispatch ships to Miami and Jacksonville for those who wanted to start anew in the land of their ancestors.[73] Support for her scheme was generally high, but several division leaders doubted the legitimacy of her propositions. Turning to the central office in New York for more information on Kofey, they demanded information on whether Garvey authorized her fundraising activities.[74] In response to the division's inquiry, Garvey denied any knowledge of Kofey's endeavors: "I have given Mrs. Kofey no authority to collect funds from members for any kind of African exodus. I authorized no one to give her authority to collect funds for such a purpose."[75] One month later, Garvey repudiated Kofey and ordered all divisions to cease their association with the woman: "No Division or Chapter of the Universal Negro Improvement Association is to entertain one Laura Coffey, alias Princess Coffey and Lady Coffey, who has for some time been collecting funds from members of the Association in the South under the guise of sending them to Africa, etc. Should she make further appeals, members should have her arrested for fraud."[76]

Immediately after Garvey's announcement in the *Negro World*, a dangerous schism developed between Garvey loyalists and Kofey followers in Miami. More than half of the Miami UNIA's membership chose to follow Kofey, who vowed to lead "the lost children of Africa" to the promise land. "They fell head over heels for her lies," James Nimmo told the *Miami Times* in 1985. "Even my sister became a follower of hers. She was a highly educated and powerful speaker. Many people begin to follow her."[77] To be sure, the Miami UNIA had many charismatic leaders, but none of them had the appeal of Kofey. Troubled by and perhaps jealous of Kofey's rising popularity, Nimmo and Claude Green, the division's president, along with several other leaders in the division, engaged in various acts of intimidation against Kofey and her followers.

Increasingly concerned about her safety, Kofey left Miami in early 1928 and temporarily moved to Jacksonville, Florida, where she formed the African Universal Church and Commercial League (AUC), which emphasized racial self-determination, African repatriation, and Christian ethics.[78] Unwilling to stay away from the city where her following was the largest, Kofey, returned to Miami and organized a local division of the AUC. A heated battle then ensued between the UNIA and Kofey's AUC when former Garveyites in the AUC attempted to hold meetings and worship services in Liberty Hall. To quell the dispute between the two groups over the use of Liberty Hall, the Miami police department padlocked the building but this only heightened the conflict between the rival parties.

The rivalry between the UNIA and the AUC turned deadly on Thursday evening, March 8, 1928. Speaking before her loyal supporters at Fox Thomson's Hall, Laura Kofey, a youthful thirty-five years of age, was fatally shot in the head. Minutes after the shooting, one group of AUC members, with revenge on their minds, seized Maxwell Cook, the captain of the UNIA's African Legions, and brutally pounded him to death with stones, bricks, and fists. Several hours after questioning AUC members, the local police arrested Nimmo and Claude Green for the murder of Laura Kofey. A tailor who worked at a dry-cleaning plant in nearby Buena Vista, Florida, Nimmo had been a respected leader in the organization. Even though he was incredibly loyal to Marcus Garvey, he denied any involvement in Kofey's murder. "I had been heckling her meetings," he admitted years later, "and I had planned to attend that one, but luckily I had to work until 8 that night."[79] Offering a completely different account, AUC members, in their discussions with the local police, stated that Nimmo had signaled for Claude Green to shoot Kofey.[80] "That's the only thing I faulted them for," Nimmo lamented, "they lied."[81] Green, a diabetic who had recently been bedridden, claimed to have been at his home at the time of the murder, but he, like Nimmo, would be arrested and indicted on first-degree murder charges.

Upset about the two men's imprisonment and deeply concerned about the future of the Miami UNIA, Parent Body representative J.A. Craigen launched a fundraising drive to help cover Nimmo and Green's legal expenses. "Every member of the organization," Craigen wrote in his appeal for funds, "knows of the value of the Miami Division to the entire organization. These men's lives are at stake. The prestige and the existence of the organization in the South are at stake. Therefore there can be no delay."[82] Sympathetic to the legal struggles of their comrades, Garveyites in New York, Detroit, Toronto, Colon, Panama, Los Angeles, and other locales generously donated to the fund. Five months after Kofey's brutal murder, the jurors of the Circuit Court of Miami acquitted Green and Nimmo of first degree murder charges. "Green and Nemo [sic] have been exonerated," Craigen rejoiced, "and the U.N.I.A. shall march on in Miami, Florida."[83] Thankful for their fellow Garveyites' support, the Miami UNIA expressed their gratitude to those who "willingly and ably assisted the division in its struggle to liberate our two brothers who were recently incarcerated, and persecuted for a crime which they did not commit."[84]

Worried about their personal safety, Nimmo briefly returned to the Bahamas while Green moved to Canada.[85] The absence of two of the organization's most effective recruiters, Nimmo and Green, created a leadership vacuum for the division and ultimately led to a decline in the branch's membership and its morale. Visiting Miami in the fall of 1928, Madame M.L.T. Ebimber, Assistant International Organizer for the UNIA found the division to be "somewhat disorganized due to the recent activities there of enemies of the organization in the Laura Kofey case."[86] No doubt, the division was in serious trouble, but the more faithful members remained optimistic amid the turmoil. "All is possible," Leon Bethel assured his fellow Garveyites, "to the man or woman who has the courage to press on until the goal is reached. We must not become discouraged and give up because the battle is hard."[87] Very few in the Miami UNIA possessed Bethel's patience as the turbulent twenties came to a close. Garveyites had to deal not only with the repercussions of the Kofey murder, but also with the economic hardships created by the onset of Great Depression.

THE GREAT DEPRESSION AND THE COLLAPSE OF THE MIAMI UNIA

Scarce employment opportunities forced many Garveyites to enter the bread lines during the Depression years. The collapse of the economy brought great suffering to laboring women and men, including those workers who had lived comfortably during the early 20s. "When the Depression came," Garveyite Albert Gibson explained, "us people who had a little money went down with the banks. At the time of President Hoover, we were standing in line for a six-pound sack of flour and a can of soup. Some days you went and stood all day, and didn't get anything."[88] All across the country, the UNIA was hobbled by its inability to develop a more activist program to address these issues. Garvey's message of economic empowerment and business enterprise had appealed to black immigrants like Albert Gibson who had achieved prosperity during the boom years of the early twenties, but now, laboring people demanded a program that would bring about more tangible results: jobs, housing, and food. No longer was the UNIA relevant to the masses of black Miamians, Bahamian or American-born, struggling to make sense of their new and much more bleak reality.

Following Kofey's murder, the Miami UNIA entered a period of stagnation and dormancy during which division leaders struggled to attract new members and retain old ones. Not until the late thirties would the Miami division officially disband; however, the Garvey movement was all but dead by 1930.[89] In an article published in the September 5, 1931 edition of the *Negro World,* an anonymous reporter for the Miami division sadly reminisced on the "by gone days when Liberty Hall was the center of attraction and served to stimulate the spirit of race pride, and respect for the standard of honor which prevails in high places."[90] Far too often, UNIA loyalists wrongly blamed the division's decline on the lack of race pride in the black community, but as was the case in most cities, the movement's disintegration in Miami was related to the economic collapse.

With the disintegration of the Miami UNIA in the late thirties, many former members pledged their allegiance to other organizations and continued their efforts to improve the quality of life for black Miamians. Committed to several institutions which aimed to provide material assistance and cultural enrichment to the black masses, Alfred Gibson, for example, actively supported St. Paul's A.M.E. Church, the Odd Fellows, the Knights of Pythias, and the Good Samaritans.[91] Other Garveyites who embraced religious black nationalism contributed to the development and expansion of St. Peter's Orthodox Church, the African Orthodox Church, and St. Francis Xavier Church, African-centered churches still in existence.[92]

Moving from nationalism to more class-based politics, several ex-Garveyites participated in the budding labor movement. One of the most important figures in the history of Miami's labor movement, James Nimmo performed an integral role in the organization of black workers in the laundry, aviation, and shipbuilding industries during the 1940s and 1950. Long after his days with the Garvey movement, Nimmo continued to be regarded as a social menace by local authorities. A brilliant labor activist who acquired important organizing skills during his years in the Garvey movement, he spearheaded the first large-scale organization of black workers in the 1940s. Very disturbed by white companies' treatment of black laundry and dry cleaning workers, Nimmo initiated the formation of the Laundry

Industry Union, which gained recognition from the American Federation of Labor (AFL) during the 1940s. Later, Nimmo provided assistance to the CIO-affiliated Transport Workers Union in their endeavors to organize workers in Miami's fledging aviation industry.[93] On account of his left-wing radicalism, the former Garveyite found himself under intensive investigation at a public hearing by the House of Un-American Activities Committee in the spring of 1953.[94] Even though Nimmo's politics shifted from black nationalism to left-wing radicalism, he continued to hold Marcus Garvey in high regards. Until his death in 1992, he praised the UNIA for its exemplary work and reminded anyone who would listen of the importance of the Garvey movement to the history of black Miami.

CONCLUSION

Garveyism was an integral component of black immigrant life in Miami during the twenties. An important institution, the UNIA provided an institutional space where Afro-Bahamians settlers could escape, if only momentarily, the racial indignities of the Jim Crow South, forge common bonds of fellowship and mutual regard with similarly situated individuals, discuss issues of importance to the liberation of black people globally, develop their leadership skills, and connect with blacks in other parts of the country and the world. Unfortunately, the movement did not always channel people toward meaningful activism against the discriminatory policies of the state. Notwithstanding their militant rhetoric and displays, Garveyites in Miami often placated rather than confronted the white power structure. This conservatism would hinder the movement as the black community started to endorse more confrontational strategies during the 1930s.

Of course, Miami was not the only place where UNIA followers accommodated white racism. In other cities, Garveyites' rhetoric and political decisions occassionally betrayed the organization's emancipatory agenda. Unconcerned about the repercussions of their actions, some conservative Garveyites in the North and South even allied with white separatists who found agreement with the UNIA's emigration policies. Exploring the history of the UNIA in Virginia, the next chapter further examines the politics of the movement's more conservative supporters, probes their relationship with white supremacists, and evaluates the extent to which the movement's conservative tendencies limited its effectiveness. Sensitive to the complexity of Virginian Garveyism, the next chapter also documents the activism of Virginia Garveyites who proposed political alternatives to the activities of their more reactionary counterparts.

Figures

Figure 1. A founding member of the Newport News, Virginia UNIA, Henry Vinton Plummer, Jr. played a critical role in the growth of the UNIA in eastern Virginia during the post-World War I years. He was the 1st Vice-President of the Newport News branch from 1918 to 1920. Moving to New York in 1920, he would be named the head of the Black Star Line Bureau of Publicity and Propaganda. A high ranking official in the New York UNIA, Plummer was also the chief of Marcus Garvey's secret service staff. (UNIA Almanac, Schomburg Center for Research in Black Culture, New York Public Library, New York)

Figure 2. Significantly contributing to the growth of the UNIA in the urban South during the 1920s were Parent Body recruiters who endured the virulent racism of the region in order to spread the political message of Garveyism. Noted recruiters included James Eason, Alaida Robertson, George Tait, Jacob Slappey, Adrian Johnson, and J.D. Brooks. Crucial to the success of the New Orleans UNIA during its formative period, Adrian Johnson (above) played a key role in the growth of the local branch in early 1921. Open to working with other organizations in the black community, Johnson brought thousands of New Orleaneans to the Garvey Movement. (UNIA Almanac, Schomburg Center for Research in Black Culture, New York Public Library, New York)

Figure 3. Another effective recruiter from New York who ventured into the South during the movement's formative years, J.D. Brooks (above) played a critical role in the expansion of Garveyism in the state of North Carolina. He assisted greatly in the growth of branches in Raleigh and Winston Salem during the early 1920s. (UNIA Almanac, Schomburg Center for Research in Black Culture, New York Public Library, New York)

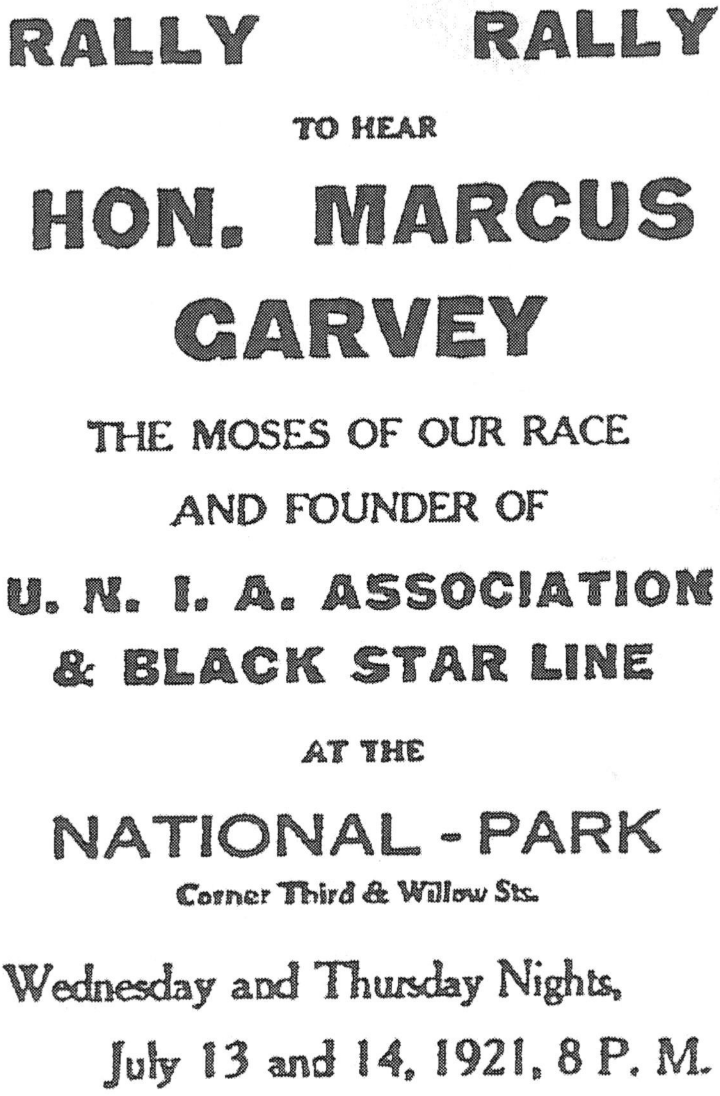

RALLY   RALLY

TO HEAR

HON. MARCUS GARVEY

THE MOSES OF OUR RACE

AND FOUNDER OF

U. N. I. A. ASSOCIATION & BLACK STAR LINE

AT THE

NATIONAL - PARK

Corner Third & Willow Sts.

Wednesday and Thursday Nights,
July 13 and 14, 1921, 8 P. M.

Figure 4. Over the period between 1920 and 1924, Marcus Garvey made several trips to the Jim Crow South. This advertisement for a Garvey lecture in New Orleans, Louisiana was found in the records of the Bureau of Investigation. Nearly two thousand blacks gathered at National Park in New Orleans, Louisiana to hear Garvey lecture on the problem of global white supremacy. Once leaders of the New Orleans UNIA received news of his trip, they distributed the above circular announcing his scheduled lectures. (National Archives, Washington, DC)

Figure 5. Over the period between 1920 and 1922, black Southerners, especially those in urban centers, purchased thousands of dollars worth of Black Star Line stock. Not enough attention has been given to BSL officials' effective use of advertising in convincing black workers to purchase BSL shares. Fully cognizant of black workers' desire to improve their economic lot, Garvey in advertisements for the shipping company specifically targeted black laborers with disposable income. Not simply promising workers better economic opportunities, advertisements presented the purchase of BSL shares as a way for black women and men to achieve respectability. (*Negro World*, February 26, 1921)

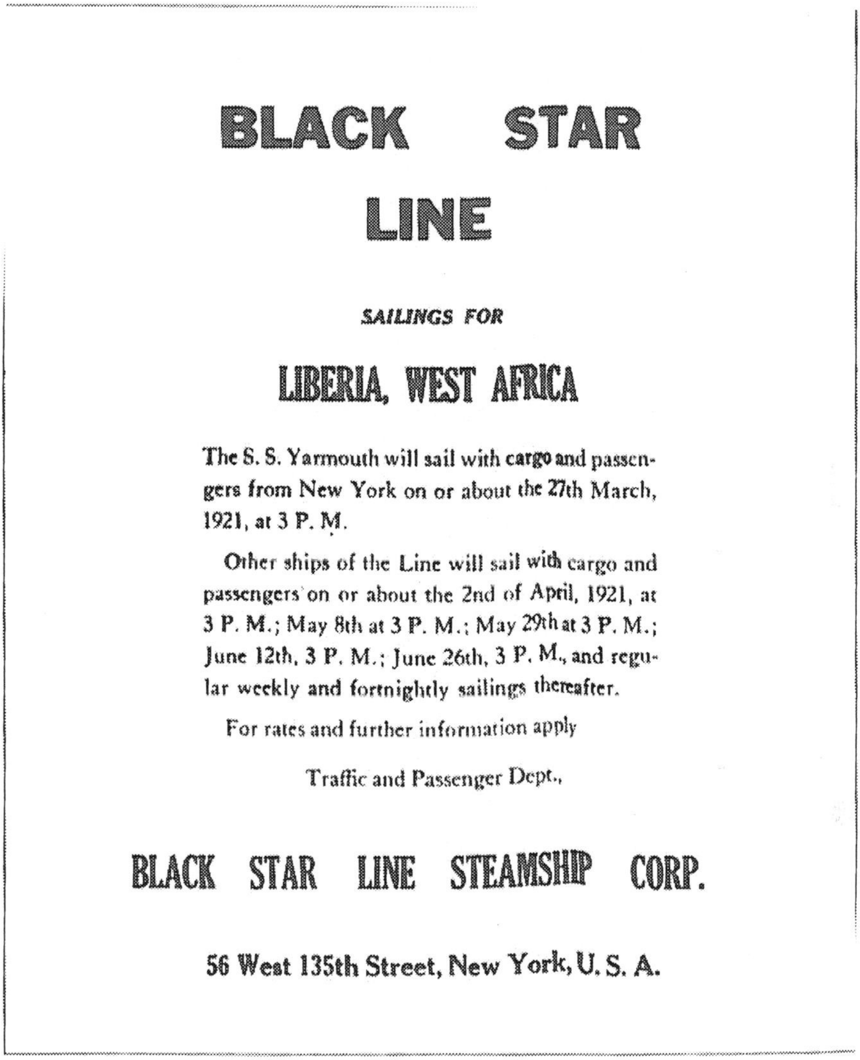

BLACK STAR LINE

SAILINGS FOR

LIBERIA, WEST AFRICA

The S. S. Yarmouth will sail with cargo and passengers from New York on or about the 27th March, 1921, at 3 P. M.

Other ships of the Line will sail with cargo and passengers on or about the 2nd of April, 1921, at 3 P. M.; May 8th at 3 P. M.; May 29th at 3 P. M.; June 12th, 3 P. M.; June 26th, 3 P. M., and regular weekly and fortnightly sailings thereafter.

For rates and further information apply

Traffic and Passenger Dept.,

BLACK STAR LINE STEAMSHIP CORP.

56 West 135th Street, New York, U. S. A.

Figure 6. A central component of the UNIA's Pan-African agenda was its effort to establish an autonomous colony in the West African country of Liberia. Negotiations between the UNIA and the Liberian government commenced in 1920. Nowhere in the United States was response to advertisements for emigration to Liberia more enthusiastic and positive than the Jim Crow South. (*Negro World*, February 26, 1921)

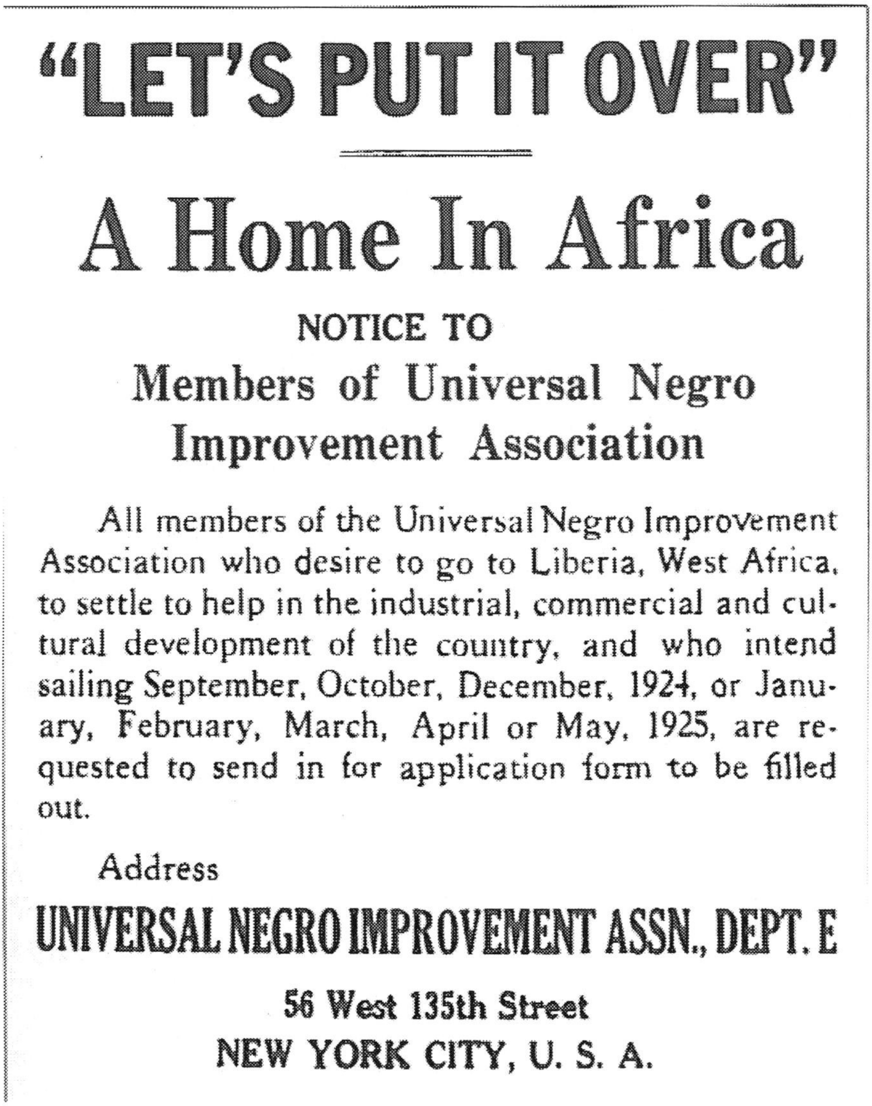

"LET'S PUT IT OVER"

A Home In Africa

NOTICE TO
Members of Universal Negro Improvement Association

All members of the Universal Negro Improvement Association who desire to go to Liberia, West Africa, to settle to help in the industrial, commercial and cultural development of the country, and who intend sailing September, October, December, 1924, or January, February, March, April or May, 1925, are requested to send in for application form to be filled out.

Address

UNIVERSAL NEGRO IMPROVEMENT ASSN., DEPT. E

56 West 135th Street
NEW YORK CITY, U. S. A.

Figure 7. Terribly frustrated with the resiliency of white supremacy in the United States, thousands of black Southerners responded enthusiastically to the UNIA's revitalization of its colonization program in 1924. Unfortunately for those interested in starting anew in Liberia, the UNIA proved unable to reach an agreement with the West African country. (*Negro World*, July 18, 1924)

Chapter Four
Virginia Garveyism, 1918–1942

Not beholden to any one political movement, Walter F. Green of Portsmouth, Virginia dedicated his time, resources, and intellect to various organizations after the close of World War I. Moved by the intense political activity in Virginia during the war, Green viewed the state's political landscape as pregnant with possibilities for revolutionary change. Few developments pleased the labor activist more than black Virginians' positive response to the formation of the National Brotherhood Workers of America (NBWA). Organized in Washington, DC on March, 21, 1919, the NBWA had launched an aggressive unionization drive in several major cities along the Atlantic Seaboard. Only three months after its formation, the NBWA claimed nearly five thousand members, of which the vast majority resided in Virginia. "Southern Negroes," Green proudly proclaimed, in the pages of the Negro World, "have begun to see that they can utilize the same methods used by white men for achieving the things they desire."[1] Terribly frustrated with the American Federation of Labor's callous disregard for black workers, Green labored diligently to transform the NBWA into a powerful force in working-class politics. Not surprising given the fluidity of race and class politics in black Virginia, the labor activist was also supportive of another organization extremely popular among African American workers in the state: the Universal Negro Improvement Association. Serving as the president of the Portsmouth UNIA in 1920, the labor activist participated in the organization's historic 1920 convention, organized local meetings, and even sold shares in the Black Star Line. Never compromising his politics, Green strategically used the institutional structures of the UNIA to draw more attention to the position of the black worker in the capitalist economy, the necessity for massive unionization, and the need for blacks to always question the prevailing authorities, powers, and hierarchies of the world. Even though many leftists criticized the Garvey movement for its race first philosophy, Green celebrated the UNIA as an organizational vehicle through which black workers could achieve political power and economic justice.

This chapter details the diverse and at times contradictory ways in which politically engaged Virginians used the UNIA to transform existing power relations at the local and international level. It focuses on those cities in Virginia where the movement was most visible: Newport News, Norfolk, Portsmouth, and Richmond. Surveying the political options available to them, thousands of blacks in these port cities viewed political unification with oppressed blacks in other parts of the world as the most viable solution to the problem of global white supremacy "There is one way," W.H. Pearson of Newport News reasoned, "in which we can improve ourselves, and take our place beside other races of the earth, and that is to develop our full power by uniting our forces and bringing about unity of action among the Negro peoples of the world. We must draw together our scattered and divided forces into one gigantic organization and act as one solid body all over the world for the amelioration and ultimate emancipation of the race."[2] An immediate concern for those committed to the internationalist agenda of the UNIA was the formation of a powerful Negro nationality in Africa. To achieve this end, some Virginian Garveyites worked with the white supremacist Earnest Sevier Cox and the Anglo-Saxon Clubs of America. A racist group based in Richmond, the Anglo-Saxon Clubs of America sought to secure the passage of legislation favoring federal support for African American repatriation to Liberia. Even though UNIA followers routinely criticized liberal integrationists and black leftists for associating with whites, some movement supporters displayed little reservations about their own collaborations with white racists. Virginian Garveyites' relationship with some of the state's leading white supremacists speaks volumes about the conservative strains within the UNIA, as well as reveals the extent to which their political decisions were significantly informed by the state's political culture. Virginia provided black nationalists with certain political options, choices, and alliances unavailable in many parts of the South. An outspoken and visible group of white supremacists in the state not only dedicated themselves to the passage of legislation providing federal support for the massive relocation of African Americans to Africa, but freely expressed their willingness to cooperate with black nationalist organizations.

Not all Virginian Garveyites, however, embraced white supremacist groups. Skeptical about Earnest Cox and his white cohorts, one group of UNIA followers proposed political alternatives to the activities of their more conservative counterparts. To more effectively counter the local, national, and global manifestations of white political and economic supremacy, they advocated the development of economic cooperatives, provided assistance to civil rights, labor, and radical groups in their community, and generally stayed away from political alliances with white racists. Thus, the UNIA in Virginia was hardly uniform with regards to its ideological focus and political activity. Noting the existence of competing traditions within the Virginia Garvey movement enables us to better understand how individuals as politically diverse as trade unionist Walter Green and white supremacist Earnest Cox could find political utility, if only briefly, in the Pan-African nationalism of the UNIA.

HAMPTON ROADS, VIRGINIA: THE BIRTHPLACE OF SOUTHERN GARVEYISM

A coastal area including the cities of Portsmouth, Newport News, Norfolk, and Jamestown, Hampton Roads, Virginia was the official birthplace of Southern Garveysim. Three months after the UNIA's incorporation in New York City, Marcus Garvey, in September of 1918, initiated an extensive membership campaign in Newport News, Virginia. Upon his arrival in the bustling port city, Garvey scheduled dinner at Gaskins Café with a group of men quite familiar with the West Indian's meteoric rise in Harlem. Intrigued by Garvey's political vision, these men immediately arranged for him to speak at First Baptist Church the following night. No record of Garvey's speech is available, but according to one eyewitness, the UNIA leader's message of black pride, Pan-African unity, and economic uplift resonated deeply with those who attended his lecture. "A division was established with over a hundred names the first night," Henry Vinton Plummer, the division's first vice-president, recalled years later, "and continuously thereafter members were enrolled to the extent of three or four thousand in less than six months."[3] Shortly after the formation of the Newport News UNIA, vibrant locals sprouted up in the nearby cities of Norfolk and Portsmouth. To recruit new members into the organization as well as strengthen the foundations of the movement in their local communities, UNIA branches held elaborate meetings, which familiarized the community with the objectives of the UNIA, provided lively entertainment, and featured some of the most recognized leaders in black America. Such well-respected community leaders as P.B. Young, editor of the largest black newspaper in the South, the *Norfolk Journal and Guide*, William Rich, president of Norfolk's Metropolitan Bank and Trust Company, and Mr. J.E. Maynor, manager of the Praiseworthy Muse Publishing Company, frequently spoke at UNIA functions in Norfolk and Newport News. Virginian Garveyites also had the opportunity to entertain northern intellectuals and activists like the noted socialist thinker, Hubert Harrison, William Ferris, Amy Ashwood Garvey, and of course, Marcus Garvey. Frequent visits by northern leaders not only strengthened Virginians' bond with blacks who lived above the Mason-Dixon Line, but also added vitality to the local political culture.[4]

Staying abreast of the UNIA's developments in New York, black Virginians were particularly interested in the movement's most heralded enterprise, the Black Star Line. Living in an area where the shipping industry employed thousands of people, many blacks in the Hampton Roads area shared Garvey's views on the potential earning power of the BSL. Writing to his New York followers in July of 1919, Garvey enthused over Afro-Virginians' interest in the BSL and their willingness to purchase shares in the fledging enterprise:

> I have been lecturing through the state of Virginia for fourteen days, and I must say that the people all through have been most responsive to the new doctrine being taught, that of preparation and action in this, the age of unceasing activity. The great enterprise of the Black Star Line is receiving great support in Virginia, and I feel sure that by the splendid start by the people in their sections that our steamship line will become one of the most prosperous ones afloat after October 31.[5]

Garvey was particularly encouraged by the people in Newport News who "responded most splendidly to the call of the Universal Negro Improvement Association." "At that end," he proudly noted, "I found an enthusiastic people anxiously waiting to receive us and to show their fullest appreciation of the work that we have started in the interest of our downtrodden people."[6]

Thrilled about the BSL's potential for success, Afro-Virginians were deeply committed to the UNIA's economic agenda, but their faith would be severely tested in September of 1919, when Robert Abbott of the *Chicago Defender* dismissed the BSL as a worthless enterprise. Writing off the BSL as a fraudulent scheme designed solely to get money from "ignorant Negroes," the editor of the most widely read weekly in black America advised against purchasing BSL stock.[7] "Garvey's proposition," Abbott explained, "is similar to the one tried on the American public a few years ago by Chief Sam, a notorious confidence man who chartered a dilapidated ship at the expense of his victims, and set out on the ocean voyage to reach the shores of Africa, but drifted aimlessly about in the waves at the mercy of the sea."[8] Needless to say, the *Chicago Defender's* commentary on the BSL deeply troubled Virginian investors. "A large number who had subscribed to stock in the Black Star line," Allen Hobbs, the president of the

Norfolk UNIA, later remembered, "demanded their money back and pro-spective investors refused to purchase stock."[9] Testifying for the UNIA in its libel case against the *Defender*, Hobbs stated that "upwards of one thou-sand people called his attention to the statement published in the *Chicago Defender* and wanted to get an explanation as to the truths and untruth of the statements."[10] Walter Green reported a similar situation in Portsmouth. One member of his church who had purchased BSL stock dismissed the line as "no good," complaining that Marcus Garvey was "taking money from them and putting it into a fake proposition."[11] Sales in the line declined considerably for about two weeks, but rebounded after Garvey visited Newport News in October of 1919.[12] Lecturing in the Hampton Roads area for nearly a week, Garvey assured his followers of the line's legitimacy. Very successful in his efforts, Garvey collected nearly ten thousand dollars, which enabled the BSL to finalize its purchase of the SS *Yarmouth*.[13] To the delight of Virginian Garveyites, the SS *Yarmouth*, rechristened as the SS *Frederick Douglass*, embarked on its first voyage to Cuba and the West Indies on November 5, 1919. Over the next year, black Virginians con-tinued to invest in the line, which purchased two additional ships, the SS *Kanawha* and the SS *Shadyside*.

A strong desire to be of service to the race definitely motivated Virgin-ian women and men to purchase shares in the line, but Garvey's promise to provide black laborers with skilled and high paying jobs was an equally important factor in their decision to invest in the enterprise.[14] Work-ing women and men found the chance to widen their economic options quite appealing. To be sure, few southern cities offered black men more employment opportunities during the World War I period than Newport News, Norfolk, and Portsmouth, but the segmentation of the labor market along racial lines still consigned most black workers to the lowest-paying and least stable jobs.[15] "Even the government," Walter Green complained to fellow Garveyites, "in the giving out of employment in the Navy Yard, discriminates against the colored man, giving preference in almost every instance to white men; not only that, but colored mechanics and work-men receive less pay from the Government than whites."[16] Viewing the BSL as an additional vehicle through which black workers could improve their material condition, Green promoted the BSL "as a great boon and benefit to the race in the future."[17] Until black laborers received fair and equal treatment from white employers and the white-controlled labor unions, he opined, the African American working class should rally behind the UNIA's race-based economic agenda.

More than a few Virginians shared Green's views. Fully supportive of the UNIA's economic nationalism, Allen Hobbs of the Norfolk UNIA encouraged others to become BSL shareholders.[18] "Let us take out shares in the Black Star Line in order that we may buy more ships, better ships, and bigger ships."[19] A common laborer at the local docks, Hobbs championed the idea of working for and investing in black-owned enterprises. "There should be no trouble," he asserted, "in making up your minds to help your race rise to a position in the maritime world that you and every other Negro could point to with pride."[20] Once their economic position was strengthened, Hobbs and other Virginian Garveyites reasoned, African Americans would be in a better position to challenge the white power structure and eventually secure their political rights. "Upon the strong arm of our commercial and industrial strength," Newport News Garveyite N. Colatus Drew asserted, "we can demand, not beg for the same rights and privileges that are meted out to others."[21]

To advance the UNIA's goals, Garveyites in the Hampton Roads area not only financed the Black Star Line, but like their counterparts in other Southern cities, they also purchased Liberian Construction Bonds to "help in the furtherance of the industrial, commercial and agricultural purposes of the association in its construction plans in Africa."[22] Thanks to the support of black workers, the Hampton Roads area supported the UNIA's economic initiatives more consistently than any other region in the South. To a large extent black workers' embrace of the UNIA was a manifestation of their growing class consciousness, which as Earl Lewis points out in his brilliant study on black Norfolk, remained imbedded in the perspective of race.[23] Frequently ignored in discussions on Garvey's spectacular rise was the extent to which he benefited from the rising militancy of the black working class. An upsurge in black proletarian activism definitely assisted his efforts in Newport News, Norfolk, and Portsmouth. A year before Garvey's arrival in the Hampton Roads area, black waterfront laborers affiliated with the Transportation Workers Association had successfully negotiated new contracts which dramatically improved their pay, working conditions, and control over the production process.[24] Entering the region at a time when black working women and men felt quite confident about their abilities to effect social change, Garvey encountered African Americans who already harbored strong ideas concerning racial solidarity, the economic roots of their political struggles, and the ability of working people to achieve success without the support of the black elite.

VIRGINIA GARVEYISM AND THE POSTWAR RECESSION

Over the period between 1918 and 1920, the Hampton Roads area distinguished itself as the undisputed center of Southern Garveyism, but in the spring of 1921, UNIA divisions in Norfolk and Newport News started to show signs of decline due to financial hardships brought on by postwar demobilization.[25] All across the country, the economic recession resulted in rising levels of unemployment and extreme cutbacks in pay for those fortunate enough to hold on to their jobs. The situation was particularly bad in the Hampton Roads area. "Industrially," N. Colatus Drew sadly reported to readers of the *Negro World,* "Newport News is almost dead. Countless of our people are walking about the streets with absolutely nothing to do."[26] Similar letters came from UNIA leaders in other parts of the country. "The city," Reverend J.J. Mumford of the Winston-Salem UNIA informed the Parent Body in early 1922, "is at present passing through a financial crisis and many who would like to connect themselves with the association cannot conviently [sic] do so at present."[27] Undoubtedly many Virginians sympathized with the struggles of their comrades in North Carolina.

Taking notice of recent developments, Marcus Garvey promoted racial self-help as the most viable prescription for blacks' economic woes:

> "What are we going to do? Should we fold our arms and sit down in this condition? Are we waiting on some imaginary savior to come and relieve the situation? Are we waiting for some spiritual being to help us? We will wait until doomsday, and the miracle will not be performed . . . By your own actions, if initiated now, shall we be saved the fate of threatened disaster. Whilst conditions are bad among a large number of our race, we through unity in America, the West Indies, Central America, and Canada, we who are employed can do something worthy of the name of the race, though which we can ward off universal want within our ranks. You men of the Negro race who have $1,000, invest at least $500 in the Black Star Line now, and right now, and help us to buy more ships, so that we can transport the unemployed from this Western Hemisphere to Africa. If every man and woman of the Negro race does this in the next thirty days, the $10,000,000 capital of the Black Star Line will be subscribed. The corporation will be able to buy bigger ships, and more ships, and then we will be able to transport from this Western Hemisphere at least 3,000 men every week for work in Africa.[28]

Garvey's proposal was fraught with contradictions and weaknesses. First, he solicited the support of a group (the black professional class) that had been rather hostile toward the organization and had not shown much interest in its economic affairs. Second, Garvey presented Africa as replete with economic opportunity but the depression had taken its toll on the global economy. Lastly, Garvey failed to understand, or perhaps accept, the extent to which the success of self-help measures depended as much upon a favorable economic climate as blacks' desire to be of service to their race.

Not altering his political course or dialogue, Garvey continued stressing the themes of economic self-help, group unity, and African redemption in his speeches in Virginia and elsewhere. "Free national existence for the Negro race of the world," he thundered before hundreds of supporters at Norfolk's Attacks Theatre in June of 1922, "is a coming realization."[29] Standing strong in the face of adverse circumstances, Garvey predicted future success for the movement; but in the months to come, the UNIA would be beset with crisis after crisis. The defection of several prominent Parent Body leaders at the UNIA convention in August of 1922, the murder of ex-Garveyite James Eason in New Orleans on New Years Day, 1923, and Garvey's conviction on mail fraud charges in May, fractured and demoralized the movement at the local and national level.[30] Even amid considerable uncertainty, many Virginian Garveyites exhibited an unwavering devotion to the Pan-African agenda of the UNIA. "We, the Negro peoples of the world," Reverend E. Godfrey instructed his comrades in Newport News, "must put our trust in God and the Honorable Marcus Garvey and follow his footprints so that we will someday take our stand among the mighty nations of the earth. We can build a government of our own to be ruled by black men. As black men ruled in the past so black men can rule in the future."[31]

True to his promise to revitalize the organization's colonization efforts, Garvey, in December, 1923, dispatched Robert Lincoln Poston, Henrietta Vinton Davis, and J. Milton Van Lowe to Monrovia, Liberia, where they negotiated with government officials over the possible acquisition of territory near the Cavilla River in Maryland County.[32] Understanding the success of the organization's Liberian plans depended on its ability to provide affordable transportation to prospective colonists, Garvey organized the Black Cross Navigation and Trading Company (BCNTC) in March, 1924. Garvey's reconstitution of the defunct Black Star Line as the BCNTC spurred a new wave of activism in Virginia. Writing to the *Negro World,* W.J. Ward, president of the Mudlin division in Norfolk, enthused over the renewed interest in the organization's work: "Many people that at one time stood up against the U.N.I.A. are now ready to embark for Africa, and many of those that were onetime members have taken on new life."[33] Virginians interested in relocation to Liberia solicited information from African students in the area. Two natives of Cameroon, J.H. Eldwive and F.H. Mingolly lectured on life in West Africa before UNIA divisions in eastern Virginia. "Their lectures," an unidentified reporter for the Compostella Division in Norfolk wrote, "were full of information and inspiration. We know now more of our motherland

than we ever knew before. On each and every occasion that these two gentle-
men spoke in the division the hall [,] was packed with an eager and anxious
crowd."[34]

Virginian Garveyites' fervid desire to leave the United States undoubtedly surprised more than a few whites. Frequently, whites portrayed Virginia
as an idyllic region where the black population had ample opportunities for
advancement,[35] but Garveyites refuted these claims by pointing out the many
proscriptive measures imposed upon the black population by the white power
structure.[36] "Colored people," one Norfolk Garveyite succinctly explained,
"are Jim-crowed, segregated, ostracized, and given everything but a square
deal."[37] So long as blacks remained in the United States, many Garveyites
believed, they would never achieve complete freedom and realize their potential. "The vast reservoir of intellect of my race in America," John Fenner, the
president of the Richmond division, opined, "is going to waste. Why waste
it when if we are granted the proper support in a country all our own we
could well develop economically, industrially and make other achievements
of merit?"[38]

To sustain Virginians' interest in the organization's colonization plans,
Garvey and his assistant William Sherrill made several trips to the state.[39] Virginians turned out in impressive numbers when Sherrill visited Norfolk and
Newport News in the spring of 1924. A *Newport News Star* reporter attending one of Sherrill's lectures in Norfolk was stunned by the large percentage
of longtime members in the crowd. "When we entered the hall in which the
meeting was being held we were struck with the fact that scattered about in
the audience were men and women who joined the association when it first
started; men and women who were just as enthusiastic now for the organization as they have ever been."[40] Virginians' enthusiasm was remarkable not
merely because of the previous failure of the BSL, but also because of recent
efforts on the part of the black clergy to undermine the movement.

Three months before Garvey announced the formation of the BCNTC,
a group of black ministers in the Hampton Roads area had counseled local
blacks to sever their ties with the UNIA. "The Garvey movement," the
Baptist Ministers Union of Norfolk, Portsmouth, and Vicinity asserted in a
paid advertisement in the *Norfolk Journal and Guide*, "does not impress us
as being a sound proposition. It has more of the appearance of mirage, or
the hallucination of an enfeebled brain."[41] To continue to support the organization, they argued, was simply foolish. "It has been sufficiently proven,"
the ministers continued, "that something has gone wrong with the people's
money collected in this Movement."[42] In these ministers' estimation, the
organization and its various ventures were "unworthy of the moral or
financial support of the Negro anywhere."[43]

Claiming to have learned from the mistakes of the Black Star Line, Garvey instructed his followers to ignore such criticisms: "Don't you pay any attention to what the Negro critic is saying in his newspaper or pulpit. Not one of them can hand you a loaf of bread. They have no provision for employing the people: they can only take away from the people. The Universal Negro Improvement Association seeks to feed the people, employ the people and to make the people independent."[44] Undeterred by the Baptist Ministers Union's criticism of the new venture, Virginian Garveyites rallied behind the Parent Body's second attempt to build a viable shipping line.

With financial assistance from blacks in Virginia and elsewhere, BCNTC's officials purchased the line's first and only ship, the SS *General Goethels,* in the fall of 1924. On January 10, 1925, the SS *General Goethels* sailed for the West Indies. Stopping through Norfolk for a short period of time, BCNTC officials received additional funds from the city's working-class community. "In Norfolk we received a tremendous welcome from the Negro workers," one of the ship's crew members later recalled in the *Daily Worker.* "Marcus Garvey collected lots of money in Norfolk, cashing in on the enthusiasm of the people."[45] Of course, Garvey's success had to do with more than the enthusiasm of the people.

An important factor in BCNTC officials' fundraising success in Norfolk was local blacks' mounting concern about their place in the political economy. A growing number of Garveyites viewed the economic initiatives of the UNIA as the only way to safeguard themselves from the deleterious effects of mechanization and capital's reorganization of labor. Not long after the *General Goethels* embarked on its first voyage, one Virginian laid bare his economic concerns. "The modern inventions," Henry Harrison of the Norfolk UNIA opined in the *Negro World,* "have the greatest tendency to obstruct the earning power of the Negro people, as the majority of our race depends upon the white race for their livelihood."[46] No group, the longshoreman asserted, was in greater danger than black women. African American women in the domestic service sector, he explained in the pages of the *Negro World,* "are constantly replaced by the electric iron, percolator, and the electrical stove. . . . Anyone can plainly see that our women are being slowly eliminated of work."[47] Looking at the experiences of black men in Norfolk and elsewhere, Harrison, who worked on the local docks in Norfolk, was equally distressed over black men's precarious economic position. Capitalists' increased reliance on machines, he noted, "has reduced the number of our men employed twenty-five or thirty per cent or more. The electrical trucks with trailers and derricks on the docks, the tractors on the farms, machinery in factories are slowly but surely obstructing the earning power of our men, and causing large numbers to be out of work, and that makes labor so cheap that it is impossible to get a salary at a rate in which we can live comfortable."[48] To achieve economic empowerment within the ever-changing capitalist system, Harrison insisted, blacks needed to financially back the "commercial and industrial enterprises of the UNIA."[49]

Unfortunately for Harrison and other black workers who contributed so generously to the line, the *General Goethels*, which was constantly detained at many ports by fines for violations previously committed by the defunct Black Star Line, suspended operations in the summer of 1925.[50] Once again, Virginian Garveyites had to deal with disappointment and failure. Seven years had passed since the formation of the first UNIA in Virginia and the organization had yet to achieve most of its objectives. Strong adherents to the organization's philosophy of economic nationalism, working women and men had contributed thousands of dollars towards the central office's various enterprises, but they failed to reap any material benefits from their investments. Even worse, the Parent Body had been unable to strike a deal with the Liberian government. Worried about the potential strength of a UNIA colony, Liberia's State Department in the summer of 1924 banned the entrance of anyone associated with the UNIA. Still hopeful that a deal could be reached between the two parties, Garvey vowed to take the necessary steps to improve the Liberia situation, but the UNIA leader's imprisonment on mail fraud charges in February, 1925 complicated his plans to mend the organization's fractured relationship with the black republic.

Unwilling to give up on his African agenda, Garvey, in what some viewed as an act of extreme desperation, opened negotiations with the Anglo-Saxon Clubs of America (ASCOA), a Virginia-based, white supremacist group that lobbied hard for the passage of legislation authorizing the federal government to finance the removal of blacks to Liberia.[51] Cynical about the possibility of blacks achieving freedom in the United States, many Virginian Garveyites backed their leader's coalition with one of the most racist organizations in the state.[52] A central theme at UNIA meetings had been the need for blacks to act without white assistance, but after Garvey's imprisonment, many Garveyites in Virginia agreed to work with racial extremists in the white community, most notably Earnest Sevier Cox.

NEW STRATEGIES: GARVEYITES, WHITE COLONIZATIONISTS, AND THE AFRICAN REPATRIATION MOVEMENT

Noted white supremacist Earnest Cox functioned as the principal liaison between UNIA divisions in Virginia and the Anglo Saxon Clubs of America. A native of Tennessee who moved to Richmond in 1920, Cox had recently gained recognition as the author of *White America* and *Let My People Go*, two racist treaties which proposed colonization as the only solution to America's racial dilemma. Cox was extremely close to John Powell and W.A. Plecker, two racist ideologues who shared most, if not all, of his views on the most pressing social issues of the day. Substantially influenced by Madison Grant's *The Passing of the Great Race, or the Racial Basis of European History*, Lothrop Stoddard's *The Rising Tide of Color Against White World Supremacy*, and R.W. Shufeldt's *The Negro: A Menace to American Civilization*, Cox, Plecker, and Powell worried incessantly about the infusion of contaminated Negro blood into the white race. Convinced that "miscegenation had been increasing since the Civil War and that more and more people of mixed racial stock were passing as whites," these men vowed to defend the integrity of the white race.[53] Saving white civilization, they insisted, required Euro-America's upper crust to remove from the "superior white race" all those individuals contaminated with inferior Negro blood. As part of his crusade for the purification of the white race, University of Virginia graduate John Powell organized the Anglo-Saxon Clubs of America in the fall of 1922. Never would the ASCOA claim a large membership, but according to historian Richard Sherman, the organization produced "effective lobbyists who warned of the horrible fate that awaited the state and nation if immediate steps were not taken to prevent further racial intermixture."[54] Skillfully manipulating the fears and concerns of the white press along with Virginia's leading legislators, ASCOA leaders convinced the Virginia Assembly to pass the Racial Integrity Act of 1924, which changed the statutory definition of white from anyone with less than one-fourth of "Negro blood" to anyone with a discernable trace of African ancestry. Under tremendous pressure from the ASCOA, legislators immediately amended the existing laws against intermarriage to correspond to this new racial configuration.[55] Leading spokespersons for the Anglo Saxon Clubs were elated but not completely satisfied. Still concerned about the purity of the white race, John Powell and Earnest Cox redirected their attention to lobbying for congressional support for the removal of blacks to Liberia.

Certain that the success of their lobbying efforts for repatriation depended on their ability to demonstrate substantial black support for their cause, Cox and Powell pursued a relationship with Marcus Garvey and his black nationalist followers. Had Garvey been able to strike a deal with the Liberian government in 1924, he probably would have rejected the white supremacists' overtures, but the collapse of his negotiations with the Liberian government coupled with his imprisonment in early 1925 pushed him to the side of the ASCOA. Even though Garvey routinely frowned upon blacks in the NAACP and the Communist Party for their close relationship with white leftists, the imprisoned leader enthusiastically cooperated with Cox and his cohorts. "The White American Society, Anglo Saxon-Clubs, and [the] Ku-Klux-Klan," Garvey admitted to Cox in a letter in 1925, "have my full sympathy in fighting for a pure white race even as we are fighting for a pure Negro race."[56] Seemingly unconcerned about the negative impact his activities could have on the organization, Garvey publicly endorsed the ASCOA's politics.

Word of Garvey's budding friendship with the ASCOA and Earnest Cox spread quickly to his followers in Virginia. Intrigued by the white racist's proposed solutions to America's race problem, many UNIA followers in Virginia corresponded regularly with Cox, purchased the white supremacist's books, and allowed him to address them at their meetings. Next to Marcus Garvey's *The Philosophy and Opinions of Marcus Garvey,* Cox's *White America* and *Let My People Go* were the most widely read books in UNIA circles.[57] To the astonishment of Cox, Garveyites in Virginia purchased his books by the dozens and waxed eloquently on how much they loved the racist's ideas.[58] Samuel Ashby, treasurer of the Norfolk division in 1925, raved over *White America* and placed an order for ten additional copies of the book. "I fell in love with it," Ashby informed Cox, "and many friends ask me to get a copy of it."[59] Although Cox's Hegelian perspective on blacks' negligible role in the development of human society contradicted many of the Afrocentric teachings of the UNIA, Cox's strong denunciation of interracial sexual relations between whites and blacks mirrored many of the ideas advanced by racial purists within the Garvey movement.

Some outsiders looked with confusion at the alliance between Virginian Garveyites and the ASCOA; however, black and white separatists were alike in several ways. Obsessed with the issue of miscegenation, black nationalists and white supremacists tended to openly advocate racial purity, express loudly their disapproval of intermarriage, and portray civil rights activists as conniving miscegenationists whose primary purpose in life was racial amalgamation. The ideological similarities between UNIA followers and the Anglo Saxon Club leaders, according to political scientist Dean Robinson, should not surprise us. "More often than not," he explains, "nationalists share conventional assumptions common to their historical periods about "race," "culture," gender, class and group mobility."[60]

More than a few Garveyites expressed sympathy with many of Cox's ideas. Writing to Cox in the summer of 1925, A.A. Boyd of Norfolk applauded the white supremacist for his stance on miscegenation, black civil rights leaders, and repatriation. Candid in his discussions about interracial marriages, Boyd reveled in the opportunity to share his views with an avowed white supremacist. "I do not believe that God intended that the two races should dwell together," the outspoken Garveyite confessed in a letter to Cox, "and while the Negro race are [sic] being deprived of the privilege of their rights in this country, I see nothing for him but the fatherland . . . where they can work out their own destiny. [T]hey have the knowledge to do so."[61] Fighting for the creation of a biracial democracy in the United States, in the minister's opinion, was not only futile but against divine providence. "This is the white man's country, and I do not exspect [sic] the full privledge [sic] here as he."[62] Boyd not only acquiesced to the government's denial of his civil rights, but in his letters to Cox, he harshly condemned those leaders who struggled to garner the protection and the privileges of American citizenship:

> There are quite a few Negro minersters [sic] who are opposed to the Garvey movement. I ask that you white people please send out a committy [sic] among the such Negroes, lecture them to at their churches and their halls, and tell them just what they must do, and just what they must not do. They are preaching to their congregation that this is his home and that he has as much rights here as the white man, and I imphatically [sic] deny any such doctrine . . . Just one word from you white people, will work wonderously [sic] toward tearing down this so called high Negro.[63]

Boyd's letter reveals not only his utter contempt for certain members of the black elite but also the extent to which he and others increasingly viewed the support of whites as an essential precondition for the movement's success. "I ask that you white people," Boyd beseeched in his closing words to Cox, "please do what you can and all you can in helping us to go home because it is from you white people that we are looking to for succor."[64]

Not everyone in the UNIA, however, was willing to embrace such a paternalistic relationship with the Anglo-Saxon Clubs. Nor did all Virginian Garveyites obsess over the question of sexual relations between the races. To some, the matter of blacks' repatriation to Africa had absolutely nothing to do with the issue of miscegenation. John J. Fenner, the president of the Richmond UNIA, endorsed *voluntary* colonization as a way for blacks to ameliorate their deplorable condition, but he took exception to Garvey and Cox's fixation on the issue of racial purity. "I do not agree with you on the "Race Question" as you write. If you and Mr. Marcus Garvey think that time will bring about the integrity of both races you are mistaken."[65] Strongly defending an individual's right to engage in sexual relations with whomsoever he or she chose, the president of the Richmond division, unlike Garvey and Cox, viewed any effort to stop interracial romances and marriages as futile. "There has been and always will be incessant intermingling of types. And this process will continue whether my race settle in a domain to itself, or remain scattered."[66] Turned off by the notions of black inferiority underlying many of Cox's arguments against intermarriage, Fenner distanced himself from Earnest Cox and the Anglo Saxon Clubs.

Not surprisingly, Fenner eventually found himself in disagreement with those Garveyites who befriended white racists. Upon hearing of Rosa Loving's decision to invite Cox to lecture at a mass gathering sponsored by the UNIA, Fenner seethed with discontent over the proposed meeting. Troubled by the idea of his division featuring a white supremacist as its guest speaker, Fenner ordered Cox to cancel his visit for the sake of those who disapproved of his politics. "As president of Richmond," he explained, "and as one largely responsible for the work here I must state to you that the proposed meeting does not meet with my approval nor the complete approval of our members."[67] Cox's visit may not have had the approval of many in the Richmond Division, but the white supremacist had the support of Marcus Garvey, his wife Amy Jacques, who was scheduled to attend the meeting, and William Sherrill, the Acting President of the UNIA. Staying true to his initial promise to Rosa Loving and the Parent Body, Cox refused to cancel his plans.[68] No major disturbance occurred at the meeting attended by Cox, but his next appearance at a UNIA-sponsored event would not go over so smoothly.

On Wednesday night, September 15, Earnest Cox arrived at the Sharon Baptist Church, where William Sherrill, was scheduled to address a large audience of UNIA supporters. Once Sherrill completed his speech, Cox approached the pulpit. Totally against the idea of Cox speaking at his church, Reverend Roger Johnson, Jr., the pastor of Sharon Baptist, ordered the white supremacist to return to his seat. Stunned by the minister's bold actions, Cox walked away from the pulpit without any verbal objections. Sensing the potential for trouble, the minister hastily adjourned the meeting without any explanations to the stunned audience. Unbeknownst to Cox, Reverend Johnson had already informed the organization of his disapproval of the UNIA's plans to allow the white supremacist to speak in his church. Folks familiar with the Anglo-Saxon Clubs' attacks on social relations at Hampton Institute had communicated to Johnson their disagreement with the proposed meeting. Days before the scheduled gathering, Johnson, the Richmond UNIA, and Parent Body officials in New York reached an agreement which would supposedly satisfy all parties: Cox would be admitted into the church but he would not be allowed to address the audience.

Johnson ordered William Sherrill to inform Cox of the new agreement, but the Acting President General refused to do so. Why Cox was not informed of the organization's compromise with the church was never discussed in later correspondence between Sherrill, Cox, and the Richmond UNIA leaders, but in all probability, Sherrill assumed that Reverend Johnson would not have taken the risk of confronting a white man in public. Standing strong in his convictions, Johnson at the meeting refused to budge, even if his actions violated the rules of racial etiquette. More than likely, Johnson's actions greatly embarrassed Cox and his white friends in attendance, but the white supremacist remained in contact with UNIA divisions in Newport News, Norfolk, and even Richmond. So desperate was Cox to win black support for his colonization efforts that he tolerated actions which would have been totally unacceptable to the average white Southerner.

Shortly after the incident at Sharon Baptist, the Richmond division started to experience a rapid decline in membership.[69] So much of the UNIA's success in urban Virginia had been built upon its image as a defender of the humanity of black people. The UNIA's alliance with the ASCOA caused the organization to lose its credibility among more than a few of its supporters. Frustrated with the direction of the Garvey movement, John Fenner, along with nearly half of the Richmond UNIA, departed the organization in the fall of 1925. Even though he endorsed African emigration, Fenner refused to consort with white supremacists and criticized those black nationalists who chose to do so. In his opinion, the UNIA's alliance with the ASCOA complicated rather than enhanced the work of those committed to the struggle for equality and freedom.

A significant number of the organization's sympathizers shared Fenner's perspective. "Negroes, not members of the Universal Negro Improvement Association, but who have entertained quite a deal of sympathy with Garvey," *Norfolk Journal and Guide* editor P.B. Young observed, "are expressing amazement at his apparent confession of sympathy with the aims and purposes of the White American Society."[70] Quite possibly, the venerable editor had himself in mind when he made this observation. Friendly towards the Norfolk UNIA, Young had spoken to the division's followers on numerous occasions, carried notices of their meetings in his newspaper, and generally supported their work. More balanced in his coverage than most black editors, Young had refrained from attacks on the UNIA and its leader during the movement's formative years. All of this changed, however, when news of the Anglo Saxon Clubs' courtship of Garvey and Virginian Garveyites became public.

Incensed by Garvey's willingness to consort with the ASCOA, Young, in a series of editorials published between August and October of 1925, excoriated the UNIA leader for his refusal to recognize the irreparable damage his alliance had done to the black freedom struggle. Very much a race man, Young certainly sympathized with black nationalists who had become disenchanted with life in America, but he was disheartened by what he perceived as Garveyites' opportunistic alliance with the Anglo-Saxon Clubs of America. Moreover, the newspaper editor had major issues with the unwillingness of repatriation proponents to seriously address the diplomatic barriers in the way of their African designs. In the August 29th edition of his *Norfolk Journal and Guide*, Young catalogued all of the weaknesses in the UNIA's emigration scheme:

> If Mr. Garvey's Richmond friends could by any stretch of the imagination succeed in removing the 12,000,000 American Negroes to Africa they would be jumping out of the frying pan into the fire, because with the exception of little Liberia, there is not a foot of land in Africa that is not under the control of and inhabited by the European white man. All of them have served official notice upon Mr. Garvey to keep out. So has little Liberia, which has had notice served upon her by the bullish British and French that if she admits Garvey or any of his fool propaganda there will be immediately trouble for Liberia and plenty of it. Now then, if Mr. Garvey's Richmond friends, including the *Times Dispatch*, will join in a sincere and practical movement to assist their idol in chasing out of Africa all of the European overlords, commandeering the United States army and navy in the process, the thoughtful Negroes in this country will consider a colonization movement. [71]

Not in agreement with Young's commentary, H.C. Midgett, a member of the Newport News UNIA, criticized the editor for his criticism of the organization's politics. "Black men," he wrote, "why divide and waste energy fighting each other? If Garvey's principles are wrong, ten angels swearing they are right will make no difference; if they are right the powers of earth and hell combined will fail to keep them from fruition in due time." Quite circumspect in his letter, Midgett steered away from any discussion of the UNIA's alliance with white advocates of black removal to Africa, but he curtly dismissed Young's comments on the UNIA's emigration scheme: "I wish to say that in my humble attempts to follow the principles advocated by Garvey, I have never been able to gather that he ever advised the wholesale deportation or emigration of American Negroes to Africa."[72]

Seemingly unfazed by all of the negative publicity surrounding his alliance with Virginia's white colonization movement, Garvey did not budge from his position on the white supremacists. Writing from his prison cell in

Atlanta, Garvey advised his followers to extend to the Anglo-Saxon Clubs of America "the courtesy and fellowship that is logical to the program of the Universal Negro Improvement Association."[73] To those within the UNIA who harbored doubts about the organization's alliance with the ASCOA, he wrote: "I feel and believe that we, the two organizations, should work together for the purpose of bringing about the ideal sought—the purification of the races, their autonomous separation and the unbridled freedom of self-development and self-expression."[74] Very clear in his instructions, Garvey ordered his followers in Virginia and elsewhere to rally behind the ASCOA's attempts to persuade the Virginia Assembly to pass a resolution in favor of governmental support for the repatriation of African Americans to Liberia.

Garvey loyalists in Virginia heeded their leader's advice. Over the course of the next fifteen years, many Garveyites in Richmond, Newport News, and Norfolk stood behind the ASCOA's efforts to convince Congress to appropriate funds for the colonization of persons of African descent. Those who placed tremendous faith in the Anglo Saxon Clubs' lobbying efforts eventually discovered the political limitations of their white allies. Facing opposition from the white business elite as well as black liberals, the Virginia Assembly rejected the ASCOA's repatriation resolution in 1926 and 1930. Saddened but undeterred by the Virginia Assembly's decision, Earnest Cox pressed ahead with his plans. Several members of the UNIA were losing faith in the repatriation movement and its white proponents, but Cox refused to give up on his African dream. "There is a possibility of achieving success in this matter," Cox explained at a mass meeting sponsored by the Norfolk UNIA. "I can marshal support from any number of influential sources. I intend to ask the State of Virginia through the next Legislature to petition the Congress of the United States to aid all Negroes in America who wish to establish themselves in Liberia." "American Negroes have a right to independence as well as the white man and I intend to see that they get it."[75]

True to his word, Cox, in 1932, resubmitted his repatriation resolution to the Virginia Assembly. Listening to legislators discuss the strengths and weaknesses of the proposal, Cox felt confident about the chances of the resolution being passed. "It seemed for a few days," Cox later recalled to Marcus Garvey, "that the Virginia legislature would commit itself favorably to the Liberian project."[76] Ostensibly impressed with the resolution, the legislature asked its sponsors to insert within the document information on earlier Virginia statesmen's involvement in various colonization movements. "While this paragraph was being prepared," Cox explained to Garvey, "Delegate Sisson, sponsor of the resolution, requested that the

Committee allow him to withdraw the resolution, saying that though it was limited to aiding volunteer colonists it did not meet the approval of certain Negroes who oppose separation of the races as the solution of the race problem."[77] Still upbeat after another defeat, Cox urged patience on the part of his black colleagues. Visiting the UNIA division in Richmond in 1932, he guaranteed the eventual success of their Liberian scheme: "A government for Negroes of Negroes, and by Negroes, is not only in the making, but will come to pass and Marcus Garvey will reign supreme."[78]

Not everyone in the UNIA, however, was willing to patiently wait for the Virginia Assembly to pass a repatriation bill. Nor were they content to place black folks' future in the hands of a white racist whose lack of political power had become increasingly obvious. A more effective strategy, several Garveyites argued, had to be developed to redress the immediate grievances of the black population, especially with the onset of the Great Depression. Recognizing the limitations of the UNIA's program, one group of Garveyites formed locally-based political unions, participated in consumer boycotts, and organized their own cooperatives.[79]

Never had the UNIA exhibited much interest in political activity, but the exigencies created by the depression resulted in a shift in several Garveyites' position on the UNIA's involvement, or lack thereof, in local politics.[80] More than one hundred Garveyites in Newport News, for example, organized a Negro Political Union (NPU) in the spring of 1929, which aimed to strengthen the political power of the local black community. Organizers envisioned the political union as a vehicle to "unify all the electorate," so as to "obtain through collective action what is impossible by individual efforts."[81] The same year, several Garveyites in Norfolk participated in an extensive campaign to encourage blacks to pay their poll taxes. Some within the division refused to "pay $1.50 just for the privilege of voting for some white man," but others deemed it necessary to work towards increasing the black electorate.[82]

Moving away from the conservative faction within the UNIA, several Garveyites also participated in mass-based movements against the white power structure. UNIA followers in the Berkley division (Norfolk), for example, participated in a community-wide consumer boycott against white businesses in the summer of 1931. Very critical of local whites' treatment of African Americans, Joseph Eaton, president of the Berkley division, played a prominent role in organizing the boycott. "We called for 'boycotting' of certain merchants in our city," Eaton informed the editor of the *Negro World*, "because of their attitude toward our race, as to politics and also, for their using certain disrespectful remarks about the Negro on election day." If whites continued to deny blacks their civil rights, Eaton reasoned, then blacks should cease their patronage of white merchants. "I have not given one week's support to a white grocer since 1899 and advocated those methods to every Negro as far as general contact is concerned."[83]

Simultaneous with their boycott, Virginian Garveyites also launched cooperatives in Norfolk and Newport News. Economic hardships had led blacks all across the country to establish cooperatives in order to better harness their resources as consumers, producers, and workers. "The only thing that we not only can but must do," W.E.B. Du Bois insisted in a controversial article in the *Crisis*, "is voluntarily and insistently organize our economic and social power, no matter how much segregation it involves."[84] Sharing Du Bois belief, Newport News Garveyites organized a laundry service in 1931. Two years later, their counterparts in Norfolk opened a grocery story which was also organized along cooperative lines. It is hard to state with any degree of certainty the success of the laundry service and the grocery store, but as late as 1936, these cooperatives were still in operation.[85] The left's influence on the Garvey Movement was evident not only in its cooperative activity, but also in some Garveyites' cooperation with the Communist Party.

A sign of the movement's political flexibility, the Berkley UNIA permitted white and black radicals in the Communist Party to use its Liberty Hall for rallies in favor of rent strikes. On October 21, 1933, more than four hundred people assembled at Liberty Hall to protest the arrest of Fred Allen and his wife, two Communist organizers who had aided a man evicted from his home.[86] It is impossible to determine the number of Garveyites sympathetic to the Communist movement during the late twenties and thirties, but when one takes into consideration the Party's strong critique of Jim Crow and the class consciousness of many Virginian Garveyites, it is not unlikely that some folks in the UNIA may have been attracted to the ideas of the Communist Party. Unfortunately, the fragmentary nature of the evidence complicates any attempt to draw definitive conclusions on the involvement of Virginian Garveyites in the Communist Party or their level of support for other civil rights initiatives. However, the scant information available suggests that a small minority within the UNIA, unlike the more single-minded repatriationists, recognized the need to develop new strategies during the trying Depression years.

To the casual observer, the UNIA appeared to be moving towards the political left, but the situation was much more complex. Notwithstanding their white collegues' numerous failures, some Virginian Garveyites remained committed to their alliance with Earnest Cox and the Anglo Saxon Clubs of America. Their perseverance would be rewarded in 1936 when the Virginia Assembly finally passed a resolution in favor of governmental support for African American repatriation to Africa.

Nearly ten years after the ASCOA submitted its first repatriation resolution, on February 27, 1936, the Virginia General Assembly adopted the Bazille resolution, which memorialized Congress "to make provision for the colonization of persons of African descent, with their own consent, in Liberia, or at any other place or places on the African continent."[87] Overjoyed by the passage of the resolution, white supremacists applauded the legislators for their actions. "True emancipation of the Negro was inaugurated by the action of the Virginia Assembly on Capital Hill today," John Powell proclaimed in the *Richmond Dispatch.* [88] Thrilled by the news of the Virginia legislature's endorsement of federal aid for repatriation, Garveyites in Richmond praised Earnest Cox for his endeavors:

> We, the undersigned colored people of Richmond, Virginia, desire that you know that we appreciate your efforts to promote the cause of Negro Nationalism as advocated by the leaders of the Universal Negro Improvement Association. We favor your resolution before the General Assembly which requests federal assistance be given to capable men and women of the Negro Race who may volunteer to continue the colonization of Liberia and develop that country into a strong nation.[89]

Signed by sixty members of the Richmond division, the letter illustrates their deep appreciation for the white racist's work on their behalf. Spirits were extremely high in UNIA circles, but the passage of the Bazille resolution was only a small step in the tedious process of trying to secure governmental funding for their endeavors. To advance their cause, Garveyites solicited the assistance of legislators in other parts of the country, but few politicians outside Virginia exhibited any interest in the bill.

Then finally, in 1938, Virginian Garveyites discovered an ally in the person of Mississippi Senator, Theodore Bilbo. Sensing a change in the nation's politics and possibly the imminence of a major civil rights revolution, Bilbo embraced the repatriation movement and its leading black advocates. Widely known in the black community for his virulent racism as well as his public approval of the lynching of African Americans, Bilbo had recently gained recognition as one of President Franklin Roosevelt's most loyal allies in the conservative South. The Senator's dogged resolve to furnish greater public services and New Deal programs to poor whites endeared him to New Deal liberals in the North, who conveniently excused his virulent racism.

Bilbo's first public endorsement of federal funding for African repatriation occurred during his filibuster of Senators Robert F. Wagner and Frederick Van Nuys anti-lynching bill.[90] Angry with the proposed legislation, Bilbo vowed to get even with the "damn Yankees" by "getting the negroes deported to Africa."[91] One year later, on April, 24, 1939, the senator presented the Greater Liberia Bill before Congress. An amalgamation of previous resolutions by white separatists and black nationalists, the bill authorized Congress to negotiate with European powers for the cession of portions of West Africa lands, in addition to whatever settlements Liberia might provide.[92] Once the United States acquired the necessary land, which Bilbo reasoned should not be a problem due to England and France's financial indebtedness to the United States, African Americans between the ages of twenty-one and fifty would be eligible to receive land grants of fifty acres and grants–in-aid until their farms or businesses were self-sustaining. A clear reflection of Bilbo's doubts about blacks' capacity to self-govern, the Greater Liberian Bill authorized the American military to "govern the cession for up to two years, setting up a civil administration that could then govern for up to four more years." The territory would then gain "complete autonomy as a commonwealth of the US, but the bill maintained US officials the option of either seeking inclusion for the commonwealth in the state of Liberia or granting it full independence."[93]

Understanding the passage of his bill depended on plausible evidence of support by blacks, Bilbo solicited assistance from several black nationalist organizations: Mittie Lena Gordon's Chicago-based group, the Peace Movement of Ethiopia, Ramon A. Martinez's Negro Nationalist Society of America, and Marcus Garvey's UNIA.[94] Living in England at the time, Garvey, who stayed abreast of Bilbo's activities, had already encouraged followers to back the bill. Conversing with delegates at the UNIA's Eighth International Convention, held in Toronto during the summer of 1938, Garvey encouraged his followers to set aside their issues with the Mississippian's racist politics: "You will all realize that Senator Bilbo's resolution stands separate and distinct from Senator Bilbo himself. Regardless of how good or how bad a man may be himself, whenever he brings something that appeals to a race or group it is up to that particular group to grasp that particular thing and carry it for their own good. The motion as we understand it does not seek to compel all Negroes to return to Africa, but those who wish to go must be given the opportunity."[95]

The only Virginian delegate at the Toronto Convention, Priscilla Giddings, president of the Norfolk Club, carried the UNIA leader's message to her constituency. Once again, she received the support of Earnest Cox. A strong supporter of Bilbo's bill, Cox stayed in close contact with UNIA divisions and branches in Richmond and the Hampton Roads area. Taking several trips to Norfolk and Newport News in 1939, Cox delivered lectures on the Liberia Bill to the various branches in the city and surrounding areas. Though Cox encouraged Virginians to press ahead with their petition drive for Bilbo's bill, he also urged them to put more pressure on Virginian politicians. "A petition from a considerable number of Virginia Negroes," Cox explained to Giddings after a visit to the Norfolk UNIA, "would have a powerful effect in our legislature."[96] Very supportive of Cox's idea, Giddings responded with considerable enthusiasm. "I think it is a grand idea. And I shall do all in my power to get as many people to sighn [sic] the petition as I can. I shall get in touch with the Newport News division at once and start them to work on the matter. I am sure we can get at least three thousand or mabe [sic] more."[97] Immediately, Giddings organized a committee to coordinate the petition drive, which was launched in Richmond, Newport News, and Norfolk.

Giddings, Rosa Loving of Richmond, and Frank Morris of Newport News canvassed their respective communities for signatures for Bilbo's petition. A leading organizer for UNIA divisions and branches in Norfolk, Giddings encountered strong opposition from the NAACP and local ministers during her efforts to rally the community behind the organization's repatriation efforts.[98] Interpreting the civil rights organization's vigorous opposition as a sign of power shift in the black community Cox instructed Giddings to remain vigilant in her activities. "The N.A.A.C.P. fear [s] your group of Negro Nationalists more than they fear anything else on the earth. They fear that you will get attention from white people and get white support for your hope of gradually building up a Negro nation."[99]

Senator Bilbo rather than the NAACP delivered the death blow to the repatriation movement. Unfortunately for those who so desperately wanted to leave the United States, the demands of World War II along with a reelection campaign in 1940 forced the Negrophobe to suspend his repatriation efforts. Observing recent developments from London, Marcus Garvey dismissed Bilbo's abandonment of the repatriation cause as inconsequential to the UNIA's future. Not one to concede defeat, Garvey encouraged his American followers to carry on the work of the UNIA.

Taking her leader's advice, Priscilla Giddings pledged to build UNIA membership in the Hampton Roads area to the level of the early twenties, but the organization no longer appealed to the masses of black people.[100] A disappointed Giddings attributed the organization's struggles to apathy on the part of blacks, but her analysis was not grounded in reality. Anything but apathetic during the 1930s and early 1940s, black Virginians, as Earl Lewis demonstrates in his study of Norfolk, engaged in various attacks on the system of Jim Crow during these years. To effectuate change in the economic and political sphere, women and men buttressed the efforts of the Communist-sponsored Unemployed Councils, the Congress of Industrial Organizations, and the NAACP. Far too conservative in their politics, Garveyites' coalition with some of the state's most notorious white supremacists had alienated many individuals in the community.

CONCLUSION

Nothing was particularly unique about the movement's decline in Virginia. Eclipsed in popularity by such organizations as the Brotherhood of Sleeping Car Porters, the Congress of Industrial Organizations, and the American Communist Party, UNIA locals across the nation struggled to attract members during the 1930s. Quite simply, UNIA leaders at the local and national level failed to develop an agenda reflective of the needs, aspirations, and goals of those working-class blacks who had once been the movement's principal supporters. Worsening economic conditions not only limited Garveyites' ability to maintain their divisions' various programs, but caused many to question the wisdom of the organization's political agenda. Not only was the UNIA's self-help strategy unpersuasive during these trying times, but the association's apolitical stance hindered its ability to recruit blacks who embraced a more activist style of politics during the depression years. Early in the UNIA's history, the organization's focus on the development of black economic cooperatives, African redemption, and race pride meshed perfectly with the political experiences and aspirations of the 1920s New Negro, but by the New Deal era, the organization's political agenda had lost much of its appeal among blacks in both the southern and northern sections of the country.

So what happened to those women and men in urban Virginia, New Orleans, Miami, and other parts of the South who had dedicated their lives to the Garvey movement and created programs which contributed to the UNIA's vitality during the 1920s? Did the collapse of the movement mark the end of their political careers? Or did they immerse themselves in various nationalist, civil rights, and labor organizations?

Taking up an issue which has been treated only sparingly in the literature on black radical politics during the Popular Front period, the next chapter considers how women and men who had actively participated in UNIA branches and divisions across the South continued their fight against white supremacist institutions and practices, economic inequities, and social injustice after the organization's decline. It examines the complex ways in which their new political commitments challenged as well as reinforced the constellation of values and ideas which had previously shaped their worldview and activities.

Chapter Five

Life after the Garvey Movement

The broken fragments of the UNIA contain some of the best rank-and-file material to be found—material which has not been corrupted by false leadership. If the organization cannot be saved, at least out of the best of the fragments something will grow that is more in line with the new tendencies.

Robert Minor, Director of the American Communist Party's Central Committee for Negro Work, 1926 [1]

A lot of people think the Garvey movement is something that used to be, but Africa for the Africans at home and abroad will live for ever. I'm sure it will live forever. And the fact that it's in my heart, and I'm eighty years old, shows that the Garvey movement is still alive, you see."

Audley Moore, 1978 [2]

Standing before an emotionally distraught crowd of black New Orleaneans on the morning of December 2, 1927, Marcus Garvey bid an emotional farewell to his American followers. Scheduled for deportation to his native land of Jamaica at 11:30 a.m., Garvey had the opportunity to say a few words to his loyal followers in New Orleans, as well as to his closest New York associates who had hurriedly rushed to the Crescent City. Very briefly, Garvey expressed his appreciation for those who had provided financial and moral support during his stay in the United States, restated his adherence to the ideology of black nationalism, and assuaged the fears of those concerned about the negative impact his deportation might have on the future of the Universal Negro Improvement Association. "Nothing that has happened has daunted my courage," Garvey assured the crowd. "I want you to be impressed that wherever I may go I shall direct the affairs of the Universal Negro Improvement Association." [3] An emotional Garvey concluded his speech and prepared for departure. As the *Saramacca* veered away from the docks with the leader of the largest black organization of the decade on board, the distraught crowd, in cinematic fashion, erupted with the singing of the first stanza of the Universal African National anthem:

Ethiopia, the tyrant's falling,

Who smote thee upon thy knees?

And thy children are lustily calling

From over the distant seas.

Jehovah the Great One has heard us,

Has noted our sights and our tears

With His spirit of Love he has stirred us

To be one through the coming years.

A profound sadness engulfed UNIA followers upon hearing news of Garvey's deportation. No other leader had commanded more admiration, respect, and loyalty from black Americans during the 1920s. "Garvey," James Weldon Johnson remarked in his brilliant study, *Black Manhattan*, "stirred the imagination of the Negro masses as no Negro ever had. He raised more money in a few years than any other Negro organization had ever dreamed of. He had great power and great possibilities within his grasp."[4] Not simply successful in Johnson's Harlem, Garvey attracted support from women and men in the Midwest, the West Coast, and the Jim Crow South.

Suffering under the most invidious forms of white supremacy, many black Southerners celebrated the Jamaican-born activist as divinely chosen to lead his people out of political bondage and economic servitude. No one articulated this position more forcefully than the president of the Newport News UNIA. "Many of our colored organizations," R.R. Taylor proclaimed in an address to a local crowd, "have broken down because they had the wrong leaders, leaders who were chosen by the white man. We have a leader [Marcus Garvey] that a white man did not put before us, we have a leader that God sent to us."[5] Steadfast in their commitment to Garvey's racial vision, many Southern Garveyites continued their stride toward freedom after the UNIA leader's deportation from the United States.

To improve their local communities, Southern Garveyites established economic cooperatives, adult night schools, employment bureaus, and political unions. Standard survey texts on African American history routinely portray Garvey's incarceration in 1925 as the beginning of the UNIA's demise, but many UNIA divisions in the South thrived during the second half of the twenties. Weakening the UNIA in the South and the North was not Garvey's imprisonment and deportation, but the Great Depression. Even though black nationalism in its varied manifestations continued to influence certain aspects of African American culture, politics, and society, the UNIA was no longer a major force in black organizational life by the mid-1930s. Southern Garveyites desirous of continuing their fight against white supremacy had to find other mediums through which to realize political and economic freedom in the United States.

Continuing one's struggle against dehumanizing white supremacy after the agonizing pain of political defeat requires enormous courage, fortitude, and an unwavering commitment to defend the interests of black people. To summon the courage to evaluate critically and honestly one's past mistakes, to reaffirm one's faith in self and others, and to declare war against a political entity whose power seems infallible constitutes one of the greatest challenges for activists committed to revolutionary change and societal transformation. Transcending the pain and disappointment of the Garvey movement's collapse was not easy but vitally important for thousands of women and men who had dedicated their time, financial resources, and spiritual energy to the UNIA during the interwar years. To move forward politically, these women and men had to acknowledge the political shortcomings and even ethical failings of leaders whom they had viewed as unassailable giants, wrestle with the painful betrayals of those whom they had once called allies, and deal truthfully with their own political mistakes.

Finding new organizational vehicles through which to continue their fight against white supremacy and economic exploitation was a way for many black women and men to recover from the profound disappointment brought about by the collapse of the UNIA. All across the country, especially in New York and Chicago, former Garveyites pledged their allegiance to such organizations as the American Communist Party, the Congress of Industrial Organizations (CIO), the American Federation of Labor (AF of L), and the Brotherhood of Sleeping Car Porters. Taking the skills and lessons acquired from the UNIA to new social movements, former Garveyites provided exemplary leadership, dedicated service, and timely theoretical contributions to various labor, civil rights, and radical organizations.

No one will ever know the exact number of Southern Garveyites who went on to endorse the radical politics of the Communist Party, participated in the protest marches of the Civil Rights era, or rallied around the Black Power slogans and programs of the late sixties and early seventies. Quantifying UNIA followers' involvement in other political organizations is impossible; however, the available evidence suggests that many civil rights, nationalist, and labor organizations benefited from the services of ex-Garveyites.

Emerging out of the southern wing of the UNIA were several gifted women and men who assumed prominent positions in such organizations as the Nation of Islam, the Southern Tenant Farmers Union, the AF of L, the NAACP, the Southern Christian Leadership Conference, the Revolutionary Action Movement, and the Republic of New Africa. Few claimed a more distinguished career than Sylvia Woods. An outspoken labor activist whose political affiliations included the UNIA, the CIO, the Communist Party, and the Free Angela Davis Committee in Chicago, Woods traced her political roots to the Garvey movement in New Orleans. The daughter of a Garveyite father, who was also actively involved in the local labor movement, Woods regularly attended UNIA meetings as a child. "I was about maybe nine or ten at the beginning of the Garvey movement. We couldn't wait for Sundays to come because we went to the big meeting in Longshoremen's Hall. The band would be playing and we would march." [6] The youngster enjoyed the pageantry, but she was also moved by the powerful female presence in the organization:

> I'll never forget, there was a little woman there and she used to speak every Sunday. When that woman got up to talk, my father would just sit thrilled and then he'd look at me: "Are you listening?" I'd say, "I'm listening." "I want you to hear ever word she says because I want you to be able to speak like that woman. We have to have speakers in order to get free." And when we got home he would say, "Now what did she say?" I could say it just like her, with her same voice, all of her movements and everything. This would please him to no end. [7]

Spending much of her life fighting for the rights of black working women and men, Woods, as the quote above indicates, was groomed at an extremely young age for an active role in the black liberation struggle. Very early, the young Garveyite developed a strong sense of pride in her race, as well as an impatience with the hypocrisy of the United States. Summoned to the principal's office for her refusal to sing the Star Spangled Banner at the start of class, the ten-year old astonished him with her rejection of the cultural symbols of the US. To the principal's question of why she had refused to honor the country's national anthem, the precocious youngster responded,

"Because it says 'The land of the free and the home of the brave' and this is not the land of the free." Frustrated by the principal's line of questions, the youngster also communicated her displeasure with pledging her allegiance to the U.S. flag. "It's not my flag," she hissed to her principal. "The flag is with freedom. If the land is free and the flag is mine, then how come I can't do like the white kids?" Even after the fall of Jim Crow, Woods still expressed disregard for the country's national symbols: "I still don't pledge allegiance to the flag and don't sing the Star Spangled Banner," she proudly told Alice and Staughton Lynd in the 1970s.[8]

Such assertiveness pleased Woods' Garveyite father, who lectured his daughter daily on such diverse topics as the economic dimensions of white supremacy, the need for black and white workers to support trade unions, and the importance of women assuming leadership roles in racial uplift organizations. Extremely active in the New Orleans UNIA as a child and teenager, Woods' involvement with the black-nationalist organization ended after moving to Chicago during the depression. A geographical center of black nationalism during the thirties and forties, the Midwestern metropolis hosted relatively vibrant chapters of the UNIA, the Peace Ethiopian Movement, and of course, the Nation of Islam; however, the woman who had been so influenced by the teachings and social activities of the New Orleans UNIA rallied behind the work of the Congress of Industrial Organizations.

Frustrated with the treatment of black workers in the aircraft industry, the New Orleans native pledged her support to the CIO-affiliated United Autoworkers. Skillfully employing the rhetorical techniques that she had picked up as a child in the Garvey movement, Woods proved to be an effective union leader for the CIO, but she initially reeled at the prospect of joining hands with white workers who labored by her side at a local aircraft factory. "I only joined the union for what it could do for black people," Woods admitted years later. "I didn't care anything about whites. I didn't care if they lined them all up and shot them down—I wished they would! I had no knowledge of the unity of white and black. The only thing that I was interested in was what happened to black people."[9] Taking into account the knowledge and experiences gained in New Orleans and Chicago, Woods thought long and hard about the benefits and dangers efficacy of uniting with oppressed white workers. Significantly, Woods never doubted the importance of class unity across racial lines; rather the daughter of a self-proclaimed "union man" struggled to overcome her understandable apprehension concerning white workers' willingness to check their racist ideology and practices at the union's door. "You have to have faith in people," she later noted. "You know, I had little faith in white people. I think I had faith in black people. But you have to have faith in people. People have to learn and they can't learn unless we give them a chance." Notwithstanding her reservations about working with whites, Woods eventually plunged into intensive organizing work with the interracial CIO. Working hard to create a vibrant political culture among workers, the trade unionist organized lively meetings which had much in common with the UNIA political gatherings she had so diligently attended as a child in New Orleans. Serious about improving the lives of workers, especially those of African descent, Woods' contributions to black radical politics extended beyond the union hall. Entering the predominantly male electoral arena after World War II, Woods later gained recognition in 1946 as the first African American woman to run for the Illinois General State Assembly.

A politician, trade unionist, and black radical, Woods was amazing woman whose political career demonstrates the ways in which various ideologies and organizations pushed activists into various directions. Moving from black-nationalism to a more class-based politics, Woods eventually changed her attitude with regards to white workers, but she never abandoned her belief in the need for racial solidarity. Nor did she question the political usefulness of such nationalist organizations as the UNIA. More than thirty years after the demise of the Garvey movement, the New Orleans native celebrated her involvement in the UNIA as "the beginning of my realizing that you have to fight for freedom."[10]

Another noted black radical with political roots in Southern Garveyism was Queen Mother Audley Moore. A dedicated grassroots activist who figured prominently in the American Communist Party, the Revolutionary Action Movement, and the Republic of New Africa, Audley Moore spent her early adult years in New Orleans, where she actively participated in the UNIA between 1920 and 1922. Even though Moore had demonstrated a strong intolerance for racial injustice as a youngster, she viewed her years in the Garvey Movement as critical to the development of her political consciousness. "Marcus Garvey," she explained, "raised in me a certain knowledge of me belonging to people all over the world, the African people, and he gave me pride."[11] Leaving New Orleans for New York in 1922, Moore had profound respect and admiration for the UNIA and its Pan-African agenda, but the social and economic dislocations brought about by the Great Depression forced her to think more critically about the relationship between capitalist exploitation and racial oppression. The Louisiana native continued to believe strongly in certain aspects of black nationalism, but in the years following her move from New Orleans to New York, Moore was increasingly attracted to the radical politics of the black Left. Moved by the Communist Party's defense of the Scottsboro Boys, its involvement in local rent strikes, and its strong anti-imperialist position, Moore identified strongly with the politics of the Harlem Communist Party and its black spokesperson James Ford. "Mr. James Ford, the Communist representative" she recalled years later, " . . . was a black man talking about imperialism in Africa, [saying] that they [the Communist Party] had a worldwide movement with the working class organized throughout the world . . . Well now, I thought, this was a wonderful vehicle. If they've got a movement like that, and they're conscious of this thing that Garvey had been speaking about, then this may be a good thing for me to get in to help free my people."[12] Intensive study with Ford and other Communist Party theoreticians, she recalled, gave her a more in-depth understanding of capitalism, imperialism, and Socialism.[13] Leaving the Communist Party in 1950, Moore founded the Universal Association of Ethiopian Women, which focused on welfare rights, anti-lynching legislation, and prisoner rights. Staying active during the Civil Rights and Black Power eras, Moore mentored many prominent black radicals during the sixties and seventies. Noted black radical Askia Toure (Max Stanford), founder of the Revolutionary Action Movement, praised Moore for providing him and other revolutionary thinkers with political, theoretical, and organizational guidance. Years after her involvement in the New Orleans UNIA, Moore continued to carry the division's spirit of grassroots activism, racial pride, and self-determination to black women and men across the country.

To a large extent, the political activities of Audley Moore and Sylvia Woods after the decline of the UNIA demonstrate the ideological shifts taking place in the black community during the 30s and 40s. Even though Woods and Moore adopted a more anti-systemic position after leaving the UNIA, their love for African-descended peoples and their commitment to the black liberation struggle never wavered. In fact, their profound love for and commitment to black people animated and informed their class politics. The same can be said about another Southern Garveyite who embraced the labor struggle after the UNIA's decline: James B. Nimmo.

A Bahamian native who had been in charge of the Miami UNIA's paramilitary group, the Universal African Legions, Nimmo performed a critical role in the mass unionization of the city's workers between 1940 and 1955. Strong in his commitment to improving the quality of life for black laborers, Nimmo worked primarily with the Laundry International Union, the Transport Workers of America (TWA), and the CIO-affiliated Shipbuilder's Union.[14] Terribly frustrated with working conditions in the laundry industry, Nimmo, employed as a tailor, initiated discussions with workers at the city's largest laundry and dry cleaning plants about the formation of a labor union in 1943.[15] To stop their organizing efforts, one laundry plant fired several workers who had attended Nimmo's weekly meetings. Infuriated by the plant's actions, employees at City Laundry, French Benzol, and Town Laundry went on strike in support of their fired comrades.[16] Thoroughly organized, these laundry workers eventually forced their employers to yield to their demands for better pay, improved working conditions, and fairer job assignments.

Well-respected in Miami's black working-class community, Nimmo eventually attracted the attention of the leading Communist organizer in the city, Charles Smolioff. Quite impressed with the black laundry workers' efforts, Smolioff frequently stopped by their meetings to encourage them in their endeavors, offer his advice on the best ways to negotiate with management, and familiarize them with some of the basic principles of the American Communist Party. He wanted Nimmo to join the CIO. Nimmo was mainly committed to the work of the CIO, but in 1945, he agreed to become a member of the Florida Communist Party.[17] Apparently, Nimmo had not internalized Garvey's negative views toward white American Communists. Nor had he listened to black leaders in Miami who denounced the Soviet Union as the evil empire. "I didn't see communism at the time as an evil," he later explained. "I frankly thought it was a good thing. I didn't think there was anything evil about it."[18]

Nimmo worked closely with Smolioff and other Party organizers in the CIO's effort to organize workers in the shipbuilding and aviation industries, yet he never exhibited a genuine commitment to the Party's agenda. Even though he was a member of the Party's executive committee, he refused to pay his membership dues and showed very little interest in keeping up with the Party's position on key political questions. Not surprisingly in 1950, Nimmo severed his ties with the CP. Fifty-two years of age at the time of his departure from the Party, Nimmo had been at the center of black Miamians' struggle for political freedom and economic justice for more than thirty years. Notwithstanding his wealth of organizing experience, Nimmo found himself on the margins of the civil rights movement in Miami. Troubled by Nimmo's black nationalist past and his radical politics, moderate civil rights leaders shunned Nimmo and many others who had aggressively pushed for labor rights during the 1940s and 1950s.

Searching for a political home after the decline of the UNIA, Nimmo, Moore, and Woods turned to more leftist-oriented organizations, but the civil rights establishment was the more suitable option for some former Garveyites. A member of the Greensboro UNIA during its heyday, Randolph Blackwell was actively involved in the NAACP, the Southern Christian Leadership Conference, and the Voter Education Project between 1940 and 1965. Very supportive of Marcus Garvey's political agenda, Blackwell's father, Walter, had preached the virtues of the movement to his young son. Quite involved in the Greensboro UNIA[19], Randolph Blackwell not only attended meetings, but he also sold the official organs of the UNIA, the *Negro World* and later the *Black Man,* to folks in his community.[20]

Up until the 1930s, the Blackwell household remained strong in their commitment to the UNIA, but as Garvey's residence in Jamaica strained his ability to communicate with his followers in America, the politically conscious family searched for organizational alternatives to the UNIA. Even though Garvey had strongly condemned the work of the NAACP, Blackwell's father came to view the civil rights organization as the most effective vehicle through which to continue his struggle for improved social conditions for American blacks. "My father," Blackwell explained, "who had not particularly liked Du Bois up to this point or the NAACP up to this point, having been highly influenced by the Garvey movement begin to ease in his attitude towards [the NAACP] and by 1938 was then beginning to feel that that which he couldn't do through the Garvey movement could possibly be done through the NAACP. So that began to become the umbrella through which he would work."[21]

The younger Blackwell also pledged his support to the NAACP; however, the UNIA's emphasis on the need to organize "the masses" would continue to have a significant impact on his political philosophy. Working in the NAACP's Youth Council (NYC) as a student at North Carolina A&T, Blackwell was bothered by the organization's inability to involve black workers in its voter registration campaigns. To gain the support of laboring people, he convinced Brodie McCauley to run for a seat on the Greensboro City Council. The manager of a popular pool room and bar, McCauley had not engaged in any illegal activities, but many black leaders regarded him as a negative influence in the black community. Not in agreement with the black elite, Blackwell and his college friends conceived the running of McCauley as a way to involve marginalized women and men in the political process. Moreover, Blackwell sought to challenge traditional constructions of the "ideal political candidate."[22] Even though McCauley lost his bid for the council position, Blackwell was ecstatic that the college students' campaign had registered folks normally excluded in political life. Without question, their work laid the foundation for the election of Greensboro's first black city councilman, William Hampton, the following year.[23]

Surveying the political options available to him after the demise of the UNIA, Blackwell viewed participation in the NAACP as the most effective way to advance the black freedom cause. Not all ex-Garveyites shared his opinion. An avid follower of Marcus Garvey during the 1920s and 1930s, James Anderson of Camden, Arkansas had serious issues with the NAACP.

"I was never a member of the NAACP. I could not accept Dr. W.E.B. Du Bois' position because he seemed to oppose Marcus Garvey's program and I was on Garvey's side."[24] Viewing the NAACP as insufficiently militant, he entertained the idea of becoming a member of the American Communist Party. "I did think that perhaps the communist could offer something because they advocated that all men were equal regardless of race," he explained.[25] Taking notice of the Party's work, Anderson admired the leftist organization for its defense of the Scottsboro boys, their tireless efforts with the Unemployed Council, and their strong critiques of American racism, but he had issues with the Party's strident anti-capitalist position. "After studying the communist philosophy I came to the conclusion that their economic system was too harsh. I believe that the individual has right of private ownership."[26]

Settling in Chicago in 1934, Anderson eventually found a political and spiritual home in Elijah Muhammad's Nation of Islam (NOI). "It did not take much convincing for me to join the Temple because it seemed Islam was what I was looking for," he later recalled.[27] Climbing high in the leadership ranks of the NOI, Anderson eventually became the Assistant Minister of the Chicago Mosque and trusted confidante of Elijah Muhammad. Although he admired Muhammad, Minister James X praised Marcus Garvey as the "greatest Negro leader in American history."[28] Speaking on the legacy of Universal Negro Improvement Association at a NOI meeting, Minister James X credited his strong race consciousness to the work and teachings of Marcus Garvey. Anderson's continued admiration for Garvey speaks volumes not only about the Pan-Africanist's charismatic personality, but the power of his nationalist ideas.

An eclectic political movement advocating race pride, pan-African unity, and economic self-sufficiency, Garveyism had a profound impact on thousands of women and men in the US during the 1920s and 1930s. Easily the most successful black nationalist organization in Southern history, the UNIA achieved a level of success in the region unmatched by the Nation of Islam, the Black Panther Party, or the Republic of New Africa. To the amazement of the white populace, federal intelligence agents, and even officials at the UNIA's headquarters in New York, black Southern women and men enthusiastically embraced the pan-African politics of the UNIA. Even though their economic situation was precarious, Southern Garveyites helped finance the UNIA's numerous economic ventures, subscribed to and read the *Negro World,* and donated generously to Garvey's legal defense funds. Working women and men in the South labored earnestly to turn Marcus Garvey's Pan-African vision into a reality while accomplishing a great deal at the local level. During the interwar years, UNIA followers in the South constructed Liberty Halls, participated in local political struggles, provided social welfare services, and most importantly created an institutional space where black women and men formulated strategies to address their most pressing problems. Southern Garveyites' strong commitment to improve the quality of life in their communities, their willingness to challenge the black leadership class, and their recognition of the international dimensions of their own struggles against white supremacy constitutes a rich legacy upon which contemporary fighters against racism, class exploitation, and social injustice can draw on in these trying political times.

Notes

NOTES TO THE INTRODUCTION

1. P-138 to Bureau agent Charles J. Scully, 16 July 1921, "Bureau Section" case file [hereafter BS] 198940–205, Records of the Federal Bureau of Investigation, National Archives [hereafter RG65, BI, NA].
2. Theodore Kornweibel, Jr., *Seeing Red: Federal Campaigns Against Black Militancy, 1919–1925* (Bloomington: Indiana University Press, 1998), 116–118.
3. P-138 to Bureau agent Charles J. Scully, 16 July 1921, file BS 198940–205, RG65, BI, NA.
4. P-138 to Bureau agent Charles J. Scully, 16 July 1921, file BS 198940–205, RG65, BI, NA.
5. Robert Hill, *The Marcus Garvey and Universal Negro Improvement Association Papers*, Vol. I, 539.
6. Over the past two decades, scholars such as Charles Payne, Tera Hunter, Earl Lewis, Michael Honey, Elsa Barkley Brown, Timothy Tyson, and Robin Kelley have richly detailed black Southerners' complex struggle for social justice, their involvement in community building projects, and their diverse strategies of resistance and survival. Crucial studies include, but are not limited to Robin D.G. Kelley, *Hammer and Hoe: Alabama Communists During the Great Depression* (Chapel Iill: University of North Carolina Press, 1990); Michael K. Honey, *Southern Labor and Black Civil Rights: Organizing Memphis Workers* (Chicago: University of Illinois Press, 1993); Tera W. Hunter, *To 'Joy My Freedom: Southern Black Women's Lives and Labors After the Civil War* (Cambridge: Harvard University Press, 1997); Timothy B. Tyson, *Radio Free Dixie: Robert F. Williams and the Roots of Black Power* (Chapel Hill: University of North Carolina Press, 1999); Charles Payne and Adam Green, eds., *Time Longer Than Rope: A Century of African American Activism, 1850–1950* (New York: New York University Press, 2003); Earl Lewis, *In Their Own Interests: Race, Class, and Power in twentieth-Century Norfolk, Virginia* (Berkeley: University

of California Press, 1991); William P. Jones, *The Tribe of Black Ulysses: African American Lumber Workers in the Jim Crow South* (Urbana: University of Illinois Press, 2005); Robert R. Korstad, *Civil Rights Unionism: Tobacco Workers and the Struggle for Democracy in the Mid-Twentieth Century South* (Chapel Hill: University of North Carolina Press, 2003); Eric Arnesen, *Waterfront Workers of New Orleans: Race, Class, and Politics, 1863–1923* (Urbana: University of Illinois Press, 1991); Chana Kai Lee, *For Freedom's Sake: The Life of Fannie Lou Hamer* (Urbana: University of Illinois Press, 1999); Lance Hill, *The Deacons for Defense: Armed Resistance and the Civil Rights Movement* (Chapel Hill: The University of North Carolina Press, 2004).

7. See Kip Vought, "Racial Stirrings in Colored Town: The UNIA in Miami during the 1920s," *Tequesta 60,* (2000): 56–76; Barbara Bair, "Renegotiating Liberty: Garveyism, Women and Grassroots Organizing in Virginia," in *Women of the American South: A Multicultural Reader.* Ed. Christine Anne Farnham (New York: New York University Press, 1997); Bair, "Garveyism and Contested Political Terrain in 1920s Virginia," *in Afro-Virginia History and Culture. Ed. John Sailant (New York: Garland Publishing, 1999).* Undoubtedly the best example of a project devoted to the study of the movement in the South is the work of Mary Rolinson. A detailed narrative of the UNIA's presence in rural Arkansas, Georgia, and Mississippi, Rolinson's dissertation, *The Garvey Movement in the Rural South,* offers invaluable insight on those agricultural workers who embraced the philosophical tenets of Garveyism, the reasons behind their support of the nationalist organization, and why particular segments of the black population favored the separatist agenda of the UNIA over the integrationist strategies of the liberal NAACP. A thoroughly researched study, Rolinson's work constitutes an important contribution to the history of black activism in the rural South. Her findings not only illuminate the ideological diversity within the black Southern community, but give voice to those Southern women and men long marginalized in the historiography on twentieth-century black nationalism. See Mary Gambrell Rolinson, "The Garvey Movement in the Rural South, 1920–1927." Ph.D. Disssertation, Georgia State University, 2002).

8. More attentive to the South than other students of the Garvey movement, Judith Stein in her book, *The World of Marcus Garvey,* had a chapter in which she discussed Garvey's efforts to win the support of black Southerners. "The nearly four hundred UNIA divisions and chapters of the South," she maintained, "testified that Garvey had been there but not much else." Judith Stein, *The World of Marcus Garvey: Race and Class in Modern Society* (Baton Rouge: Louisiana State University 1986), 161.

9. Cedric J. Robinson, *Black Marxism: The Making of the Black Radical Tradition* (Chapel Hill: University of North Carolina Press, 1999; reprint (Verso: Zed Press, 1983), 215.)

10. *Messenger,* January 1923.

11. *Messenger,* January 1923.

12. For additional analysis on black leftists' response to and relationship with Marcus Garvey and the UNIA see Tony Martin, *Race First*, 221–272; Mark Solomon, *The Cry Was Unity: Communists and African Americans, 1917–1935* (Jackson: University Press of Mississippi, 1998), 22–37. See also A. Philip Randolph, *Messenger*, September 1921; George Padmore, "The Bankruptcy of Negro Leadership," *Negro Worker*, December 1931; Cyril V. Briggs, "How Garvey Betrayed the Negroes," *Negro Worker*, August 15, 1932.

13. Chandler Owen to Harry Daughtery, case file 198940–283, obtained by the author from the Federal Bureau of Investigation through the Freedom of Information Act (Hereafter FBI-FOIA).

14. Cyril Briggs, *The Communists*, June 1931. Strangely enough, Briggs published this article at a time when new recruits into the Communist Party included hundreds of farm hands in rural Alabama. See Robin Kelley's *Hammer and Hoe* (Chapel Hill: University of North Carolina Press, 1990).

15. *Negro Worker*, December 1931.

16. *Negro World*, November 17, 1927.

17. *Negro World*, November 17, 1927.

18. Barbara Foley, *Spectres of 1919: Class Nation in the Making of the New Negro*, Chicago: (University of Illinois Press, 2003), 7.

19. Rod Bush, *We Are Not What We Seem: Black Nationalism and Class Struggle in the American Century* (New York: New York University Press, 1999), 9.

20. An interesting analysis of leftists' critique of black nationalism can also be found in the work of the African American philosopher, Lucius Outlaw. See Lucius Outlaw, *On Race and Philosophy* (New York: Routledge Press, 1996); Lucius Outlaw, *Critical Social Theory in the Interest of Black Folk* (New York: Rowman and Littlefield Publishers, 2005).

21. Scholars interested in black nationalist organizations' anti-systemic thrust and revolutionary potential, of course, must never turn a blind eye to the profoundly conservative strains and tendencies within these same organizations. Southern Garveyism drew not only women and men vehemently opposed to white racism and economic injustice, but also reactionary elements within the black community willing to defend and even embrace the most regressive ideas and movements of racist whites.

22. See Timothy B. Tyson, *Radio Free Dixie: Robert F. Williams and the Roots of Black Power* (Chapel Hill: University of North Carolina Press, 1999); Lance Hill, *The Deacons for Defense: Armed Resistance and the Civil Rights Movement* (Chapel Hill: University of North Carolina Press, 2004); James Edward Smethurst, *The Black Arts Movement: Literary Nationalism in the 1960s and 1970s* (Chapel Hill: University of North Carolina Press, 2005); Winston A. Grady-Willis, *Challenging U.S. Apartheid: Atlanta and Black Struggles For Human Rights* (Durham: Duke University Press, 2006), 114–211.

23. The term "black transnational interaction" is used in Brent Hayes Edwards' *The Practice of Diaspora: Literature, Translation, and the Rise of Black Internationalism* (Cambridge: Harvard University Press, 2003), 5.

24. Theodore Vincent, *Black Power and the Garvey Movement* (Berkley: Rampart Press, 1971), 251.
25. Vincent, *Black Power and the Garvey Movement*, 251–252.
26. A central figure in the development and maturation of black nationalist historiography has been Wilson Moses. Nearly thirty years have passed since the publication of his pioneering study, *The Golden Age of Black Nationalism*, but his work remains a foundational text in the fields of American history and Africana studies. *Golden Age's* influence permeates the work of such recent studies as Stephen Howe's *Afrocentricism: Mythical Pasts and Imagined Homes*, Eddie Glaude's *Exodus*, Dean Robinson's *Black Nationalism in American Thought and Politics*, and Tommie Shelby's *We Who Are Dark: :The Philosophical Foundations of Black Solidarity*. A tour-de-force in intellectual history, *Golden Age* pointed out black nationalism's authoritarian tendencies, its indebtedness and contributions to Western intellectual history, and its connection to other political theories. Such themes and issues would be explored in Moses' later work: *Alexander Crummell: A Study of Civilization and Discontent*, *Black Messiahs and Uncle Toms: Social and Literary Manipulations of a Religious Myth*, and *Afrotopia: The Roots of African American Popular History*. See Wilson J. Moses, *The Golden Age of Black Nationalism, 1850–1925* (New York: Oxford University Press, 1988); Wilson J. Moses, *Afrotopia: The Roots of African American Popular History* (Cambridge: Cambridge University Press, 1998); Wilson J. Moses, *Alexander Crummell: A Study of Civilization and Discontent* (New York: Oxford University Press, 1989).

Of course, other scholars have made important contributions to the literature on black-nationalism. Especially noteworthy has been the recent explosion of studies on the Black Power era. For critical reassessments of Black Power's influence on African American politics and culture see Komozi Woodard, *A Nation Within a Nation: Amiri Baraka (Leroi Jones) and Black Power Politics* (Chapel Hill: University of North Carolina Press, 1999); Jerry Watts, *Amiri Baraka: The Politics and Art of a Black Intellectual* (New York: New York University Press, 2001); Eddie S. Glaude Jr., ed., *Is It Nation Time: Contemporary Essays on Black Power and Black Nationalism* (Chicago: University of Chicago Press, 2002); Scot Brown, *Fighting for US: Maulana Karenga, the US Organization, and Black Cultural Nationalism* (New York: New York University Press, 2003); Robert O. Self, *American Babylon: Race and the Struggle for Postwar Oakland* (Princeton: Princeton University Press, 2003); Jeffrey O.G. Ogbar, *Black Power: Radical Politics and African American Identity* (Baltimore: John Hopkins University Press, 2004); Bill V. Mullen, *Afro-Orientalism* (Minneapolis: University of Minnesota Press, 2004); Peniel E. Joseph, *Waiting 'Til the Midnight Hour: A Narrative History of Black Power in America* (New York: Henry Holt and Company, 2006); Peniel Joseph, ed., *The Black Power Movement: Rethinking the Civil Rights-Black Power Era* (New York: Routledge, 2006); Algernon Austin, *Achieving Blackness: Race, Black Nationalism, and Afrocentrism in the Twentieth Century* (New York: New York University Press, 2006).

27. Several feminist scholars have pointed out black nationalism's conservative tendencies with regards to gender politics. E. Frances White, Patricia Hill Collins, Michele Mitchell, and more recently Charise L. Cheney in *Sexual Politics in the Golden Age of Rap Nationalism* have elaborated on the ways white, bourgeois notions of gender roles undermined the emancipatory potential of black nationalist politics. See E. Francis White "Africa on My Mind: Gender, Counter Discourse, and African-American Nationalism," *Journal of Women's History* 2, no. 1 (Spring 1990): 73–97; Michele Mitchell, *Righteous Propagation: African Americans and the Politics of Racial Destiny after Reconstruction* (Chapel Hill: University of North Carolina Press, 2004); Kimberly Springer, *Living for the Revolution: Black Feminist Organizations, 1968–1980* (Durham: Duke University Press, 2005); Charise L. Cheney, *Sexual Politics in the Golden Age of Rap Nationalism*; Patricia Hill Collins, *From Black Power to Hip Hop: Racism, Nationalism, and Feminism* (Philadelphia: Temple University Press, 2006).

28. Algernon Austin and Dean Robinson explore this issue in their discussion on contemporary black nationalist politics. Of particular interest to them was black nationalists' response to the myriad social, political, and economic problems faced by black people during the 1980s and 1990s. During these two decades, stagnation in wages, deindustrialization, the retrograde policies of the Reagan/Bush regimes, and the crack-cocaine trade unleashed numerous hardships on the black and brown people occupying economically devastated neighborhoods in cities across the United States. Solving these problems consumed the energy of many academicians, self-described activists, journalists, and cultural workers in the black nationalist community. Seeing the struggles of the black poor and working poor as rooted in behavioral/personal shortcomings rather structural transformations, many black nationalists championed a reform in cultural values, individual and group behavior, community infrastructures. "The black nationalism which emerged during this era," Austin asserts, "was partially a response to this conservative politics, but interestingly it also absorbed some of the dominant conservative ideas." Conspicuously absent from most nationalist platforms was any serious critique of the political economy of capitalism. Dean Robinson does not find this particularly surprising. "The most consequential feature of black nationalism," Robinson boldly asserts, "is its apparent inability to diverge from what could be considered the "normal" politics of its day." Austin, *Achieving Blackness*, 130; Dean Robinson, *Black Nationalism in American Politics*, 1.

29. Ula Y. Taylor, *The Veiled Garvey: The Life and Times of Amy Jacques Garvey* (Chapel Hill: University of North Carolina Press, 2002); Ula Taylor, "Intellectual Pan-African Feminists: Amy Ashwood Garvey and Amy Jacques-Garvey," in *Time Longer Than Rope: A Century of African American Activism, 1850–1950*. eds, Charles M Payne and Adam Green (New York: New York University Press, 2003),179–195; Barbara Bair, "Renegotiating Liberty: Garveyism, Women and Grassroots Organizing in Virginia," in *Women of the American South: A Multicultural Reader*. Ed. Christine Anne Farnham (New York: New York University Press, 1997); Ibrahim

Sundiata, *Brothers and Strangers: Black Zion, Black Slavery, 1914–1940* (Durham: Duke University Press, 2003).

NOTES TO CHAPTER ONE

1. Robert Hill, *Marcus Garvey and the Universal Negro Improvement Association Papers* [Hereinafter *Marcus Garvey Papers*], Vol. 1, (Los Angeles: University of California Press, 1983), 452.
2. *Negro World*, March 26, 1927.
3. *Negro World*, March 26, 1927.
4. To gain more insight into the life of Marcus Garvey see Tony Martin, *Race First: The Ideological and Organizational Struggles of Marcus Garvey and the Universal Negro Improvement Association* (Dover: The Majority Press, 1976); Judith Stein, *The World of Marcus Garvey: Race and Class in Modern Society* (Louisiana State University Press, 1986); Wilson Moses, *Creative Conflict in African American Thought: Frederick Douglass, Alexander Crummell, Booker T. Washington, W.E.B. Du Bois, and Marcus Garvey* (Cambridge : Cambridge University Press, 2004), 231–283.
5. Hill, *Marcus Garvey Papers*, Vol. I, 15.
6. Amy Jacques Garvey, *Garvey and Garveyism* (London: Collier-Macmillan, 1970), 6.
7. Amy Jacques Garvey, *Garvey and Garveyism*, 7.
8. Martin, *Race First*, 5; Stein, *The World of Marcus Garvey*, 28.
9. Hill, *Marcus Garvey Papers*, Vol. I, 27–35.
10. Tony Martin, *Race First*, 5–6; Hill, *Marcus Garvey Papers*, Vol. I, 57–61.
11. John Henrik Clarke, ed., *Marcus Garvey and the Vision of Africa* (New York: Vintage Books, 1974), 48.
12. Hill, *Marcus Garvey Papers*, Vol. I, 62.
13. Hill, *Marcus Garvey Papers*, Vol. I, 141.
14. Hill, *Marcus Garvey Papers*, Vol. I, 68.
15. Hill, *Marcus Garvey Papers*, Vol. I, 71.
16. The Tuskegee Institute founder denied Garvey's request for financial assistance, but encouraged the young man to "come to Tuskegee and see for yourself what we are striving to do for the colored young men and women of the South." Hill, *Marcus Garvey Papers*, Vol. I, 141.
17. Hill, *Marcus Garvey Papers*, Vol. I, 186.
18. Hill, *Marcus Garvey Papers*, Vol. I, 191–192.
19. Hill, *Marcus Garvey Papers*, Vol. I, 195–202.
20. Hill, *Marcus Garvey Papers*, Vol. I, 202.
21. Hill, *Marcus Garvey Papers*, Vol. 1, 198.
22. Hill, *Marcus Garvey Papers*, Vol. 1, 199.
23. For an analysis of Marcus Garvey's relationship with Hubert Harrison and the Liberty League of Negro Americans see Jeffrey B. Perry, ed., *A Hubert Harrison Reader* (Middletown: Wesleyan University Press, 2001), 85–92, 182–200.

24.   Hill, *Marcus Garvey Papers*, Vol. II, 225. Rod Bush, *We Are Not What We Seem: Black Nationalism and Class Struggle in the American Century* (New York: University Press, 1992). Few, if any, members of Harlem's radical community would have disagreed with the black-nationalist about the need for blacks to strengthen their economic position. There was, however, considerable debate about the best way to achieve economic security and independence in the black community. Any attempt to draw generalizations on postwar black thinkers' views about political economy runs the risk of simplification, but generally speaking, one can classify New Negro radicals' approaches to the problem of black economic advancement under three broad categories: reformist socialism, revolutionary black internationalism, and black nationalism. Opposed to the "race-first" position of Marcus Garvey's UNIA, reformist socialists energetically promulgated the "class first" view of the Socialist Party. Viewing any form of nationalism as an obstacle to the class struggle, not all but many socialists theorized class as an economic category without any cultural, racial, or social limitations. No individual articulated this position more forcefully than A. Philip Randolph. Identified by the Bureau of Investigation as one of the most dangerous Negroes in the United States, Randolph was very outspoken in his support of socialist principles, endorsement of black involvement in trade union politics, and disregard for those advocates of racial solidarity over class solidarity. The founder of the Brotherhood of Sleeping Car Porters, according to sociologist Rod Bush "supported a Kautskian brand of Marxist reforms, wherein socialism would come about as a result of a series of economic reforms between management and labor, gradually increasing the decision-making role of labor in the workplace." True to his socialist teachings and understandings, Randolph called for the elimination of private property, state ownership of the means of production and distribution, the nationalization of the land, and the elimination of all barriers standing in the way of the complete enfranchisement of all working people. Zealous government officials branded Randolph a Communist, but the activist viewed the Comintern as incapable of leading a worldwide revolution. See Rod Bush, *We Are Not What We Seem*, 92.

A different view was offered by black radicals frequently identified in the scholarly literature as revolutionary nationalists. Like Randolph, revolutionary nationalists in the black community recognized the economic roots of the Negro problem, but their views about the Soviet Union and black-nationalism differed markedly from Randolph. Led by such individuals as Cyril Briggs, Hubert Harrison, W.A. Domingo, revolutionary black socialists urged blacks to ally with "the oppressed Irish, the oppressed Indian and all other oppressed people, and with the friend of the oppressed and enemy of our enemies, SOVIET RUSSIA." Inspired by V.I. Lenin's work (particularly his "Theses on the National and Colonial Questions,") on the relationship between national liberation movements and the Comintern's revolutionary agenda, revolutionary socialists welcomed the opportunity to establish meaningful relationships with the Communist Party. To advance the black freedom and class struggle, these revolutionaries advocated the formation of workers' cooperatives, involvement in labor politics, and support of the Soviet Union's international agenda. Less sectarian than scientific socialists, black internationalists defended national liberation movements as beneficial and complementary to the class struggle.

25. Hill, *Marcus Garvey Papers*, Vol. III, 55.
26. Only blacks could buy stock in the Black Star Line and shareholders could not purchase more than two hundred dollars worth of stock.
27. *Negro World*, November 13, 1920.
28. The best analysis of the UNIA's relationship with the Liberian government can be found in Elliot Skinner's *African Americans and U.S. Policy Toward Africa* and Ibrahim Sundiata's more recent study, *Brothers and Strangers*. See Elliot P. Skinner's *African Americans and U.S. Policy Toward Africa, 1850–1924: In Defense of Black Nationality* (Washington: Howard University, 1992), 381–469; Ibrahim Sundiata, *Brothers and Strangers: Black Zion, Black Slavery, 1914–1940* (Durham: Duke University Press, 2003), 10–78.

    Specifically calling for the emigration of a technocratic elite/ urban artisan class to the African nation, the UNIA's President General viewed the contributions of Western blacks as integral to the country's political, economic, and social development. "The doctrine of going "Back to Africa" must be clearly understood," Garvey told an audience at Liberty Hall in New York. "We are not preaching any doctrines to ask all of the Negroes of Harlem and of the United States to pack up their trunks and to leave for Africa . . . But we are asking you to get this Organization to do the pioneering work. The majority of us may remain here, but we must send our scientists, our mechanics, and our artisans, and let them build the great Educational and other institutions necessary." *Negro World*, August 14, 1920.

29. Ultimately, Garvey and his officials proved unable to strike an agreement with the government for creation of an UNIA colony Liberia. A Pan-Africanist who unequivocally condemned Western colonialism, Garvey envisioned Liberia as a potential launch pad for future attacks on colonial rule in Africa. Concerned about the territorial integrity of his country, President King refused to allow Liberia to be made a center of aggression or conspiracy against other sovereign states. Another concern of the Liberian government was the UNIA's relationship with the indigenous peoples of Liberia who worked as virtual slaves on the plantations of the Americo-Liberian ruling class. In many ways, the democratic thrust of the UNIA clashed with the exploitative practices of the Americo-Liberian ruling class. Unfortunately for Garvey, President King and other members of the Liberian elite were unwilling to sacrifice their class interests at the diasporan altar. Co-operation with diasporan blacks in the political and economic realm was secondary to the government's efforts to maintain its territorial integrity and political sovereignty. Not surprisingly, negotiations between the UNIA and the Liberian government officially ended in 1924 with the government's banning the entrance of anyone affiliated with the Garvey movement.
30. See Hill, *Marcus Garvey Papers*, Vol. I, 331, 338.
31. Hill, *Marcus Garvey Papers*, Vol. III, 494.

32. Hill, *Marcus Garvey Papers*, Vol. III, 530.
33. For detail on Garvey's visit to these cities see Agent J.M. Toliver to Bureau, July 16, 1921, case file 198140–198, Record Group 59, Department of State, National Archives [hereafter RG59, DS, NA]; Howard Wright to General Intelligence Division, 14, April 1921, BS 202–600–10, RG 65, BI, NA; Robert Hill, Marcus Garvey Papers, Vol. I, 452; *The Spokesman*, May 1927; *Negro World*, March 5, April 16, April 30, 1921.
34. Fragmentary evidence points to Newport News, Virginia as the birthplace of Southern Garveyism. *The Spokesman*, May 1927.
35. *Negro World*, November 1, 1919.
36. *Negro World*, June 25, 1921. Eason's work in North Carolina was also impressive. A couple of months after Raleigh Garveyites accused J.D. Brooks, the UNIA's Secretary- General, of stealing funds from their treasury, Garvey pleaded with Eason to assist him in his efforts to restore the confidence of disgruntled women and men who had left the organization. To revitalize the movement in Raleigh, Eason conducted a series of lectures. A masterful orator, Eason drew crowds of more than six hundred in Raleigh for four consecutive nights. Thanks to the service of Eason, the Raleigh division achieved a greater degree of stability and remained active until Garvey's deportation in 1927. *Negro World*, April 16, 1921.
37. *Negro World*, February 4, 1922.
38. *Negro World*, August 25, 1923.
39. Moved by Alaida Robertson's oratorical talents, Samuel A. Haynes nominated her for the post of Fourth Assistant-President General—a position specifically created for the elocutionist Henrietta Vinton Davis, the most visible and powerful woman in the association—at the Third Annual UNIA Convention in New York during the summer of 1922. A high ranking position in the central office eluded Robertson during her fifteen-year tenure with the UNIA, but she effectively parlayed her strong oratorical skills into a long-time, salaried position as a UNIA recruiter in the Midwest. Oddly enough, despite her own work as a field organizer and her extensive travel for the association, Robertson in a debate at the 1922 convention frowned upon the selection of women as field representatives and recruiters on the dubious grounds of incompetent women "losing the respect of the men" in the organization and destroying the morale of the movement. Her objection to the selection of women as field representatives appears to have stemmed from both traditional gender conventions and genuine concerns with the dangers of travel for black women in the South. Robertson, despite her comments, maintained a highly visible, public presence in the organization in the twenties and early thirties. Hill, *Marcus Garvey Papers*, Vol. IV, 1038.
40. Central office leaders recognized the importance of the *Negro World* as a recruitment tool. Bishop George Alexander McGuire of the African Orthodox Church identified the weekly as the "greatest missionary in building up divisions and making converts to the cause outside of New York City." *Negro World*, April 2, 1921.
    The *Negro World*'s unequivocal critique of racism in the Jim Crow South and its condemnation of the horrific practice of lynching

undoubtedly sharpened the newspaper's appeal in the region. The weekly was not as fiercely anti-South as Robert Abbott's *Chicago Defender*, but definitely more critical of the racial status quota than many southern black newspapers.

41. The weekly's importance to the creation and cultivation of a diasporan and nationalistic consciousness was quite apparent to Marcus Garvey: "If there is to be a united sentiment among all the people, if there is to be unity of action in everything, then there must be a medium through which this sentiment must be created, and the greatest medium for creating sentiment in the world today is that of the newspaper," Garvey explained to readers of the *Negro World*.Hill, *Marcus Garvey Papers* I, 383.

42. *Negro World*, July 4, 1925.

43. *Negro World*, April 11, 1925.

44. *Negro World*, May 24, 1924.

45. *Negro World*, July 12, 1930.

46. *Negro World*, March 4, 1922, December 25, 1926, June, 8, 1929, October 19, 1929, June 18, 1932.

47. George Washington to Attorney General Harry Daugherty, April 28, 1921, DNA, RG 60, file 198940–123.

48. George Washington to Attorney General Harry Daugherty, April 28, 1921, DNA, RG 60, file 198940–123.

49. Special Agent C.B. Treadway to Assistant Bureau Chief, Frank Burke, 11 Aug. 1919, 185161, RG 65, BI, NA.

50. E.J. Kerwin to Bureau, 12 Mar. 1919, OG185161, RG65, BI, NA.

51. See W.W Bailey to Bureau, December 31, 1919, case file 267600, RG 65,BI, NA.

52. *Negro World*, June 3, 1922.

53. *Chattanooga Times*, August 9, 1927.

54. *Negro World*, November 26, 1927; *Chattanooga Times*, August 9, 1927.

55. Workers for a local railroad company, Ira Johnson, Emory Bailey, James Jackson, and Louis Moore had been members of the UNIA since its inception. Even though two of the men had been wounded during the riot, they all denied any involvement in the shootout. "At the time of the raid," they explained, "we were singing religious songs in the hall, with no thought of creating a disturbance or a riot." Certain that these men had been involved in the shootout, the CPD charged Johnson, Bailey, Jackson, and Moore with attempted murder and set their bond at $10,000 apiece. Writing in the pages of the *Negro World*, the imprisoned men pleaded for assistance in their fight for their freedom. "We are laboring men," they explained. "We have no money and the organization at Chattanooga has been practically dissolved and disbanded and its leaders scattered." Fortunately, Parent Body representative William Ware was committed to raising the necessary funds to provide these men with solid legal counsel. Thanks to the services of attorney George W. Chamlee, the four men were acquitted of attempted murder charges in March, 1928. *Negro World*, November 26, 1927, March 3, 1928.

56. *Negro World,* August 20, 1927.
57. *Negro World,* March 3, 1928.
58. *Chattanooga Times,* August 6, 1927.
59. Hill, *Marcus Garvey Papers,* Vol. III,
60. *Negro World,* November 19, 1921.
61. *Negro World,* February 23, 1925; Hill, *Marcus Garvey Papers,* Vol. V, 652.

NOTES TO CHAPTER TWO

1. *Negro World,* November 12, 1927.
2. The absence of comprehensive year-by-year statistics on UNIA membership coupled with the tendency of the movement's leaders to inflate membership totals has made it rather difficult to draw definitive conclusions on the actual number of dues-paying members in the New Orleans UNIA. However, fragmentary records in the *Negro World,* the Administrative Files of the UNIA Central Division in New York, and Bureau of Investigation reports suggest that support for Marcus Garvey and the UNIA was quite substantial between 1920 and 1930. The New Orleans UNIA's membership swelled from fifteen to four thousand persons between 1920 and 1921. Internal dissension within the division produced a significant decline in membership in late 1922, but New Orleans remained an important center of Southern Garveyism. In fact, not until the Great Depression did membership in the New Orleans UNIA fall below five hundred. See *Negro World,* April 12, 1921, October 29, 1921; UNIA Central Office, Administrative Files, Box 2, Folder 16, Manuscripts, Archives, and Rare Books Division, Schomburg Center for Research in Black Culture (New York Public Library, New York); Agent J.M. Toliver to Bureau, July 16, 1921, case file 198140–198, Record Group 59, Department of State, National Archives [hereafter RG59, DS, NA]; Harry Gulley to Bureau, 24 January 1923, case file 61–50–195, obtained by author from FBI through Freedom of Information Act (hereafter FBI-FOIA).
3. *Negro World,* February 19, 1921, March 11, 1922; Toliver to Bureau, July 16, 1921, 198140–198, RG59, DS, NA; Harry Gulley to Hoover, 24 January 1923, 61–50–195, FBI-FOIA.
4. Sylvester Robertson, held in high esteem for his organizing skills, was given the responsibility of organizing branches of the UNIA in Louisiana, Alabama, Tennessee, and Mississippi in early 1921. Quite impressed with Robertson's work in these areas, Garvey appointed the Louisiana native to the position of High Commissioner for the states of Louisiana, Alabama, and Mississippi in 1923. Three years later he was named president of the UNIA division in Cleveland, where he worked as a sanitation worker and supervised the affairs of the division until his death in 1931.
5. *Negro World,* April 12, 1921.
6. *Negro World,* April 12, 1921.

7. *Negro World*, April 12, 1921.
8. Toliver to Bureau, 16 July, 1921, 198140–198, RG59, DS, NA.
9. *Negro World*, October 29, 1921.
10. Felix Alexander interview with Millie Charles, July 12, 1994, Behind the Veil Collection: Documenting African American Life in the Jim Crow South, Oral History Project, Special Collections Department (William R. Perkins Library, Duke University: Durham).
11. Felix Alexander interview with Millie Charles. July 12, 1994, Behind the Veil Collection
12. New Orleans was deeply divided along social, cultural, and neighborhood lines. Generally, Creoles of Color lived in the downtown section of the city, practiced the Catholic faith, attended parochial schools in the Seventh Ward, and participated in their own social clubs. On the other hand, American blacks, the term generally used to describe blacks living in uptown New Orleans, largely attended Protestant churches, patronized the social clubs and public schools in their own neighborhoods, and seldom came into contact with Creoles in downtown. For an analysis of the intraracial politics in New Orleans see Arnold Hirsch and Joseph Logson, eds., *Creole New Orleans: Race and Americanization* (Baton Rouge: Louisiana State University Press, 1992).
13. *Negro World*, March 24, 1923. Garvey's diatribes against "Negro hating mulattoes" and their aloofness from the masses of black folk, in the opinion of his many critics, especially those of mixed racial ancestry, were not attuned to the realities of black life in the United States. W.E.B. Du Bois in an article on Garvey wrote: "American Negroes recognize no color line in or out of the race, and they will in the end punish the man who attempts to establish it." Quoted in David Levering Lewis, *W.E.B. Du Bois: The Fight for Equality and the American Century, 1919–1963* (New York: Henry Holt, 2000), 67.
14. *Negro World*, January 30, 1926.
15. Robert Hill, *The Marcus Garvey and Universal Negro Improvement Association Papers* [hereafter Marcus Garvey Papers], Vol. III, (Los Angeles: University of California Press, 1984), 115.
16. Eric Arnesen, *Waterfront Workers of New Orleans: Race, Class, and Politics, 1863–1923* (Urbana: University of Illinois Press, 1991), 218.
17. *Negro World*, February 19, 1921.
18. Harry Gulley to Hoover, January 24, 1923, case file, 61–50–195, FBI-FOIA.
19. For Elie Garcia's account of his activities in Liberia see Hill, *Marcus Garvey Papers*, Vol. II, 660–672.
20. Special Agent 800 to George F. Ruch, DJ-FBI, file 61–826.
21. Hill, *Marcus Garvey Papers*, Vol. III, 81.
22. Hill, *Marcus Garvey Papers*, Vol. III, 114.
23. *Negro World*, October, 29, 1921.
24. The foundational scripture for Ethiopianism was Psalms 68: 31, "Princes shall come out of Egypt and Ethiopia shall soon stretch forth her hands unto God." A diverse group of African Americans, including working people, intellectuals, and ministers, interpreted the text as a prediction of Africa and Africans' eventual rise in global affairs. "This biblical prophecy,"

Randall Burkett notes, "has been cited by Black churchmen in America at least since the eighteenth century, to specify God's special concern for men of African descent." Randall K. Burkett, *Garveyism as a Religious Movement: The Institutionalization of a Black Civil Religion* (Metuchen: The Scarecrow Press, 1978) 34.

25. According to historian Judith Stein, T.A. Robinson served as a delegate at the 1921 International Longshoremen Convention in Buffalo, New York. See Judith Stein, *The World of Marcus Garvey,* 182.
26. *Negro World,* October 29, 1921.
27. J.M. Toliver, 16 July, 1921, 198140–181, RG 59, DS, NA.
28. *The Crisis,* July 1921.
29. Stein, *The World of Marcus Garvey,* 61–107; Tony Martin, *Race First,* 151–173.
30. Hill, *Marcus Garvey Papers,* Vol. IV, 529.
31. Hill, *Marcus Garvey Papers,* Vol. III., 540.
32. *Negro World,* March 11, 1922.
33. *Negro World,* February 19, 1921, April 2, 1921, October 29, 1921, December 10, 1921, March 11, 1922; P-138 to Bureau agent Charles J. Scully, 16 July, 1921, file BS 198940–205, RG65, BI,NA.
34. *The Nation,* August 18,1926.
35. *Negro World,* November 17, 1927.
36. Hill, *Marcus Garvey Papers,* Vol. IV, 694.
37. On June 22, Garvey had a two-hour meeting with Edward Clarke, Acting Imperial Wizard of the KKK. Having read Garvey's speech on the benefits of Jim Crow segregation, Edward Clarke informed the president of the Atlanta UNIA of his desire to talk with the black nationalist. Supposedly concerned about the KKK's physical and verbal assaults on UNIA followers in the South, Garvey agreed to meet with the white supremacist. No reporters were allowed to observe the meeting, but according to Garvey, the two had the opportunity to explain the true intent of their organizations, their hostility towards integration, and their belief in the emigration of blacks to Africa as the most effective solution to America's racial dilemma. Garvey was satisfied with the meeting, but he received strong critiques from within and outside the UNIA
38. For a detailed examination of some of the major debates at the 1922 convention see *Marcus Garvey Papers,* Vol. IV, 782–1060.
39. *Negro World,* August 1922; Hill, *Marcus Garvey Papers,* Vol. IV, 921.
40. *Negro World,* June 10, 1922.
41. Hill, *Marcus Garvey Papers,* Vol. IV, 822.
42. Hill, *Marcus Garvey Papers* Vol. IV, 944.
43. Already angry with Garvey over his handling of other controversial issues at the convention, several delegates who voted against Eason's expulsion viewed the suspension as unduly harsh and driven more by personal animosity than genuine concern for the organization. See Hill, *Marcus Garvey Papers,* Vol. IV, 943, 988.
44. *New York Age,* September 16, 1922.
45. Gulley to Bureau, 24 January, 1923, 61–50–195, FOIA-FBI.

46. Gulley to Bureau, 24 January, 1923, 61–50–195, FOIA-FBI; *New York Age*, September 16, 1922; *Negro World*, October 2, 1922.
47. *Negro World*, October 14, 1922.
48. *Negro World*, October 28, 1922; Gully to Bureau, 16 January, 1923, 190–1781–6, FBI-FOIA.
49. *New York Age*, October 14, 1922; Gully to Bureau, 16 January, 1923, 190–1781–6, FBI-FOIA.
50. *New York Age*, October 14, 1922.
51. *Negro World*, October 28, 1922.
52. Hill, *Marcus Garvey Papers*, Vol. V, 45.
53. Marcus Garvey to William Phillips, November 9, 1922, 61–50–195, FOIA-FBI.
54. Hill, *Marcus Garvey Papers*, Vol. V, 45; *Negro World*, October 14, 1922.
55. Gulley to Bureau, 24, January, 1923, case file 61–50–195, RG65, BI, NA
56. Hill, *Marcus Garvey Papers*, Vol. V, 45.
57. Hill, *Marcus Garvey Papers*, Vol. V, 45. An important link between the New Orleans UNIA and the Parent Body in New York, Thomas Anderson served as the Commissioner of Louisiana in 1922. Viewing Anderson as too loyal to Garvey, many NOD members believed he disregarded the needs of the movement's rank and file.
58. Hill, *Marcus Garvey Papers*, Vol. V, 153–154.
59. Mortimer J. Davis to Bureau, 26 February, 1923, 190–1781–6, FOIA-FBI.
60. Mortimer J. Davis to Bureau, 26 February, 1923, 190–1781–6, FOIA-FBI.
61. *New Orleans Times Picayune*, January 2, 1923. Gully to Bureau, 16 January, 1923, 190–1781–6, FOIA-FBI.
62. *New Orleans Times Picayune*, January 2, 1923; Gully to Bureau, 16 January, 1923, 190–1781–6, FOIA-FBI.
63. Gulley to Bureau, 16 January, 1923, 190–1781–6, FOIA-FBI.
64. Coroner's Office, State of Louisiana, Parish of Orleans, City of New Orleans, January 4, 1923.
65. A day after Eason was shot, W.A. Thomas, a former member of the New Orleans UNIA, identified Dyer and Shakespeare as two of the three men whom he had chased on the night of the shooting.
66. Eventually Ramus was apprehended in Detroit, but the NOPD refused to pay extradition costs for his return to New Orleans. Gulley to Bureau, 24 January, 1923, 61–50–195, FBI-FOIA; Mortimer J. Davis to Bureau, 26 February, 1923, 190–1781–6, FOIA-FBI; Hill, *Marcus Garvey Papers*, Vol. V, 230–231.
67. Gulley to Bureau, 24 January, 1923, 61–50–195, FBI-FOIA.
68. *New York Age*, January 27, 1923.
69. *New York Age*, January 27, 1923.
70. George Lucas to Robert Bagnall, January 10, 1923, Branch Files, G-81, NAACP Papers, (Library of Congress); *Negro World*, April 19, 1921.
71. Gulley to Bureau, 24 January 1923, 61–50–195, FBI-FOIA.
72. John Cary, Thomas Anderson, Isaac Whitmore, Thomas Franklin, Henry Lee, James Hamilton, Hezekiah Griffith, William Phillips, and Lawrence

Davis were formally charged with attempting to incite a riot. See Gulley to Bureau, 24 January 1923, 61–50–195, FBI-FOIA.

73. *Negro World*, March 10, 1923.
74. Gulley to Bureau, 24, January, 1923, case file 61–50–195, RG65, BI, NA
75. Hill, Marcus Garvey Papers, Vol 1, 269.
76. *New York Age*, January 27, 1923.
77. A high school teacher with a deep commitment to improving the material conditions of the black poor, Chambers would eventually gain the respect of the local people, however, Whitmore left the organization in a matter of months.
78. *New York Age*, October 14, 1922.
79. *New York Age*, January 27, 1923.
80. Two of the letter's signatories, Essie Hathaway and Florence Watterhouse, had been arrested during the second raid on the division. *Negro World*, March 24, 1923.
81. *Times Picayune*, June 30, 1924, July 31, 1924, August 1, 1924.
82. *Negro World*, April 25, 1925, May 9, 1925, December 18, 1926.
83. *Negro World*, May 31, 1924, June 21, 1924, November 8, 1924, April 25, 1925.
84. *Negro World*, March, 22, 1924.
85. Hill, *Marcus Garvey Papers*, Vol. V, 756–757.
86. *Negro World*, June 21, 1924; Central Office Files, Black Cross Navigation and Trading Company, Salesman's Report, 1925, Schomburg Center for Research in Black Culture New York Public Library.
87. Hill, *Marcus Garvey Papers*, Vol. V, 744.
88. *Negro World*, August 7, 1926.
89. Florence Borders, Felix Alexander interview, Behind the Veil Collection: Documenting African American Life in the Jim Crow South, Oral History Project, Special Collections Department, William R. Perkins Library, Duke University.
90. *Negro World*, November 8, 1924; Ted Vincent, *Keep Cool: The Black Activists Who Built the Jazz Age* (London: Pluto Press, 1995), 123, 131.
91. Small's harmonica solos, according to one report in the *Negro World*, always "visibly moved the audience" at Liberty Hall. An avid follower of Marcus Garvey, Hall would usually say a few words about the association before he belted out the latest blues tune. *Negro World*, August 30, 1924; Vincent, *Keep Cool*, 122.
92. *Negro World*, December 19, 1931.
93. *Negro World*, April 9, 1927.
94. According to historian Theodore Vincent, the period after Garvey's imprisonment was an exciting time for many regionalists within the movement who "wanted to involve the movement, more than ever before, in the struggles for political rights, employment, housing, and other immediate issues." Theodore Vincent, *Black Power and the Garvey Movement*, 219.
95. "New Orleans Convention," Earnest S. Cox Papers, Box 2, Special Collections Department, William R. Perkins Library, Duke University.

96. *The Nation*, June 24, 1927; Walter White, *A Man Called White: the Autobiography of Walter* White (Athens: University of Georgia Press, 1948, 1995), 80–81; *Crisis*, February, 1928; Clyde Woods, *Development Arrested: The Blues and Plantation Power in the Mississippi Delta* (New York: Verso, 1998), 117–120.

97. *Negro World*, July 9, 1927.

98. *Negro World*, July 9, 1927, July 27, 1927.

99. *Negro World*, October 29, 1921.

100. *Negro World*, May 14, 1927.

101. For an analysis of the role of women and gender in the movement's history see Winston James, *Holding Aloft the Banner of Ethiopia: Caribbean Radicalism in Early Twentieth-Century America* (London: Verso, 1998), 137–155; Barbara Bair, "True Women, Real Men: Gender, Ideology, and Social Roles in the Garvey Movement," in Dorothy O. Helly and Susan M. Reverby, eds., *Rethinking Public and Private in Women's History*, (New York: Cornell University Press, 1992); Ula Yvette Taylor, *The Veiled Garvey: The Life and Times of Amy Jacques Garvey* (Chapel Hill: University of North Carolina Press, 2002).

102. The NOD was quite progressive with regards to the promotion of women to leadership positions. Of the major divisions in the South, the New Orleans UNIA was alone in its election of women to the office of president. A nurse at a local convalescent home, Grace Davis was elected as the division's president in the spring of 1925. An effective recruiter, Davis performed an integral role in the revitalization of the division after the Eason murder. "The membership" wrote Philip Clinton in the *Negro World*, "is increasing rapidly under the guiding hand of Mrs. Davis." Another powerful female president was Beulah McDonald. One of the NOD's more active workers in its community uplift programs, McDonald served as the division's president in the late thirties. Other influential women in the division included Odella Spears, Doris Bush, Mrs. R.J. Wall, Nellie Uter Crawford, Ida Vollison Thompson, and Estella Berryman. *Negro World*, October 31, 1925.

103. *Negro World*, May 14, 1927.

104. *Negro World*, July 16, 1927.

105. Donald E. De Vore "The Rise From the Nadir: Black New Orleans Between the Wars, 1920–1940" (M.A. thesis, University of New Orleans, 1983), 16–43.

106. Adam Fairclough, *Race and Democracy: The Civil Rights Struggle in Louisiana, 1915–1972* (Athens: University of Georgia, 1995), 19.

107. *New Orleans States*, December 31, 1928.

108. Walter White to George Lucas, letter undated, Box G-81, NAACP Papers.

109. In an unprecedented decision, the two men were found guilty and sentenced to life in prison. George W. Lucas to Walter White, April 22, 1929, Box G-81, NAACP Papers.

110. In fact, delegates at the UNIA's 1924 convention passed a resolution forbidding dual membership in the NAACP and the UNIA on account of the

NAACP's alleged involvement in the federal government's mail fraud case against Garvey. See Hill, *Marcus Garvey Papers*, Vol. V, 814.

111. For greater detail on Garvey's aversion to the NAACP and his many conflicts with W.E.B. Du Bois. See Tony Martin, *Race First*, 273–333; David Levering Lewis, *W.E.B. Du Bois: The Fight for Equality and the American Century*, 50–84, 148–152.

112. Amy Jacques Garvey, *Philosophy and Opinions* (Dover: The Majority Press, 1925, 1986), 316.

113. *Century*, February, 1923.

114. *Messenger*, March 1923.

115. The relationship between the UNIA and NAACP branches in Key West was quite contentious. "The U.N.I.A. organization," the officers for the NAACP branch in Key West, Florida, complained in a letter to Robert Bagnall, "did all that they could to destroy us. They characterized us as a white man's American organization that was only working for social equality, etc. That we were opposed to the Garvey movement simply because he was as a foreigner." Theresa Lang and Leonia Adams to Robert Bagnall, January 15, 1924, Box G-41, NAACP Papers.

116. NAACP Papers, Box G-81 and G-82; *City Directories of the United States*, New Orleans, 1920, Reel 10, Library of Congress.

117. Quite a few of Garvey's disciples in South Africa followed a similar course. African National Congress leader Sol Plaatje, for example, embraced the work of the UNIA and the NAACP. See George M. Fredrickson, *Black Liberation: A Comparative History of Black Ideologies in the United States and South Africa* (New York: Oxford University Press, 1995), 163.

118. Michelle Mitchell, *Righteous Propagation: African Americans and the Politics of Racial Destiny After Reconstruction* (Chapel Hill: University of North Carolina Press, 2004), 220.

119. Quite possibly, New Orleans Garveyites' awareness of the ways in which color divisions had divided their own communities pushed them away from simplistic discourses equating racial degeneration with miscegenation.

120. U.S. Bureau of the Census, Department of Commerce, *Mortality Rates, 1910–1920, with Population of the Federal Censuses of 1910 and 1920 and Intercensal Estimates of Population,* (Washington: Government Printing Office, 1923), 268; *Louisiana Weekly*, September 22, 1928.

121. See George Lucas to Robert Bagnall, December 14, 1926, Box G-81, NAACP Papers; *Louisiana Weekly*, September 22, 1928. So concerned was George Lucas about the health crisis in the black community that he suspended much of New Orleans NAACP's civil rights activity during a drive to raise funds to build a hospital in uptown New Orleans. Not surprisingly, his decision created problems between him and the national office in New York.

122. *Negro World*, January 21, 1928.

123. *Negro World*, September 15, 1928.

124. *Louisiana Weekly*, September 22, 1928.

125. Unfortunately, NOD reports in the *Negro World* do not offer much information on the operations of the clinic. In fact, the last mention of the clinic was in March of 1929.
126. *Negro World*, March 9, 1929.
127. *Negro World*, January 26, 1929. Black Cross Nurses also performed case work in uptown New Orleans. Most of the recipients of their services were black, but local whites occasionally benefited from the services of the BCN. For example, during a flu epidemic in early 1929, Black Cross Nurses provided medical attention to whites in the community.
128. *Negro World*, November 3, 1928. Garveyites in Port Limon, Costa Rica, Colon, Panama, and New York City also built schools in their respective communities. Of course, the Parent Body purchased the Smallwood-Cory Institute in Claremont Virginia in 1926, renamed it Liberty University, and ran it for three academic years under the presidency of the West Indian educator J.C. St. Clair Drake.
129. Tony Martin, *Race First*, 83.
130. U.S. Department of Commerce, *Abstract of the Fifteenth Census of the United States* (Washington: United States Government Printing Office, 1933), 287.
131. James D. Anderson, *The Education of Blacks in the South, 1860–1935* (Chapel Hill: University of North Carolina Press, 1988), 211–221.
132. *Negro World*, November 23, 1929.
133. *Negro World*, March 9, 1929.
134. *Negro World*, January 12, 1929.
135. *Negro World*, November 23, 1929.
136. During the 1920s, blacks of all classes exhibited a strong interest in their African identity and past. "The search for a personality for the New Negro," writes historian Nathan Huggins, "necessitated the rediscovery of a heritage. As much as the young Negro intellectuals wanted to proclaim a new day and to inter all vestiges of the old image, they felt a need to find justification in the past. The heritage was to serve the image." Until Africa was reconstructed as a symbol of pride instead of shame, many reasoned, blacks would continue to battle with feelings of self-hatred, self-doubt, and insecurity. Nathan Irvin Huggins, *Harlem Renaissance* (New York: Oxford University Press, 1971), 72.
137. *Negro World*, January 21, 1928.
138. *Negro World*, November 23, 1929.
139. *Negro World*, October 29, 1929.
140. *Negro World*, September 15, 1928.
141. *Negro World*, March 9, 1929.
142. George Lucas to Walter White, June 9, 1930, Box G-82, NAACP Papers.
143. De Vore, "The Rise From the Nadir," 56.
144. Douglas L. Smith, *The New Deal in the Urban South* (Baton Rouge: Louisiana State University Press, 1988), 20.
145. Roger Biles, "The Urban South in Great Depression," *Journal of Southern History* 56, no. 1 (February 1990), 80.

146. *Negro World*, December 14, 1929.
147. *Negro World*, September 15, 1928.
148. Hill, *Marcus Garvey Papers*, Vol. VI, 591, 597.
149. *Louisiana Weekly*, December 1, 1928,
150. *Negro World*, January 26, 1929.
151. *Negro World*, January 31, 1931.

NOTES TO CHAPTER THREE

1. *Negro World*, December 31, 1929.
2. Paul S. George, "Brokers, Binders and Builders: Greater Miami's Boom of the Mid-1920s," *Florida Historical Quarterly 55*, no. 2, (July 1986), 27–55.
3. Howard Johnson, *The Bahamas from Slavery to Servitude, 1783–1933* (Gainesville: University Press of Florida), 98–118.
4. Johnson, *The Bahamas from Slavery to Servitude,* 151–164. By 1920, Miami claimed a population of roughly thirty thousand, of which approximately five thousand were of Bahamian descent. The total black population was roughly nine thousand. See Raymond Mohl, "Black Immigrants: Bahamians in Early Twentieth-Century Miami," *Florida Historical Quarterly 65*, no. 3 (January 1987), 271–297.
5. Paul S. George, "Colored Town: Miami's Black Community, 1896–1930, *Florida Historical Quarterly 46*, no. 4, (April 1978), 432–447.
6. Ira De A. Reid, *The Negro Immigrant: His Background, Characteristics and Social Adjustment, 1899–1937* (New York: Columbia University Press, 1939), 189.
7. *The Miami Times*, February 21, 1985.
8. "Testimony of James B. Nimmo," in HUAC, *Investigation of Communist Activities in the State of Florida*, November 29-December 1, 1954 (Washington, D.C., 1955), 7426–7427.
9. Marvin Dunn, *Black Miami in The Twentieth Century* (Gainesville: University of Florida, 1997), 124
10. *Negro World*, August 20, 1921. Agent William Sausele to Bureau, 23 November, 1920, BS 202600–10-7 RG65, BI, NA. In many ways, the formation of the UNIA was a seminal moment in black Miami politics. It represented the first time blacks in the city joined a national political organization. Seemingly content to support such locally based advocacy groups as the Colored Board of Trade or the Negro Uplift Society, community activists, Bahamian born and African America, had not established local branches of either the National Association for the Advancement of Colored People (NAACP) or the Urban League. In 1916, leaders for the Colored Board of Trade, which primarily protested against residential segregation and police brutality, discussed the formation of a local chapter of the NAACP, but their plans never materialized.
11. Agent William Sausele to Bureau, 23 November, 1920, BS 202600–10-7 RG65, BI, NA].

12. Agent Leon Howe to Bureau, 8 July 1921, BS 198940–183, RG65, BI, NA; City directories of the United States, Miami, Reel 3, 1921; Manuscript Census Schedules, Dade County, 1920, Roll #216, U.S. Bureau of the Census, Record Group 29, National Archives. To be certain, women in the Miami UNIA contributed immensely to the vibrancy of the division, but their involvement in key policy-making decisions was minimal.

13. Howe to Bureau, 8 July 1921, BS 198940–183, RG65, BI, NA.

14. *Negro World*, August 20, 1921.

15. Finding employment in the fruit and vegetable fields of Coconut Grove, Bahamians constituted the primary labor force in the city's rapidly growing agricultural sector. Immigrants not employed in the agricultural sector worked mainly in the fishing, construction, and maritime industries—industries which seldom hired African-Americans.

16. Dunn, *Black Miami*, 97.

17. Howe to Bureau, 4 August, 1920, BS 202905, RG65, BI, NA.

18. Only a handful of African Americans became members of the Miami UNIA, but the local division was not alone in its inability to attract native blacks. Founded around the same time as the Miami division, the Key West UNIA, also predominantly Bahamian, failed miserably in its efforts to augment the number of African Americans in the division. Native blacks in Key West not only avoided the organization but they assisted local police officers and federal intelligence agents in their efforts to weaken the division. As a result, local Garveyites launched several verbal attacks on native blacks and the organizations in which they comprised the majority. "The U.N.I.A. organization," Theresa Lang and Leonia Adams of the Key West NAACP branch complained in a letter to Robert Bagnalll, "did all that they could to destroy us." "They characterized us as a white man's American organization that was only working for social equality, etc. That we were opposed to the Garvey movement simply because he was as a foreigner." See Theresa Lang and Leonia Adams to Robert Bagnall, January 15, 1924, Box G-41, NAACP Papers, Manuscript Collection, Library of Congress.

19. Howe to Bureau, 8 July, 1921, 198940–183, RG65, BI, NA.

20. Howe to Bureau, 8 July, 1921, BS 198940–183, RG65, BI, NA.

21. An outspoken critic of American injustices whose presence at UNIA meetings ruffled the feathers of the Bureau of Investigation, Holly spoke frequently at division gatherings. Threatened by the Ku Klux Klan on numerous occasions, Holly garnered much respect in the Bahamian community for his sharp criticism of American racism, the United States' occupation of Haiti, and the dehumanizing ways in which white Miamians treated blacks. A native of Port-au Prince, Haiti, Holly, the first black homeopath in Miami, moved to South Florida in 1909 after spending extensive time in Haiti, the Barbados, England, and New York City. Usually, Holly's speeches focused on the "revolutionary activities" of blacks in Haiti and the need for black international unity. See William C. Sausele, 11 November 22, 1920, BS 202600–10-7, RG65, BI, NA; *Negro World*, September 5, 1931.

22. A subscription agent for A. Philip Randolph and Chandler Owen's *Messenger*, Nishada during his lecture at the Miami UNIA discussed the strengths

of the socialist movement as well as assessed the future of the Garvey movement. "His talk to Bahama Negroes," Howard P. Wright noted in an April report on Nishada's brief visit to Miami, "was of such character as to cause dissension and to inflame them against the white race." Nishada encouraged his audience to continue their fight for freedom and draw inspiration from the "sufferings of the Russians." Howard Wright to General Intelligence Division, 14, April 1921, BS 202–600–10, RG65, BI, NA.

23. William C. Sausele, 11 November 23, 1920, BS 202600–10–7, RG65, BI, NA.

24. *Negro World*, June 14, 1924, October 6, 1928.

25. Stopping in Key West before an extended tour of the Caribbean and Central and South America, Marcus Garvey along with future wife Amy Jacques Cleveland arrived in the city on Saturday morning, February 25. Later in the day, Garvey lectured at Samaritan Hall, which, according to one UNIA reporter, "was overflowing with hundreds of eager and enthusiastic Negroes." Thrilling his audiences with his oratorical brilliance, Garvey, who spoke in the city for three consecutive nights, touched on issues and themes routinely covered in most of his speeches: the need for the development of black-owned enterprises and cooperatives, the association's Liberian colonization efforts, and pan-African unity. Specifically, he pleaded with his followers to purchase shares in the organization's leading economic venture, the Black Star Line Steamship Company, which was in serious financial trouble. Strong believers in the principle of economic self-sufficiency, UNIA followers responded well to his request for financial support. Samuel A. Mounts, corresponding Secretary of the division, in a discussion with an undercover agent for the Bureau of Investigation, claimed that "about thirty persons subscribed for stock at each meeting, each subscription from five to thirty dollars each." *Negro World*, April 30, 1921. Howard Wright to General Intelligence Division, 14, April 1921, 202–600–10, RG65, BI, NA. .

26. Howe to Bureau, 8 July, 1921, BS 198940–183, RG65, BI, NA; Kip Vought, "Racial Stirrings in Colored Town: The UNIA in Miami during the 1920s," *Tequesta* 60, (2000), 68.

27. *Negro World*, April 2, 1927.

28. Leon E. Howe to Bureau, July 8, 1921, BS 198940–183, RG65, BI, NA.

29. *Negro World*, March 26, 1927.

30. City directories of the United States, Miami, Reel 3, 1921; Manuscript Census Schedules, Dade County, 1920, Roll #216, U.S. Bureau of the Census, Record Group 29, National Archives.

31. *Miami Herald*, March 9, 1928.

32. *Miami Herald*, February 10, 1975.

33. Agent William Sausele to Bureau, 23 November, 1920, BS 202600–10–7 RG65, BI, NA; Howe to Bureau, 29 June, 1921, BS 198940–175, RG65, NA; Howe to Bureau, 8 July 1921, 198940–183, RG65, BI, NA.

34. *Miami Herald*, July 2, 1921.

35. Dunn, *Black Miami*, 120

36. *Miami Herald*, July 2, 1921.

37. *Miami Herald*, February 10, 1975.
38. *Miami Herald*, July 2, 1921.
39. *Miami Herald*, February 10, 1975.
40. Whites' abduction of Higgs was not an isolated event designed solely to weaken the UNIA, but intricately related to a larger pattern of white intimidation and violence against the black community during the tumultuous twenties. In fact, two weeks after the Ku Klux Klan kidnapped Higgs, they abducted and then tarred and feathered an Episcopalian minister named Philip Irwin who worked closely with local blacks. Leon E. Howe to Bureau, July 8, 1921, BS 198940–183, RG65, BI, NA; Howe to Bureau, 15 Sept. 1920, RG 65,BI, NA].
41. *Miami Herald*, July 3, 1921.
42. See Howe to Bureau, 29 June, 1921, BS 198940–175, RG65, NA; Howe to Bureau, 8 July 1921, 198940–183, RG65, BI, NA.
43. *Miami Herald*, July 3, 1921.
44. Dunn, *Black Miami*, 126.
45. *Negro World*, June 14, 1924.
46. Kip Vought, "Racial Stirrings in Colored Town," 66–67.
47. *Negro World*, August 20, 1921.
48. *Negro World*, October 14, 1922. It is difficult to discern the extent to which their statements reflected their ideological beliefs or were simply part of their efforts to placate local whites. Across the political spectrum, many black activists denied any interest in the matter of "social equality," which was the code world for interracial marriage or sexual relations.
49. *Negro World*, August 20, 1921.
50. *Negro World*, August 20, 1921.
51. *Negro World*, August 20, 1921.
52. Kip Vought, "Racial Stirrings in Colored Town," 67.
53. Barbara Bair, "True Women, Real Men: Gender, Ideology, and Social Roles in the Garvey Movement" in Susan M. Reverby and Dorthy O. Helly, eds., *Gendered Domains: Rethinking Public and Private in Women's History* (Ithaca: Cornell University Press, 1998), 158.
54. Kip Vought, "Racial Stirrings in Colored Town," 67.
55. *Negro World*, June 14, 1924.
56. *Negro World*, March 26, 1927.
57. Dunn, *Black Miami*, 126.
58. William W. Rogers, "Fortune and Misfortune: The Paradoxical Twenties" in Michael Gannon, ed., *The New History of Florida* (Gainesville: University of Florida, 1996), 294. See also Michael Gannon, *Florida: A Short History* (Gainesville: University of Florida Press, 1993) 81.
59. Dunn, *Black Miami*, 128.
60. *Miami Herald*, February 10, 1975.
61. *Miami Herald*, February 10, 1975.
62. *Negro World*, April 9, 1927.
63. *Negro World*, May 16, 1925.
64. *Negro World*, May 19, 1928.
65. *Negro World*, May 19, 1928.

66. *Negro World*, May 19, 1928.
67. The most detailed analysis of Laura Kofey's political career is Richard New-man, "Warrior Mother of Africa of the Most High God: Laura Adorker Kofey and the African Universal Church," in Richard Newman, ed., *Black Power and Black Religion: Essays and Reviews*, (West Cornwall: Locust Hill Press, 1987), 131–145.
68. *Negro* World, June 11, 1927.
69. *Negro* World, June 11, 1927.
70. *Negro* World, June 11, 1927.
71. *Negro World*, April 9, 1927, June 23, 1927. Kofey also achieved much suc-cess in Mobile and the nearby town of Pritchard. More than twelve hundred blacks became members of the local chapters during her stay in Mobile. "Negroes," Parent Body representative Joseph A. Craigen informed readers of the *Negro World*, "were leaving the churches so fast that the ministers of Mobile sought to have the authorities of the city order Mrs. Koofey [sic] to leave town." Several leaders in New York had issues with Kofey, but Craigen hoped the organization could benefit from the excitement created by her lectures. *Negro World*, April 9, 1927.
72. Hill, *Marcus Garvey Papers*, Vol. VII, 169.
73. *Negro World*, June 23, 1927.
74. Several folks had issues not only with Laura Kofey's fundraising schemes, but also with her negative comments about the division's social activities. Kofey criticized the Miami UNIA for its nightly dances, which she con-demned as too worldly. Instead, she suggested, the division should sub-stitute prayer meetings in their place. UNIA followers not only defended their right to use their bodies for personal enjoyment, but they also pointed out the usefulness of these dances to the organization's larger work. Unbe-knownst to Kofey, dances were not only a source of entertainment for the division's members, but the money accrued from cover charges at certain dances often financed the division's political activities. In 1925, for exam-ple, the Miami UNIA sponsored a dance in order to pay the repair fees of the UNIA's SS *General Goethels*. Moreover, dances and other social func-tions increased outsider's interest in the movement. Unfazed by Kofey's criticism, Garveyites in Miami held dances until the movement's demise in the late thirties. Richard Newman, "Warrior Mother of Africa," 134.
75. Hill, *Marcus Garvey Papers*, Vol. VI, 594.
76. In addition to their criticism of Kofey's fundraising scheme, the central office disputed Kofey's claims about her African origins. Stating that Kofey was actually an African American who had been born in Athens, Georgia, lived in Detroit from 1920 to 1924, and spent time in London and Africa as a Red Cross Nurse, J.A. Craigen dismissed the idea of her connection with any African government. *Negro World*, October 22, 1927. *Negro World*, April 7, 1928.
77. *The Miami Times*, February 21, 1985.
78. Newman, "Warrior Mother of Africa," 132.
79. *The Miami Times*, February 21, 1985.
80. *The Miami Times*, February 21, 1985.

81. *The Miami Times*, February 21, 1985.
82. *The Negro World*, May 5, 1928.
83. *The Negro World*, July 21, 1928.
84. *Negro World*, August 4, 1928.
85. Newman, "Warrior Mother of Africa," 133.
86. *Negro World*, October 6, 1928.
87. *Negro World*, December 15, 1928.
88. *Miami Herald*, February 10, 1975.
89. *Miami Times*, February 21, 1985; Dunn, *Black Miami*, 126.
90. *Negro World*, September 5, 1931.
91. *Miami Herald*, February 10, 1975.
92. Dunn, *Black Miami*, 117, 126.
93. "Testimony of James Nimmo," Investigation of Communist Activities in the State of Florida," 7426–7448.
94. "Testimony of James Nimmo," Investigation of Communist Activities in the State of Florida, 7426–7448.

NOTES TO CHAPTER FOUR

1. Robert Hill, *Marcus Garvey Papers*, Vol. I, (Berkley: University of California Press, 1983), 467.
2. *Negro World*, November 27, 1926.
3. *The Spokesman*, May 1927. Henry Plummer's tenure with the Newport News branch was rather short. Moving to New York in the summer of 1920, Plummer was named the head of the Black Star Line Bureau of Publicity and Propaganda. He was also the chief of Garvey's secret service staff. Hill, *Marcus Garvey Papers*, Vol. II, 292.
4. *Negro World*, October 14, 1922; *Spokesman*, May, 1927.
5. Robert Hill, *Marcus Garvey Papers*, 452.
6. Hill, *Marcus Garvey Papers*, Vol. I, 452.
7. Abbott was one of Garvey's most persistent critics. Viewing the UNIA as a dangerous organization, Abbott readily assisted the Bureau of Investigation in its effort to gather information on Garvey's activities. FBI agents in Chicago agents identified Abbott as a Negro leader "who has been ever ready to cooperate with this office on all investigations pertaining to Negro radical activities." Agent J.O. Peyronnin to Bureau, 3 Oct. 1919, OG329359, RG65, BI, NA.
8. *Chicago Defender*, September 20, 1919.
9. Hill, *Marcus Garvey Papers*, Vol. II, 366.
10. Hill, *Marcus Garvey Papers*, Vol. II, 366.
11. Hill, *Marcus Garvey Papers*, Vol. II, 368.
12. Noting that blacks in Philadelphia and New York had contributed immensely to the BSL in recent weeks, Garvey asked his Virginian followers to increase their contributions to the line. "New York is supplying its quota to the Black Star Line and so is Philadelphia. I have taken the chance to come to Newport News to find out if you are going to supply your quota towards the Black Star Line." "I want you to understand,"

Garvey continued, "that the opportunity is now knocking at your door. The Black Star Line is opening industrial and commercial avenues that were heretofore closed to Negroes." Hill, *Marcus Garvey Papers*, Vol. II, 112.

13. *The Spokesman*, May 1927; Hill, *Marcus Garvey Papers*, Vol. II, 366, 368.

14. *Chicago Defender*, September 20, 1919; Hill, *Marcus Garvey Papers*, Vol. II, 366, 368.

15. For an analysis of the economic opportunities available to black laborers in the Hampton Roads area see Earl Lewis, *In Their Own Interests: Race, Class, and Power in Twentieth-Century Norfolk, Virginia* (Berkeley: University of California Press, 1991), 29–65.

16. Hill, *Marcus Garvey Papers*, Vol. II, 535.

17. Hill, *Marcus Garvey Papers*, Vol. II, 366.

18. *Negro World*, February 19, 1921. Bureau of Investigation officials made an attempt to stop the sale of BSL shares. Late in 1920, Lewis Bailey, Chief of the Richmond Bureau of Investigation, queried the Norfolk office on whether the UNIA had been licensed to sell stock in the line. Taking advantage of a state law prohibiting the sale of stock without a license, Bureau officials ordered law enforcement officials across the state to arrest anyone selling shares in the Company. Once UNIA officials received word of the Bureau's designs, Elie Garcia, the secretary for the BSL, hurried to Richmond for the purpose of securing the necessary license. Scheduling a meeting with Mr. Dunford, the Chief Clerk of the State Corporation Commission, Garcia admitted to having sold stock in Newport News and Norfolk without the proper license. Wanting to undermine the movement, Bureau officials ordered the State Corporation Commission to refuse the UNIA the necessary license. Hill, *Marcus Garvey Papers*, Vol. II, 102–103.

19. *Negro World*, February 19, 1921.

20. *Negro World*, February 19, 1921.

21. *Negro World*, September 3, 1921.

22. *Negro World*, February 21, 1921.

23. Earl Lewis, *In Their Own Interests*, 58.

24. Earl Lewis, *In Their Own Interests*, 51.

25. A sign of the movement's decline, the Hampton Roads area was able to send only three delegates to the UNIA's 1921 Convention in New York City; in 1920, divisions in the area had seven representatives attending the First Annual Convention Hill. *Marcus Garvey Papers*, Vol. IV, 1075.

26. *Negro World*, September 3, 1921.

27. *Negro World*, February 4, 1922.

28. Hill, *Marcus Garvey Papers*, Vol. III, 168.

29. Still able to draw a large audience, Garvey in June of 1922, according to the *Norfolk Journal and Guide*, "packed the house to the doors." *Norfolk Journal and Guide*, July 1, 1922.

30. See Hill, *Marcus Garvey Papers*, Vol. IV and V.

31. *Negro World*, May 24, 1924.

32. Several Liberian government officials viewed the settlement of Garveyites in this area as a way to deal with its ongoing struggles with indigenous groups near the region. See Ibrahim Sundiata, *Brothers and Strangers: Black Zion, Black Slavery, 1914–1940* (Durham: Duke University, 2003), 32–36

33. *Negro World,* July 12, 1924.

34. *Negro World,* June 21, 1924.

35. "Emphasizing civility and their friendship for black Virginians," writes historian J. Douglass Smith in his description of the nature of black-white relations in the state, "paternalists promised to provide a modicum of basic services and even encouraged a certain amount of black educational and economic uplift. In return, white elites demanded complete deference and expected blacks to seek redress of their grievances only through channels deemed appropriate by whites." J. Douglass Smith, *Managing White Supremacy: Race, Politics, and Citizenship in Jim Crow Virginia* (Chapel Hill: University of North Carolina Press, 2002), 4.

36. For an analysis of race relations in urban Virginia see Charles E. Wynes, "The Evolution of Jim Crow Laws in Twentieth Century Virginia," *Phylon,* XXVII (1970), 416–418; Andrew Buni, *The Negro in Virginia Politics, 1902–1965* (Charlottesville: University of Virginia Press, 1967); Earl Lewis, *In Their Own Interests*; Smith, *Managing White Supremacy.*

37. Hill, *Marcus Garvey Papers,* Vol. II, 534.

38. Fenner to Cox, June 17, 1925, Earnest Cox Papers, Special Collections Department, William R. Perkins Library, Duke University. Fenner was hardly alone in his views on the emigration question. All across the urban and rural South, Garveyites enthused over the opportunity to start anew in Liberia. Carlise D. Arsenburg of New Orleans welcomed the opportunity to move to West African country: "I am greatly enthused over the movement with its great cause and success. I had been taught about Africa since I was fourteen years old by my mother, and I had always lived in hopes that the time would come that her words would come to pass. Surely that time has come. It is now." Only through emigration, many black southerners increasingly believed, could African Americans achieve full emancipation. Until blacks established a strong Negro nationality in Africa, many Garveyites reasoned, full emancipation would remain an elusive dream. "The Negro needs a flag and a country of his own," Sara Maclin of Memphis, Tennessee reasoned. "He can never expect to get any protection or recognition without a government of his own to back up his demands." *Negro World,* July 25, 1925.

39. *Negro World,* May 24, 1924; *Norfolk Journal and Guide,* September 27, 1924.

40. *Negro World,* May 24, 1924.

41. *Norfolk Journal and Guide,* January 17, 1924. Hill, *Marcus Garvey Papers,* Vol. V, 757.

42. *Norfolk Journal and Guide,* January 17, 1924.

43. *Norfolk Journal and Guide,* January 26, 1924.

Nothing was particularly unique about these ministers' attack on the organization. Ever since the formation of the Newport News UNIA in 1918, preachers in the Hampton Roads area had worked to undermine the movement's influence. Opposing ministers refused to allow UNIA meetings in their church, reported the activities of Garveyites to the local police, and condemned the organization from their pulpits on Sunday morning. Virginian Garveyites who brought news of their divisions' progress to the UNIA summer conventions frequently complained about the actions of their local ministers. "The preachers," W.H. Johnson of Norfolk, complained at the UNIA convention in 1920, "preach against the organization to their people telling them that it is nothing that is worthwhile." Shortly after the formation of the Black Star Line, many ministers instructed UNIA followers in the Hampton Roads area to cease their support of the line, but most Garveyites continued to support the line.

44. Hill, *Marcus Garvey Papers*, Vol. V, 757.
45. Hill, *Marcus Garvey Papers*, Vol. VII, 426.
46. *Negro World*, March 21, 1925.
47. Negro World, March 21, 1925.
48. *Negro World*, March 21, 1925.
49. *Negro World*, March 21, 1925.
50. Hill, *Marcus Garvey Papers*, Vol. VI, xxxvii.
51. Garvey, of course, had supported white supremacist politicians before. Early in 1922, Garvey had endorsed the emigration plans of noted white supremacist and Mississippi Senator McCallum. A strident segregationist, Senator McCallum was responsible for introducing into the Mississippi Senate a resolution authorizing congress to "secure by treaty, purchase, or other negotiation a piece of Africa where the Afro-American could move toward independence under the tutelage of the Untied States government." Tony Martin, *Race First*, 347.
52. See Ethel Wolfskill Hedlin, "Earnest Cox and Colonization: A White Racist's Response to Black Repatriation, 1923–1966" (Ph.D. dissertation, Duke University, 1974). Correspondence between Earnest Cox, Garvey, and UNIA followers in Virginia can be found in Cox's personal papers, which are housed at University of North Carolina.
53. Richard B. Sherman, "The Last Stand: The Fight for Racial Integrity in Virginia in the 1920s," *Journal of Southern History* 56, no. 1 (February 1988), 70.
54. Richard Sherman, "The Last Stand," 77.
55. Two years after its legislative victory, the ASCOA, upset with Hampton University's indiscriminate seating policy during public functions, launched a very controversial campaign for the passage of legislation outlawing integrated seating at public assemblages. Notwithstanding having misgivings about the bill, the state legislature passed the 1926 Public Assemblage Act, which sanctioned racial segregation in all places of public assemblages. For a detailed examination of the career of some

of the leading figures in the ASCOA see J. Douglass Smith's *Managing White Supremacy: Race, Politics, and Citizenship in Jim Crow Virginia* (Chapel Hill: University of North Carolina Press, 2002), 77–106.

56. Hill, *Marcus Garvey Papers,* Vol. VI, 211.

57. J.R. Johnson to Cox, June 23, 1925, Cox Papers.

58. It should be noted that many black intellectuals engaged in discussions with white supremacists. Noted white supremacist Theodore Lothrop Stoddard, for example, initiated correspondence with Hubert Harrison after the black socialist thinker wrote a favorable review of *The Rising Tide of Color against White World Supremacy* in the May 29, 1920 edition of the *Negro World.* See Jeffrey B. Perry, ed., *A Hubert Harrison Reader* (Middletown: Wesleyan University Press, 2001), 306–319.

59. Samuel Ashby to Cox, June 30, 1925, Cox Papers.

60. Dean E. Robinson, *Black Nationalism in American Politics and Thought* (Cambridge: Cambridge University Press, 2001), 5.

61. Reverend A.A. Boyd to Earnest Cox, July 7, 1925, Cox Papers.

62. Boyd to Cox, July 7, 1925, Cox Papers.

63. Boyd to Cox, July 7, 1925, Cox Papers.

64. Boyd to Cox, July 7, 1925, Cox Papers.

65. Boyd to Cox, July 7, 1925, Cox Papers.

66. Fenner to Cox, June 17, 1925, Cox Papers.

67. Fenner to Cox, June 17, 1925, Cox Papers.

68. *Norfolk Journal and Guide,* August 29, 1925; Fenner to Cox, September 19, 1925, *Cox Papers.*

69. Fenner to Cox, September 19, 1925, Cox Papers.

70. *Norfolk Journal and Guide,* August 29, 1925.

71. *Norfolk Journal and Guide,* August 29, 1925.

72. *Negro World,* September 5, 1925; *Norfolk Journal and Guide,* September 19, 1925.

73. Hill, *Marcus Garvey Papers,* Vol. 6, 252.

74. Hill, *Marcus Garvey Papers,* Vol. VI, 252.

75. *Negro World,* November 28, 1931.

76. Cox to Marcus Garvey, May 25, 1933, Cox Papers.

77. Cox to Garvey, May 25, 1933, Cox Papers.

78. *Negro World,* July 16, 1932.

79. *Negro World,* November 28, 1931; June 17, 1933; Hill, *Marcus Garvey Papers,* Vol. VII, 670.

80. Starting in 1924, many Garveyites in the North involved themselves more in political activities as a result of Marcus Garvey's decision to create the Universal Negro Political Union. "Our duty,' he explained in an October 26 speech, "was to put in office men who we believe will serve the interests of the Negro race." UNIA locals in Detroit, New York, Cleveland, and Philadelphia campaigned for several politicians, but the organization never became a powerful force in local politics. *Negro World,* November 2, 1924.

81. *Negro World,* June 15, 1929.

82. Earl Lewis, *In Their Own Interests,* 147.

83. *Negro World,* June 13, 1931.
84. The Crisis, April, 1934.
85. *Negro World,* November 28, 1931; June 17, 1933; Hill, *Marcus Garvey Papers,* Vol. VII, 670.
86. *Norfolk Journal and Guide,* October 22, 1933.
87. Gordon to Cox, March 6, 1936, Cox Papers.
88. Gordon to Cox, March 6, 1936, Cox Papers.
89. "To the Honorable Earnest Sevier Cox,"1936, Cox Papers.
90. Fitzgerald, " 'We Have Found a Moses' ": Theodore Bilbo, Black Nationalism, and the Greater Liberia Bill of 1939," *The Journal of Southern History* 63, no. 2 (May 1997): 296–297.
91. Fitzgerald, "We Have Found a Moses," 297.
92. Fitzgerald, "We Have Found a Moses," 307.
93. Fitzgerald, "We Have Found a Moses," 306.
94. Fitzgerald, "We Have Found a Moses," 307.
95. Hill, *Marcus Garvey Papers,* Vol. VII., 855.
96. Cox to Giddings, October 11, 1939, Cox Papers
97. Giddings to Cox, October 17, 1939, Cox Papers.
98. Giddings to Cox, December 26, 1939, Cox Papers.
99. Cox to Giddings, December 13, 1939, Cox Papers.
100. Giddings to Cox, June 6, 1942, Universal Negro Improvement Association, Central Division, New York Records, 1918–1959 (Manuscript, Archives, and Rare Books Division, Schomburg Center for Research in Black Culture, New York Public Library, microfilm).

NOTES TO CHAPTER FIVE

1. *Workers Monthly,* June 1926.
2. Ruth Edmonds Hill, *The Black Women Oral History Project,* Vol. 8, (London: Meckler, 1991, 173).
3. *Negro World,* December 17, 1927.
4. James Weldon Johnson, *Black Manhattan,* (New York: Da Capo Press, 1930), 256.
5. Robert Hill, *Marcus Garvey Papers,* Vol. II, 113; UNIA Central Office, Administrative Files, Box 2, Folder 16, Manuscripts, Archives, and Rare Books Division, Schomburg Center for Research in Black Culture; Agent J.M. Toliver to Bureau, July 16, 1921, case file 198140–198, Record Group 59, Department of State, National Archives [hereafter RG59, DS, NA];Harry Gulley to Bureau, 24 January 1923, case file 61–50–195, obtained by author from FBI through Freedom of Information Act (hereafter FBI-FOIA); . William C. Sausele to Bureau, 11 November 22, 1920, BS 202600–10–7, RG65, BI, NA; Agent Leon Howe to Bureau, 8 July 1921, BS 198940–183, RG65, BI, NA.
6. Alice and Staughton Lynd, *Rank and File: Personal Histories by Working-Class Organizers.* Boston, Beacon Press, 1973), 114.
7. Lynd, *Rank and File,* 114.

8. Lynd, *Rank and File*, 116.
9. Lynd, *Rank and File*, 125.
10. Lynd, *Rank and File*, 114.
11. Hill, *The Black Women Oral History Project*, Vol. 8, 123.
12. Hill, *The Black Women Oral History Project*, Vol. 8, 132.
13. Hill, *The Black Women Oral History Project*, Vol. 8, 124.
14. Few southern cities experienced a more profound economic restructuring during the World War II period than Miami. Ever since the city's incorporation in 1896, the local economy had revolved principally around the tourist industry, but the city became more industrialized after the onset of World War II. No small factor in the diversification of the city's economy was the emergence of commercial aviation and ship building as major industries in Miami. Serving as the hub for Eastern, Delta, and Pan-American airlines, Miami became an important center for the commercial aviation industry during the late 1940s and early 1950s. These dramatic transformations in Miami's economy had profound implications for labor-capital relations in the city. Determined to benefit from the wartime prosperity, white and black laborers increasingly demanded a greater collective voice within Miami's workplaces.
15. Interestingly enough, Nimmo held meetings at the former gathering place for the UNIA, which was located on 4th Avenue and 19th Street. No data on the exact number of Garveyites involved in these discussions is available, but in his interview with the House of Un-American activities he identifies a few ex-Garveyites as members of union. "Testimony of James Nimmo," 7428.
16. "Testimony of James Nimmo,," 7428.
17. "Testimony of James Nimmo," 7430.
18. "Testimony of James Nimmo," 7443.
19. A major UNIA stronghold in North Carolina, Greensboro hosted a vibrant division, which benefited tremendously from the contribution of the local community's black college students. Looking for political avenues to express their disgust at existing race relations, these students involved themselves in the work of the UNIA. Like the civil rights leaders of the 1960s, UNIA leaders in Greensboro capitalized on the youthful energy and intellectual talent of the city's black collegiate and high school students. To the delight of the older members, Garvey's representative Samuel Haynes, in the summer of 1928, organized a group of students from Bennett College, the local high school, Sedalia Institute, and North Carolina A & T into the Garvey Club. Sharing their knowledge with the other members in the division, these college students recited the most popular Negro poetry at the division's meetings, engaged in intensive political debates, and suggested ways to make the movement more appealing to the broader black community. *Negro World*, July 14, 1928.
20. Interview with Randolph Blackwell, March 5, 1973. Duke University, Oral History Project
21. Interview with Randolph Blackwell, March 5, 1973. Duke University, Oral History Project.

22. Interview with Randolph Blackwell, March 5, 1973. Duke University, Oral History Project

23. Interview with Randolph Blackwell, March 5, 1973. Duke University, Oral History Project. Blackwell became an influential member of both the Southern Christian Leadership Conference and the Voter Education Project (VEP). Charles Payne, *I've Got the Light Freedom: The Organizing Tradition and the Mississippi Freedom Struggle* (Berkeley: University of California Press, 1995), 108.

24. E.U. Essien-Udom, *Black Nationalism: A Search for an Identity in America*, (New York: Dell Publishing:, 1962), 113.

25. Essien-Udom, *Black Nationalism*, 113.

26. Essien-Udom, *Black Nationalism*, 113.

27. Essien-Udom, *Black Nationalism*, 113.

28. Essien-Udom, *Black Nationalism*, 373.

Bibliography

PRIMARY SOURCES

Manuscript Collections

Durham, North Carolina

Rare Book, Manuscripts, and Special Collections Library, Duke University

Earnest Sevier Cox Papers
William Chafe Oral History Collection
Behind the Veil Collection

Washington, D.C.

Library of Congress
National Association for the Advancement of Colored People Papers
American Colonization Society Papers
City Directories of the United States, Miami, Reel 3, 1921
National Archives,
United States Department of Justice, Record Group 60
United States Pardon Attorney, Record Group 204: 42–793
Manuscript Census Schedules, Dade Council, U.S. Bureau of the Census, Record Group 29
Federal Bureau of Investigation

New York City, New York

Schomburg Collection, New York Public Library
Universal Negro Improvement Association, Records of the Central Division (New York), 1918–1959,

Newspapers

African Repository
A.M.E. Church Review

A.M.E. Zion Quarterly Review
Amsterdam News
Baltimore Afro-American
Blackman
Chattanooga Times
Chicago Defender
Crisis
Crusader
Daily Gleaner
Florida Times Union
Louisiana Weekly
Messenger
Miami Times
Miami Herald
Negro Worker
Negro World
New York Age
New York Times
Norfolk Journal and Guide
Pittsburgh Courier
Richmond Dispatch
Spokesmen
Times Picayune
The Messenger

SECONDARY SOURCES

Abraham, Kinfe. *Politics of Black Nationalism From Harlem to Soweto*. Trenton: African World Press, 1991.

Adekele, Tunde. *Un-African Americans: Nineteenth-Century Black Nationalists and the Civilizing Mission*. Lexington: University Press of Kentucky Press, 1998.

Adi, Hakim. *West Africans in Britain, 1900–1960: Nationalism, Pan-Africanism, and Communism*. London: Lawrence and Wishart, 1998.

Akpan, M.B. "Black Imperialism: Americo-Liberian Rule over the African Peoples of Liberia, 1841–1964." *The Canadian Journal of African Studies 7*, (1973): 217–36.

———. "Liberia and the Universal Negro Improvement Association: The Background to the Abortion of Garvey's Scheme for African Colonization. *Journal of African History 14*, I (1973): 105–27.

Anderson, Benedict. *Imagined Communities: Reflections on the Origin and Spread of Nationalism*. New York: Verso, 1983.

Anderson, James D. *The Education of Blacks in the South, 1860–1935*. Chapel Hill: University of North Carolina Press, 1988.

Anderson, Robert Earle. *Liberia: America's African Friend*. Chapel Hill: University of North Carolina Press, 1952.

Angell, Stephen Ward. *Bishop Henry McNeal Turner and African-American Religion in the South.* Knoxville: The University of Tennessee Press, 1992.

Appiah, Kwame Anthony. *In My Father's House: Africa in the Philosophy of Culture.* New York: Oxford University Press, 1992.

Arnesen, Eric. *Waterfront workers of New Orleans: Race, Class, and Politics, 1863-1923.* Urbana: University of Illinois Press, 1994.

Austin, Algernon. *Achieving Blackness: Race, Black Nationalism, and Afrocentrism in The Twentieth Century.* (New York: New York University Press, 2006).

Baldwin, Kate. *Beyond the Color Line and the Iron Curtain: Reading Encounters Between Black and Red, 1922–1963.* Durham: Duke University Press, 2003.

Bates, Beth Tompkins. *Pullman Porters and the Rise of Protest Politics in Black America, 1925–1945.* Chapel Hill: University of North Carolina Press, 2001.

Beardsley, Edward H. *A History of Neglect: Health Care for Blacks and Mill Workers in the Twentieth-Century South.* Knoxville: The University of Tennessee Press, 1987.

Bell, Howard H. *A Survey of the Negro Convention Movement.* New York: Arno Press and New York Times, 1969.

Bilbo, Theodore G. "An African Home for Our Negroes." *Living Age* 358, 4451 (June (1940): 327–35.

Bixler, Raymond W. *The Foreign Policy of the United States in Liberia.* New York: Pageant Press, 1957.

Blyden, Edward W. *Christianity, Islam, and the Negro Race.* 1887. Edinburgh: University of Edinburgh Press, 1967.

Bracey, John H. Jr., August Meier, and Elliot Rudwick, eds. *Black Nationalism in America.* Indianapolis: Bobbs-Merrill, 1970.

Brotz, Howard. *African American Protest Thought, 1850–1920.* New Brunswick: Transaction Publishers, 1992.

Brundage, W. Fitzhugh. *Lynching in the New South: Georgia and Virginia, 1880–1930.*Urbana: University of Illinois Press, 1993.

Buni, Andrew. *The Negro in Virginia Politics, 1902–1965.* Charlottesville: University Press of Virginia, 1967.

Burkett, Randall K. *Black Redemption: Churchmen Speak for the Garvey Movement.*Philadelphia: Temple University Press, 1978.

———. *Garveyism as a Religious Movement: The institutionalization of a Black Civil Religion.* New Jersey: Scarecrow Press, 1978.

Burkett, Randall and Richard Newman, eds. *Black Apostles: Afro-American Clergy Confront the Twentieth Century.* Boston: G.K. Hall and Company, 1978.

Bush, Rod. *We Are Not What We Seem: Black Nationalisms and Class Struggle in the American Century.* New York: New York University Press, 1999.

Cell, John W. *The Highest Stage of White Supremacy: The Origins of Segregation in South Africa and the American South.* New York: Cambridge University Press, 1982.

Chafe, William. *Civilities and Civil Rights: Greensboro, North Carolina, and the Black Struggle for Freedom.* New York: Oxford University Press, 1980.

Clarke, John Henrik. Marcus Garvey and the Vision of Africa. . New York: Random

House, 1974.

———. *Africans at the Crossroads: Notes for an African World Revolution*. Trenton: Africa World Press, 1991.

Clegg, Claude Andrew. *An Original Man: The Life and Times of Elijah Muhammad*. New York: St. Martin's Press, 1997.

Cohen, William. *At Freedom's Edge: Black Mobility and the Southern White Quest for Racial Control, 1861–1915*. Baton Rouge: Louisiana State University Press, 1991.

Cronon, Edmund David. *Black Moses: The Story of Marcus Garvey and the UniversalNegro Improvement Association*. Madison: University of Wisconsin Press, 1955.

Cruse, Harold. *The Crisis of the Negro Intellectual*. New York: William Morrow and Company, 1967.

Deburg, William L. Van. *New Day in Babylon: The Black Power Movement and American Culture, 1965–1975*. Chicago: University of Chicago Press, 1992.

———., ed. *Modern Black Nationalism: From Marcus Garvey to Louis Farrakhan*. New York: New York University Press, 1997.

Dittmer, John. *Black Georgia in the Progressive Era, 1900–1920*. Urbana: University of Illinois Press, 1977.

Drake, St. Clair. *The Redemption of Africa and Black Religion*. Chicago: Third World Press, 1970.

Draper, Theodore. *The Rediscovery of Black Nationalism*. New York: Viking, 1970.

Dunn, Marvin. *Black Miami in the Twentieth Century*. Gainesville: University of Florida Press,1997.

Eschen, Penny Von. *Race Against Empire: Black Americans and Anticolonialism, 1937-1957*. Ithaca: London, 1997.

Esedebe, P. Olisanwuche. *Pan-Africanism: The Idea and Movement, 1776–1963*. Washington, D.C.: Howard University Press, 1982.

Essien-Udom, E.U. *Black Nationalism: A Search for an Identity in America*. New York: Dell, 1969.

Fabre, Michel. *Black American Writers in France, 1840–1980*. Urbana: University of Illinois Press, 1991.

Farajaje-Jones, Elias. *In Search of Zion: The Spiritual Significance of African in Black Religious Movements*. New York: P. Lang, 1991.

Fairclough, Adam. *Race Democracy: The Civil Rights Struggle in Louisiana, 1915–1972*. Athens: University of Georgia Press, 1995.

Favor, J. Martin. *Authentic Blackness: The Folk in the New Negro Renaissance*. Durham: Duke University Press, 1999.

Fax, Elton. *Garvey: The Story of a Pioneer Black Nationalists*. New York: Dodd, Mead, 1972.

Fierce, Milfred C. *The Pan-African Idea in the United States, 1900–1919*. New York: Garland Publishing, 1993.

Fitzgerald, Michael W. "We Have Found a Moses': Theodore Bilbo, Black Nationalism, and the Greater Liberia Bill of 1939," *Journal of Southern History* 63 (May 1997): 293–320.

Foley, Barbara. *Spectres of 1919: Class Nation in the Making of the New Negro.* Chicago: University of Illinois Press, 2003).

Foley, Neil. *The White Scourge: Mexicans, Blacks, and Poor Whites in Texas Cotton Culture.* Berkeley: University of California Press, 1997.

Foner, Philip S. *Organized Labor and the Black Worker, 1619–1973.* New York: International Publishers, 1974.

Franklin, V.P. *Black Self-Determination: A Cultural History of African-American Resistance.* New York: Lawrence Hill Books, 1992.

Frazier, E. Franklin. "Garvey: A Mass Leader," *The Nation,* August 19, 1926, 147–148.

Freire, Paulo. *Pedagogy of the Oppressed.* 1970. Reprint. New York: The Continuum Company, 1997.

Gaines, Kevin. *Uplifting the Race: Black Leadership, Politics, and Culture in the Twentieth Century.* Chapel Hill: University of North Carolina Press, 1996).

Gannon, Michael. *Florida: A Short History.* Gainesville: University of Florida Press, 1993.

———. Ed., *The New History of Florida.* Gainesville: University of Florida, 1996.

Garvey, Amy Jacques. *The Philosophy and Opinions of Marcus Garvey,* 1925. Reprint, Dover: The Majority Press, 1986.

Geiss, Imanuel. *The Pan-African Movement.* Trans. Ann Keep. New York: Africana Publishing Company, 1974.

George, Paul S. "Brokers, Binders and Builders: Greater Miami's Boom of the Mid-1920s," *Florida Historical Quarterly* 55, no. 2 (July 1986): 27–55.

———. "Colored Town: Miami's Black Community, 1896" *Florida Historical Quarterly* 65, no. 3 (January 1987): 271–297.

Gilroy, Paul. *The Black Atlantic: Modernity and Double Consciousness.* Cambridge: Harvard University Press, 1993.

Glaude, Eddie S, Jr. *Exodus!: Religion, Race, and Nation in Early Nineteenth-Century Black America.* Chicago: University of Chicago Press, 2000.

———. Ed. *Is It Nation Time? Contemporary Essays on Black Power and Black Nationalism.* Chicago: University of Chicago, 2002.

Goings, Kenneth and Raymond A. Mohl.,eds. *The New Urban History.* California: Sage Publications, 1996.

Goldberg, David J. *Discontented America: The United States in the 1920s.* Baltimore: The John Hopkins University Press, 1999.

Greenfield, Liah. *Nationalism: Five Roads to Modernity.* Cambridge: Harvard University Press, 1992.

Grossman, James R. *Land of Hope: Chicago, Black Southerners, and the Great Migration.* Chicago: University of Chicago Press, 1989.

Grubbs, Donald H. *Cry from the Cotton: The Southern Tenant Farmers' Union and the New Deal.* Chapel Hill: The University of North Carolina Press, 1971.

Griffin, Farah Jasmine. *"Who Set You Flowin'?:" The African-American Migration Narrative.* New York: Oxford University Press, 1995.

———. "Ironies of the Saint:" Malcolm X, Black Women, and the Price of Protection." In *Sisters in the Struggle: African American Women in the Civil Rights-Black Power Movement*, ed. Bettye Collier Thomas and V.P. Franklin, 214–229. New York: New York University Press, 2001.

Hair, William Ivy. *Carnival of Fury: Robert Charles and the New Orleans Race Riot of 1900*. Baton Rouge: Louisiana State University Press, 1976.

Hale, Grace Elizabeth. *The Making of Whiteness; The Culture of Segregation in the South, 1890–1940*. New York: Pantheon Books, 1998.

Harlan, Louis. *Booker T. Washington: The Wizard of Tuskegee, 1910–1915*. New York, Oxford University Press, 1983.

Harris, Joseph E. *African-American Reactions to War in Ethiopia, 1936–1941*. Baton Rouge: Louisiana State University Press, 1994.

———., ed. *Global Dimensions of the African Diaspora*. Washington, D.C.: Howard University Press, 1982.

Harris, William H. *The Harder We Run: Black Workers since the Civil War*. New York: Oxford University Press, 1982.

Harrison, Hubert H. *When Africa Awakes: The "Inside Story" of the Stirrings and Strivings of the New Negro of the Western World*. New York: Porro Press, 1920.

Haywood, Harry. *Negro Liberation*. New York: International Publishers, 1948.

Hedlin, Ethel Wolskill. Earnest Cox and Colonization: A White Racists Response to Black Repatriation, 1923–1966. Ph.D. diss., Duke University, 1974.

Henri, Florette. *Black Migration: Movement North, 1900–1920*. Garden City, New York: Doubleday, 1975.

Hill, Lance. *The Deacons for Defense: Armed Resistance and the Civil Rights Movement*. Chapel Hill: University of North Carolina Press, 2004.

Hill, Robert A., ed. *Marcus Garvey: Life and Lessons*. Berkeley: University of California Press, 1987.

Hill, Robert A., ed. *Universal Negro Improvement Association and Marcus Garvey Papers*, Vol. 1–7. Berkeley: University of California, Press, 1983.

Hine and McLeod, ed., *Crossing Boundaries*. Bloomington: Indiana University Press, 1999.

Honey, Michael K. *Southern Labor and Black Civil Rights: Organizing Memphis Workers*. Urbana: University of Illinois Press, 1993.

Hopkins, A.G. *An Economic History of West Africa*. New York: Columbia University Press, 1973.

Howe, Stephen. *Afrocentricism: Mythical Past and Imagined Homelands*. New York: Verso, 1998.

Hunter, Tera W. *To 'Joy My Freedom: Southern Black Women's Lives and Labors After the Civil War*. Cambridge: Harvard University Press, 1997.

Huggins, Nathan Irvin. *Harlem Renaissance*. New York: Oxford University, 1974.

Richard Iton. *Solidarity Blues: Race, Culture, and the American Left*. Chapel Hill: The University of North Carolina Press, 2000.

Jacobs, Sylvia. *The African Nexus: Black American Perspectives on the European Partitioning of Africa, 1880–1920*. Westport: Greenwood Press, 1981.

———.ed. "The Historical Role of Afro-Americans in American Missionary Efforts in Africa." In. *Black Americans and the Missionary Movement in Africa.* Westport: Greenwood Press, 1982.

James, Winston. *Holding Aloft the Banner of Ethiopia: Caribbean Radicalism in Early Twentieth-Century America.* New York: Verso, 1998.

Johnson, Howard. *The Bahamas From Slavery to Servitude, 1783–1933.* Gainesville: University Press of Florida, 1996.

Jordan, Winthrop. *The White Man's Burden: Historical Origins of Racism in the United States.* New York: Oxford University Press, 1974.

Kelley, Robin D.G. Kelley. *Hammer and Hoe: Alabama Communists During the Great Depression.* Chapel Hill: University of North Carolina Press, 2001.

———. *Race Rebels: Culture, Politics, and the Black Working Class.* New York: Free Press, 1994.

———. *Freedom Dreams: The Black Radical Imagination.* Boston: Beacon Press, 2002.

Kornweibel, Theodore. *Seeing Red: Federal Campaigns against Black Militancy, 19191925.* Bloomington: Indiana University Press, 1998.

———. *No Crystal Stair: Black Life and the Messenger, 1917–1928. Westport, Conn: Greenwood Pres, 1975.*

Knought, Kip. "Racial Stirrings in Colored Town: The UNIA in Miami during the 1920s," *Tequesta* 60, (2000).

Levine, Lawrence. *Black Culture and Black Consciousness: Afro-American Folk Thought From Slavery to Freedom.* New York: Oxford University Press, 1977.

———. "Marcus Garvey and the Politics of Revitalization." In *Black Leaders of the Twentieth-Century,* ed. J.H. Franklin and A. Meier, 104–138. Urbana: University of Illinois Press, 1986.

Lewis, David Levering. *When Harlem Was in Vogue.* New York: Penguin Books, 1979.

———. *W.E.B. Du Bois: The Fight for Equality and the American Century, 1919-1963.* New York: Henry Holt and Company, 2000.

Lewis, Earl. *In Their Own Interests: Race, Class, and Power in Twentieth-Century Norfolk, Virginia.* Berkeley: University of California Press, 1991.

Lewis, Rupert. *Marcus Garvey: Anti-Colonial Champion.* Trenton: African World Press, 1988.

Lewis, Rupert, and Patrick Bryan, eds. *Marcus Garvey, His Work, and Impact.* Trenton: African World Press, 1991.

Link, William. A. *The Paradox of Southern Progressivism, 1880–1930.* Chapel Hill: The University of California Press, 1992.

Litwack, Leon F. *Trouble in Mind: Black Southerners in the Age of Jim Crow.* New York: Vintage Books, 1998.

Locke, Alain. *The New Negro.* 1925. Reprint, New York: Atheneum, 1969.

Manning, Marable. *Black Leadership: Four Great American Leaders and the Struggle for Civil Rights.* New York: Penguin Books, 1998.

———. "The Divided Mind of Black America: Race, Ideology and Politics in the Post-Civil Rights Era," in Manning Marable, ed., *Beyond Black and White: Transforming African-American Politics.* New York: Verso, 1995.

———. *Speaking Truth to Power: Essays on Race, Resistance and Radicalism*. New-York: Westview Press, 1996.

Martin, Tony. *Race First: The Ideological and Organizational Struggles of Marcus Garvey and the Universal Negro Improvement Association*. Connecticut: Greenwood Press, 1976.

———. *Literary Garveyism*. Dover: The Majority Press, 1983.

———. *The Pan-African Connection: From Slavery to Garvey and Beyond*. Dover: The Majority Press, 1983.

Marx, Anthony W. *Making Race and Nation: A comparison of the United States, South Africa, and Brazil*. New York: Cambridge University Press, 1997.

McMillen, Neil R. *Dark Journey: Black Mississippians in the Age of Jim Crow*. Urbana:University of Illinois Press, 1990.

Meier, August. *Negro Thought in America, 1880–1915: Racial Ideologies in the Age of Booker T. Washington*. Ann Arbor: The University of Michigan, 1963.

Meier, August. *Negro Thought in America, 1880–1915: Racial Ideologies in the Age of Booker T. Washington*. Ann Arbor: University of Michigan Press, 1969.

Miller, Floyd J. *The Search for a Black Nationality: Black Emigration and Colonization, 1787–1863*. Urbana: University of Illinois Pres, 1975.

Mitchell, Michele, Righteous Propagation: African Americans and the Politics of Racial Destiny after Reconstruction. Chapel Hill: University of Carolina Press, 2004.

Mohl, Raymond A. "The Pattern of Race Relations in Miami since the 1920s." In *African American Heritage of Florida*, ed. David R. Colburn and Jane L. Landers, 326–365. Tallahassee: University Press of Florida, 2000.

———. "Black Immigrants: Bahamians in Early Twentieth-Century Miami," *Florida Historical Quarterly* 46, no. 4, (April 1978): 432–447.

Montgomery, David. *The Fall of House of Labor: The Workplace, the State, and American Labor Activism, 1865–1925*. Cambridge: Cambridge University Press, 1987.

Morgan, Chester M. *Redneck Liberal: Theodore G. Bilbo and the New Deal*. Baton Rouge: Louisiana State University Press, 1986.

Moses, Wilson Jeremiah. *The Golden Age of Black Nationalism, 1850–1925*. New York: Oxford University Press, 1978.

———. *Black Messiahs and Uncle Toms: Social and Literary Interpretations of a Religious Myth*. University Park: Pennsylvania State University Press, 1982.

———. *Afrotopia: The Roots of African American Popular History*. New York: Oxford University Press, 1978. Cambridge University Press, 1998.

———. *The Golden Age of Black Nationalism, 1850–1895*. New York: Oxford University, 1978.

———. *Classical Black Nationalism: From the American Revolution to Marcus Garvey*. New York: New York University Press, 1996.

———. Creative Conflict in African American Thought: Frederick Douglass, Alexander Crummell, Booker T. Washington, W.E.B. Du Bois, and Marcus Garvey. Cambridge: Cambridge University Press, 2004.

Mudimbe, Valentine Y. *The Invention of Africa: Gnosis, Philosophy, and the Order of Knowledge*. Bloomington, IN: Indiana University Press, 1988.

Mulzac, Hugh. *A Star to Steer By*. New York: International Publishers, 1963.

Naison, Mark. *Communists in Harlem During the Depression*. Urbana: University of Illinois Press, 1983,

Nelson, Bruce. *Divided We Stand: American Workers and the Struggle for Black Equality*. Princeton: Princeton University Press, 2001.

Newman, Richard. "Warrior Mother of Africa's of the Most High God: Laura Adorker Kofey and the African Universal Church." *Black Power and Black Religion: Essays and Reviews*. West Cornwall: Locust Hill Press, 1987.

Osofsky, Gilbert. *Harlem: The Making of a Ghetto: Negro New York, 1890–1930*. New York: Harper Torchbooks, 1968.

Ottley, Roi. *"New World A-Coming": Inside Black America*. Boston: Houghton Mifflin, 1943.

Outlaw, Lucious. *Critical Social Theory in the Interest of Black Folks* (New York: Rowan and Littlefield Publishers, 1996).

Padmore, George. *Pan-Africanism or Communism? The Coming Struggle for Africa*. London: Dobson, 1956.

Painter, Nell Irvin. *The Narrative of Hosea Hudson: The Life and Times of a Black Radical*. New York: W.W. Norton, 1979.

———. *Southern History across the Color Line* (Chapel Hill: University of North Carolina Press, 2002.

Payne, Charles. *I've Got the Light of Freedom: The Organizing Tradition and the Mississippi Freedom Struggle*. Berkeley: University of California Press, 1995.

Perry, Jeffrey B. *A Hubert Harrison Reader*. Middletown: Wesleyan University Press, 2001.

Pfeffer, Paula F. *A. Philip Randolph, Pioneer of the Civil Rights Movement*. Baton Rouge: Louisiana State University Press, 1990.

Phillips, Kimberly. *Alabama North: African-American Migrants, Community, and Working-Class Activism in Cleveland, 1915–1945*. Urbana: University of Illinois Press, 1999.

Plummer, Brenda Gayle. *Rising Wind: Black Americans and U.S. Foreign Affairs, 1935-1960*. Chapel Hill: University of North Carolina Press, 1996.

Powdermaker: Hortense. *After Freedom: A Cultural Study in the Deep South*. New York: Atheneum, 1968.

Robinowitz, Howard. *Race Relations in the Urban South, 1865–1890*. Urbana: University of Illinois Press, 1980.

Redkey, Edwin S. *Black Exodus: Black Nationalists and Back-to-Africa movements, 1890–1910*. New Haven: Yale University Press, 1969.

Reid, Ira De A. *The Negro Immigrant: His Background, Characteristics and Social Adjustment, 1899–1937*. New York: Columbia University Press, 1939.

Robinson, Cedric J. *Black Marxism: The Making of the Black Radical Tradition*. 1983 Reprint. Chapel Hill: University of North Carolina Press, 2000.

Robinson, Dean E. *Black Nationalism in American Politics and Thought*. New York:Cambridge University Press, 2001.

Rolinson, Mary G. *The Garvey Movement in the Rural South, 1920–1927*. Ph.D. Dissertation, Georgia State University, 2002.

Scott, James C. *Domination and the Arts of Resistance: Hidden Transcripts.* New Haven: Yale University Press, 1990.

Scott, William R. *The Sons of Sheba's Race: African–Americans and the Italo-Ethiopian War, 1935–1941.* Indiana University Press, 1993.

Shepperson, George. "The American Negro and Africa." *British Association for American Studies* 8 (June 1964): 3–20.

———. "Notes on Negro American Influence on the Emergence of African Nationalism. *Journal of African History 1 (1960): 299–312.*

Sherman, Richard B. "The Last Stand: The Fight for Racial Integrity in Virginia in the 1920s." *Journal of Southern History 56,* no 1 (February 1988):

Skinner, Elliott P. *African Americans and U.S. Policy toward Africa, 1850–1924: In Defense of Black Nationality.* Washington, D.C.: Howard University Press, 1992.

Solomon, Mark. *The Cry Was Unity: Communists and African Americans, 1917, 1936.* Jackson: University Press of Mississippi, 1998.

Smethhurst, James Edward. *The Black Arts Movement: Literary Nationalism in the 1960s and 1970s.* Chapel Hill: University of North Carolina Press, 2005.

Smith, J. Douglass. *Managing White Supremacy: Race, Politics, and Citizenship in Jim Crow Virginia.* 2002.

Stein, Judith. *The World of Marcus Garvey: Race and Class in Modern Society.* Baton Rouge: Louisiana State University Press, 1986.

Stoddard, Lothrop. *The Rising Tide of Color against White World-Supremacy.* New York: Scribner, 1920.

Stuckey, Sterling. *Slave Culture: Nationalist Theory and the Foundations of Black America.* New York: Oxford University Press, 1987.

———. *The Ideological Origins of Black Nationalism.* Boston: Beacon Press, 1972.

Sundiata, Ibrahim. *Brothers and Strangers: Black Zion, Black Slavery, 1914–1940.* Durham: Duke University, 2003.

Taylor, Ula Yvette. *The Veiled Garvey: The Life and Times of Amy Jacques Garvey.* Chapel Hill: University of North Carolina Press, 2002.

Trotter, Joe William Jr. *River Jordan: African American Urban Life in the Ohio Valley.* Lexington: University Press of Kentucky, 1998.

———. *The Great Migration In Historical Perspective: New Dimensions of Race, Class, and Gender.* Bloomington: Indiana University Press, 1991.

Vincent, Theodore. *Black Power and the Garvey Movement.* Berkeley: Ramparts Press, 1971.

———. *Keep Cool: The Black Activists Who Built the Jazz Age.* London: Pluto Press, 1995.

White, Deborah Gray. *Too Heavy a Load: Black Women in Defense of Themselves, 1894-1994* (New York: W.W. Norton& Company, 1999.

Williamson, Joel. *New People: Miscegenation and Mulattoes in the United States.* New York: New York University Press, 1984.

Willis-Grady, Winston. *Challenging U.S. Apartheid: Atlanta and Black Struggles for Human Rights, 1960–1977.* Durham: Duke University Press, 2006.

Zieger, Robert H. *The CIO: 1935–1955.* Chapel Hill: University of North Carolina Press, 1995.

Index